Space Between the Stars

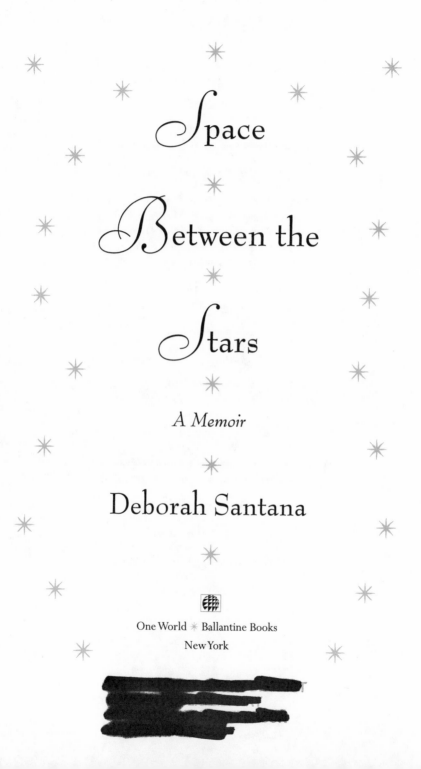

Space

Between the

Stars

A Memoir

Deborah Santana

One World ✳ Ballantine Books

New York

A One World Book

Published by The Random House Publishing Group

Copyright © 2005 by Cadestansa, LLC

www.oneworldbooks.net

Library of Congress Cataloging-in-Publication Data

Santana, Deborah, 1951–
Space between the stars : a memoir / by Deborah Santana.—
1st hardcover ed.
p. cm.
ISBN 0-345-47125-3
1. Santana, Deborah, 1951– 2. Santana, Carlos. 3. Rock musicians—United
States—Biography. 4. Musicians' spouses—Biography. I. Title.

ML420.S226A3 2005

787.87'164'092—dc22   2004050146

Manufactured in the United States of America

First Edition: March 2005

2   4   6   8   9   7   5   3   1

Book design by Mercedes Everett

For Carlos,

Salvador,

Stella, and

Angelica,

who hold my heart

Truth burns up error.

—Sojourner Truth

$\mathcal{C}$ontents

Contents

Preface

When I was in the third grade, my teacher stood in front of the blackboard and asked each one of us what we wanted "to do." I answered, "Write." And I began then—with poems, short stories, and a diary. Simple. Unpretentious. Through adolescence, through my first heartbreak, while traveling on trains, and after childbirth—I wrote about it all. It was my way of taking my stuffed-down yearnings and releasing them like butterflies in the sky.

I married at twenty-two, and in the thirty-one extraordinary years of my union with Carlos Santana, I have moved turbulently between two images: the feminist culture of the 1970s that told me I did not need a man to make me whole, and the provincial Christian teachings of my youth that said woman is helpmeet to her husband. While Carlos played music around the world believing that his art could transform human consciousness with positive energy and molecules of light, I studied

Spanish and creative writing, managed a vegetarian restaurant, answered fan mail, and taught meditation.

When our children dropped like flowers from my womb, I became guide, healer, and teacher, their lives giving me true meaning along the way. I stayed home to raise the lives that had come through us: volunteering in the children's schools; raising money for music and sports programs; surviving field trips; and watching our three children interact with a young version of humanity. I purchased real estate; took over our corporation, managing twenty employees; sat on the board of a nonprofit before we developed our own Milagro Foundation; and, with Carlos, decided on his career choices and direction.

Many people see me only in the context of Carlos's life. This concept of being known through my connection with someone famous contradicts all that I value about people. I am Carlos's wife, but I am first myself—a body of cells, emotions, beliefs, perspectives, and intelligence. Together, Carlos and I are sure-footed visionaries united by our devotion to spiritual truths, our family, and the betterment of the human condition. *Space Between the Stars* explains who I am and how I have struggled to maintain my identity. I hope that what I have learned in finding and defining myself can give voice and hope to others. My memoir exposes the rugged, uneven terrain of my discoveries and glories, as well as the impact of society's racism on my growth. Each sentient being has a story, a fascinating journey with family and friends, of awakenings and disappointments. My story represents the power of every life. I wrote my memoir because I am interested in this sacred unfolding, and I have learned to value myself through introspection and hard work. My goal is to give others encouragement and stamina to soar.

My parents were legally denied the right to marry in 1947 because they were not the same "race" (human race did not count). They were vilified and hated for loving each other, yet they chose to stand in their love. Society evolves by people risking to live what they believe is right for them. Slowly, so slowly, acceptance dawns in our culture because a group of rebels fights for their rights. I still find my parents' convictions and courage remarkable, and tell their story, with mine, as a symbol of thousands of people who willingly fight to liberate us all. My mother's amazing acceptance and love of people taught me that each person is unique and special in the eyes of God. She was never impressed by fame. Mom's interest in someone was sparked if they were kind, had faith in God, or said something that allowed her to glimpse their character.

Looking back, I have gathered the beauty and completeness of these years—the strength of my parents and the exquisiteness of my life with Carlos. I have been to Paris, London, Tokyo, Osaka, Barcelona, Madrid, Sydney, Melbourne, Acapulco, Puerto Vallarta, Puerto Rico, Kingston, Tobago, Geneva, Zurich, Moscow, New York, and Taos. I have visited El Prado, the Duomo, Britain's Natural History Museum, and Zen temples—learning sacred history and cultural customs. I have met famous people and people working in anonymity with great humility and power. Carlos's musical mission was always our focus, and our experiences have been sublime.

If I had designed my own existence, I may have lit on a

course of study, seeking a depth of knowledge in one area, or I may have served as a hospice worker helping children and adults come to terms with the power of their transition from this life to the next. I definitely would have chosen to be seen as an individual.

In writing this memoir, I have followed a labyrinth to my heart and have become aware that the wholeness I saw in others existed in the struggles and triumphs of my life and my marriage, in the loving-kindness of years survived and cherished. The words in this book are my remembrance of what I have lived on my journey, a prayer to my amplified life, nuggets of truth from my soul. May each reader see their own life as sacred, every experience as holy.

Space
Between the
Stars

1

Skin

San Francisco, California, 1960

✳

The summer I was nine I climbed to the top of our hill, grabbing handfuls of dry sweet grass to pull me over jagged rocks. I stood looking out at San Francisco unfurled before me, a mix of winding streets that trailed into the sky, or tipped into the soft, blue bay. Sunlight strained to warm me through the fog, and people drifted like watercolors on a page, hues of dark and light, diverse as the world. We lived on Majestic Avenue, a cul-de-sac whose name fit perfectly with our family surname, King. Feeling crystalline and ever so shaky in the gusting wind, I stood at the top of our street and waved my arms to the city, queen of it all.

My sister, Kitsaun, almost two years older than me, thought *she* was queen. She climbed ahead of me to the top of the bluff, holding stalks of anise toward the sky, the scent of licorice sifting down to me. Sitting on a ledge, I could see our little house with red stairs that led to the front door, a mean cactus century plant with two-inch thorns growing near the driveway. Once, Kitsaun had fallen off the porch onto the spiny arms and I thought she was dead. She had long scratches and cuts that bled, and Mom laid her on the couch so I could touch her face and bring her food. "She's a fainter," Mom said. "She'll be fine." The next day she was back on the hill, waving her royal stems.

Kitsaun and I shared a bedroom at the front of the house. Every night I slept with my head under the covers, clutching my stuffed dog, Brownie. I tried to fall asleep right after prayers because I did not want to be awake by myself in the dark. Kitsaun's bed was next to mine. She slept soundly under her flowered comforter—unafraid of the night. Morning light rose over the mountains of the East Bay and through the branches of a tall Monterey pine outside our window, and we could see the tip of the Bay Bridge glinting in the sun. We played hide-and-seek and "mother may I" with the kids on our block and some evenings we filled balloons with water and hid behind parked cars and bushes that poked us while we ran and smacked one another with wet, rubbery fun. We rode on coasters we made from planks of wood nailed to ball bearings, shrieking wildly as we careened down the smooth sidewalk, our hands clasping a circle of rope, a close-knit passel of friends.

My father, Saunders King, was a flinty observer of life, a man who spoke only when necessary. Singing was his language. He carried society's racism and his personal view of right and wrong a knife's blade beneath his steely control. His life as a guitarist and singer fulfilled him, and he tried to never compromise his art by working a nine-to-five job. Mom was an outspoken Irish-English woman who fell in love and married Dad, an African-American man, in the 1940s. She worked full-time in an era when it was acceptable, if not expected, that women stay at home with their children and sublimate their dreams and desires to help their husbands reach theirs. Mom loved working, and Dad loved being at home with Kitsaun and me during the day before going to his gigs at nightclubs. Our family was not at all defined by the traditional American mores of 1951, the year I was born.

Sundays, Dad would drive Mom, Kitsaun, and me across the Bay Bridge for church. Dad's brother Ulysses was pastor of Christ Holy Sanctified Church, the Pentecostal house of worship started by their father, Judge King, and Sarah, their mother. Dad would dress up in a shiny fitted suit with a wide tie like he was going to work. He smelled of Ivory soap and lime aftershave. Mom wore suits with stockings and heels. My favorite was pink mohair that felt like a rug. Kitsaun and I wore dresses with white socks and saddle shoes that made our legs look like toothpicks in boats. We both had hair that looked like we were in a perpetual wind. I wore a scarf tied tight around my head, pressing my waves flat. My bangs sat like a Tootsie Roll across my forehead. Kitsaun's black hair curled around her face. She was taller and lankier than me, smart and funny, too. She enjoyed yelling and singing, often combining the two, like opera. Mom would laugh and tell her to quiet down, which she did while making dramatic faces of rejection.

Church service began at eleven in the morning with the choir marching through the front doors in their white robes with red satin collars. My eyes followed their feet as they stepped forward with one foot, held it for two counts, and then pulled up the foot in back, tapping lightly. The choir bounced like springs, singing about the holiness of God. And I believed. Church grounded me in the heavens, telling me through sermons that life was full of strife, but that God was a present help in times of trouble. *Call on Him and you will find peace,* their powerful voices sang.

Every summer, a few days after school let out, Mom and Dad took us to Grandmother King's farm in Chowchilla, where the land lay out flat and dry, and when we walked down the road, a mirage of water shimmered in the distance. Grandmother wore a dress with a flowered apron over it. She spoke with a crinkle in her voice—never a bad word, either. She was not much taller than Kitsaun, even with her sturdy black shoes on, but strong spirited with a quietness that concealed her courage. Grandmother looked across her yard to the farmlands, as if she could see farther than the fields and pastures. I recognized a fire inside her, but she never spoke in a tone that was not gentle. She made a cup of hot water every morning, stirring in two heaping teaspoons of sugar and a splash of evaporated milk. She sat in a wooden rocking chair, her brown leather Bible open in her lap as she read and rocked, sipping her hot water. It was so scorching hot in Chowchilla that Grandmother never let us play outside between eleven in the morning and four in the afternoon. Every slow and sizzling day, Grandmother had Kitsaun and me wash and dry the dishes, dust the dining table, and fold tea towels. If we giggled and made fun of someone, Grandmother scolded our meanness—she didn't believe in gossip or swearing. She had a funny way of saying "excuse me" after she coughed, but nothing after a loud belch—which may have been a custom from Louisiana, where she was born. Dad's brother Judge lived with her, caring for the farm, because Grandfather King had died years before. Uncle Judge rose long before our dreams were done, to milk the two cows that lived in the tiny pasture. After our breakfast of Cream of Wheat or grits and eggs, Kitsaun and I followed Uncle Judge out to the chicken coop to toss corn feed to the hens and roosters. Once, when a chicken pecked my thigh, Uncle Judge wrung its neck and cooked it for dinner. I was grateful for the revenge, feeling the tender puncture where the beak had poked into my leg, but I could not swallow the meat that steamed on my plate. Where were the feathers, the head, the beady eyes?

At night, Grandmother put her teeth in a jar of water on the bathroom sink. It took me a long time to go to the bathroom without Kitsaun: The teeth looked so big in the glass. I would sit on the toilet and squeeze my eyes closed until I saw stars, wipe myself, and run out of the bathroom while pulling up my pajamas. Kitsaun and I slept on the sofa bed in the living room, the window open wide, without a prayer of a breeze— only crickets singing in the dark.

I learned about the peace of God in that house. Grandmother prayed morning and night, hummed hymns, and taught us Bible verses. On the dining table was a tiny wooden box that held little rectangular pieces of cardboard with scriptures that we read out loud before each meal. No matter how young, we were to pick out a pink, blue, or green card and stumble through a verse. No food passed our lips without a blessing. No sleep came until we said the Lord's Prayer. Kitsaun and I had memorized John 3:16 before we knew how to tie our shoes: ". . . that God so loved the world, He gave His only begotten son that whosoever believeth on Him shall not perish, but have eternal life." We grew up knowing we were expected to live up to Grandmother's image of a spiritual human being, praying for others and choosing good over bad. I still love the smell of cow pies when I drive in the country, because they remind me of hot, quiet days watching Grandmother's cows chew their cuds while I turned cartwheels through sprinklers on the crabgrass with my sister. I still can't fall asleep until I have said good night to God.

Every August, three of Mom's four sisters converged on our house in San Francisco—Aunt Nita and Aunt Ginger from Chicago and Aunt Nomi from South San Francisco. Our living room, with the Sears Roebuck sofa, and a black-and-white TV beside the upright piano, became a land of stories and bebop music. Mom reminisced about picking cotton with her sisters in Arizona when she was five, how raw and pricked their fingers got. Dad remembered his first singing lessons with Mrs. Forsythe in Oakland. She had taught him to enunciate his words and sing from his diaphragm. Aunt Ginger had introduced Mom to Dad in 1947 when Dad's band, the Saunders King Orchestra, was playing at the Café Society in Chicago. She and Uncle Stan had become Dad's fans listening to him in San Francisco at the Club Savoy. Our scrapbook had a photo of Dad in a sleek, dark suit and black bow tie, his white shirt stark against his smooth, charcoal skin. His eyes glimmered with starry light, his teeth straight and white beneath his mustache. He sang and played the guitar with his sextet, and often sat in with Billie Holiday, Charlie Mingus, and T-Bone Walker.

Dad played Ella Fitzgerald and Louis Armstrong on the turntable in our living room. Aunt Nita, Aunt Ginger, and Mom laid out cards for group solitaire in the kitchen. Aunt Daisy, Dad's sister who lived in Berkeley, came over with fried chicken, collard greens, and sweet potato pies that she had made at her apartment late at night.

Dad smiled big, listening to the music and playing his guitar along with the records. He would curl his lip and shake his head if he didn't like the intonation or choice of his notes. Our aunts snapped their fingers to the beat, and Daisy moved her head side to side, her arms bent upward like a funky Egyptian dancer. Our aunts said what they thought about each other and the world while pinching our cheeks and hugging us into their soft breasts. Kitsaun and I adored them and loved how alive our house became when we were all together. Late at night, voices buzzed, ice cubes were plunked into drinks, and Dad's velvety tenor serenaded us through our bedroom door. Mom was the only one who didn't drink, because her father drank and smoked himself to death. That didn't seem to bother her sisters, who loved to make cocktails while Dad kept the music hot.

My first lesson in who I was came on a Saturday when I was nine. I had just come in from playing on the hill, and I was waiting for Mom to take Kitsaun and me to the Stonestown Library for our weekend ritual of borrowing books to read during the week. Mom devoured Agatha Christie and Ian Fleming; Kitsaun and I, Nancy Drew and young fiction. Mom, Aunt Nita, Aunt Ginger, and Dad were in the kitchen, sitting around the wooden table that I had poked my name into with a fork. Aunt Ginger pulled me onto her lap, her pedal pushers smooth against my legs. Her hair was a rusty red, and she wore it swept up into a French twist, which made her nose look pointy and her ears very small. I folded my hands across my tummy, and she rubbed her palms over my fingers. Mom sat across the table, her brunette hair falling softly onto her high cheekbones. She looked like a model in her navy blue dress with small white polka dots and a thin belt that showed off her tiny waist. Dad sat near the window, his legs crossed and a toothpick between his lips. Sunlight cut across his broad nose and high forehead. His shoulders were straight, the muscles in his arms showed through his shirt. His skin shone like the wet earth that slid down our street in hard rain. Aunt Nita stood at the sink in her ruffled housedress, pouring hot water over Lipton tea bags and stirring sugar into the pitcher. Her bleached hair was flattened in curls that were twisted with bobby pins; her blond wig sat on a Styrofoam head on my dresser. "Remember when they stretched the rope down the center of the dance floor, Saunders?" Aunt Nita asked. "Where was that?"

"That was a big night," Dad said. "It was in Tennessee. Nashville, Tennessee."

I wondered how a jump rope could reach across a dance floor. I had watched *Dance Party* on TV. Teenagers danced in a big crowd, jerking their arms and shaking their butts.

"Damn prejudiced Southern fools!" Aunt Ginger said. "Saunders didn't allow them to separate whites and Negroes in the nightclubs he played."

My throat tightened. Who wanted to separate the Negroes and whites? It wasn't three o'clock yet, so I knew Aunt Ginger hadn't poured her drink, but her voice spit with the same sneering drawl she often had by nightfall when she listened to Dad's 78 rpm records over and over, drinking vodka and orange juice, hanging her head, and nodding while trying to sing along to "Summertime" or "Danny Boy."

Mom folded the *San Francisco Chronicle* in half, Herb Caen's column facing up so Aunt Ginger could read it later.

"Here, Jody." Aunt Nita handed Mom a plastic tumbler of iced tea. "What happened that night, Saunders?"

"Well, we were touring the South. My manager and valet drove with me in the Lincoln. The other band members were in another car. When we arrived in Nashville, my manager paid the Musicians' Union so we could play. But when we reached the nightclub, something wasn't right."

"Wasn't Eddie Taylor in your band then?" Nita stood in the archway, clutching her glass of tea, her nails painted red like fire. "I sure loved the way he played that sax."

Dad smiled. "Yes, Eddie was there. His was the first face I saw when we walked into the room. That's how I knew something was wrong. He pulled me aside and told me the owner of the club, Mr. Casey, was going to put a rope down the center of the dance floor to separate the whites and Negroes."

"What year was that, Saunders?" Mom liked to know numbers.

"Let's see." Dad whistled. "1944, 1945." His eyes trailed off, and then settled on me. "You took your life in your hands going down South for any reason. That's why my mother and father left Louisiana. I would rather raise Cain than take a backseat because of my race. They had to give it to me right, or not at all."

Aunt Nita sat down at the end of the table. "What did you do, Saunders?" She made her eyes bug out as she did when Dad sang her favorite songs, and big tears plopped into her martini.

"My manager was still back at the hotel and I was too hot to wait for him. I told Eddie I was going to talk to Casey. He wanted to go with me. We walked to the office in back, and I set my guitar on the floor. Casey asked what I wanted. I told him, 'Mr. Taylor tells me you're thinking about stretching a rope across the dance floor to segregate the Negroes.' I stared deep into his eyes to let him know I could see his soul. I told him, 'I don't play to segregated audiences. Never have. Never will.' "

"What if he had told you to take your band and leave?" Nita's voice was soft.

"I knew he could throw me out or call the police. But we could work in other cities. We didn't need to stay in Tennessee. It wasn't the first time I had to stand up to racism. I had almost been shot in El Paso when the sheriff called me off a Greyhound bus because I wasn't sitting in the back."

I swallowed hard and shifted in Aunt Ginger's arms. She squeezed me around the waist, and I could smell the sweet scent of her Juicy Fruit gum. "Are you okay?" she whispered in my ear.

Mom looked over and waved me to her lap. I ran to her and snuggled into her arms, my body trembling.

Dad made a clicking sound with his tongue against his teeth and said, "Mr. Casey just stared at me, so I picked up my guitar and walked back across the dance floor. Eddie Taylor followed close behind. I took long, slow steps so Casey could catch up if he wanted. 'Saunders!' he called. He was excited, all right. He told me, 'We have two hundred people arriving in an hour. You can't leave.' I stopped. I was too mad to turn around. I wanted to take a swing at him. I could feel perspiration dripping down my back. I turned to Casey and said, 'Man, I don't play to segregated audiences anywhere. You want my band—no rope.' "

Dad pulled a white handkerchief out of his pants pocket and patted his forehead. Every word stuck right to my heart. I knew that what had happened to Dad in Tennessee was a lesson for me.

Aunt Nita's voice cut in: "If you hadn't gone back, your musicians would have followed you."

"Oh yes," Dad said, "they surely would have left with me. They were watching the action. Their rights were hanging, too."

Mom hugged me tighter. "I hate these stories about the South. The 'Jim Crow' laws were horrible. Saunders, you had too many close calls."

"Quite a few serious close calls," Dad said. "I had a terrific temper, too. But we wanted to work, we wanted to play."

"So, what happened?" Aunt Nita swirled her ice cubes and stared at Dad.

He smiled. "They took the rope down. We made the place jump that night, and we got out of there."

"Let's have a drink," Aunt Ginger said. She and Aunt Nita stood up to make their afternoon cocktails.

I sat ice-cold in Mom's lap. My heart pounded in my chest.

Dad's story reminded me of something that had happened to me. Hearing how those people had wanted to separate blacks and whites made me remember a bad experience I'd had last semester. I had been skipping into the yard at San Miguel Elementary School, going to my third-grade class. I waved good-bye to Kitsaun, and she turned to go across the playground. A group of older kids leaned against the fence. After I passed them, a girl hissed in the meanest voice I had ever heard: "Your mama's as white as day, and your daddy's as black as night."

Then one of them snorted, and there was a burst of evil laughter.

I skipped faster. My legs wobbled, but I didn't look back. I ran into school, hot tears pooling in my eyes as I pictured Mom and Dad.

"Your mama's as white as day. Your daddy's as black as night." What was wrong with Mom and Dad being different skin colors? I stumbled into the back of my classroom and leaned into my cubby, shaking. I closed my eyes and imagined Mom's brown eyes crinkled in love when she brushed my hair, as I watched in the mirror. Her skin—yes, now I see—her skin is white. No, not white; it's creamy, like French vanilla ice cream. Dad's skin is dark like nighttime, his white teeth like starlight. He's the color of songs.

Outside, the principal rang the hand bell. Kids' voices came closer. I wanted the cubby to swallow me, to make the fire exploding in my heart go away. I rubbed my sleeve across my face. *Your mama's as white as day. Your daddy's as black as night.*

I hated those kids. I had never thought of my parents as colors. They were Mom and Dad. Mysteries and music.

My classmates had come into the cloakroom with me. Steven Chin hung his jacket on a hook, pushed his glasses up on his nose, and walked to his desk on the other side of our cubbies. Sharon Rodgers tossed her thick braids over her shoulders and smiled at me. Her skin was light brown—like mine. I untied the knot beneath my chin and slid my scarf off my head, wadding the fabric into a soft ball like the one in my stomach. I dropped it on the floor next to my lunch and carried my schoolbooks to my desk. The teacher was calling roll.

"Deborah King."

"Here," I murmured, sitting tall in my chair—a picture of night meeting day hanging before me.

The whole day, I careened through space, unable to stop trembling, feeling as though I were spinning round and round. Every child became a color: my best friend, Karmen, brown; Janet, white; Steven, ivory.

Kitsaun and I walked home from school. I quietly stepped where she stepped, but I didn't tell her what had happened. I didn't ask her to interpret the mean words, and I didn't want her to feel the crushing pain of the realization that Mom and Dad were different from everyone else's parents. I felt like those kids were going to beat me up because of my parents' skin colors.

Dad was sitting on the couch when we arrived home. He told us to wash our hands, and he gave Kitsaun and me red apples. Mom cooked hamburger patties for dinner. Nothing was different at home except my vision of every color in my life. When Mom tucked me in, I told her what the kids had said to me. She sat on the edge of my bed, her soft hands tracing my eyebrows, my cheeks. Kitsaun was brushing her teeth in the small bathroom between our room and Mom and Dad's. I tried not to cry, but my lips quivered and my eyes watered.

"Oh honey," Mom said, "people see things very differently. Your father and I married because we love each other, not because of what we look like. Those children don't know the first thing about love. Don't let their ignorance hurt you."

Kitsaun ran into our room and jumped onto her bed, her dark curls flying. She had heard everything: "Show me who said it," she said, raising her fists like a fighter and punching the air. "I'll tell them a thing or two."

The next day, Dad came to school to pick me up. I saw him standing in the schoolyard outside the principal's office as I came down the stairs. He looked taller than usual. His black skin glistened like cold lava. His mouth was pulled tight, his eyes dark.

"Dad!" I called out. His lips opened, showing those bright white teeth. He walked his cool strut toward me as kids half his height poured out through the doorways.

"Hi, Dobs," he said, taking my hand in his.

"What are you doing here, Dad?"

"I wanted to see if those children had anything else to say to you today. Do you see any of them here? Did they bother you this morning?" Mom must have told Dad what happened.

"No, Dad. I don't even know who said it." I didn't tell him that I had stayed close to a teacher all day.

"Well, if anyone ever says anything like that to you again, or tries to hurt you, just pick up a brick and hit 'em over the head." Dad always told Kitsaun and me to pick up a brick if anyone tried to harm us, as though bricks lay along every San Francisco street, ready for our use.

I looked up into his face. His mustache twitched, and he squeezed my hand. "Let's get you and your sister some ice cream, okay?"

We waited for Kitsaun to come out. Dad began to whistle

in a full, beautiful, bird-like warble that rose above the school yard and carried me with it.

Dad's Tennessee story showed me that those kids had tried to stretch a rope down the center of me. They had tried to divide me in half because my parents had two different skin colors. Now I knew I did not need to feel less human or ashamed of being different. Like Dad, I was going to have to stand up to racism and unfairness. I wished I had been brave like Dad and had marched up to them and looked straight into their ugly, crossed eyes and said, "You're ignorant. What somebody looks like on the outside doesn't have anything to do with who they are inside."

But, even if I had said it, I would not have been able to make the picture of my family colorless again. One side was black. One side was white. I stood in the middle.

I never forgot what those children said to me. Their judgment tainted how I looked at the world and taught me how the world looked at me. Every night our family watched news reports of failed attempts to integrate the South. The violence confirmed white America's objection to my heritage. I sought to make my biracial identity an asset to my philosophy of life, to rise above the perception that it was a negative. With passing years, I strongly believed that my soul had chosen my mixed ethnicity to share with others a conviction of equality for all. I identified with my African-American ancestors who were brutally and inhumanely treated through slavery, segregation, and Jim Crow laws. I felt compassion and oneness with my Irish ancestors—more than one million had perished in the potato famine. Which survivor, through her blood, had passed on to me the will to live? My grandparents had been persecuted because of their color, my parents spat upon for crossing an invisible color line. Kitsaun and I were asked "What are you?" more than "What's your name?" or "How are you?" People wanted us to label ourselves as something they could understand.

When my daughter, Stella, turned eight, she was invited to a birthday party on our street. One of the children asked the girl who had invited Stella why she had invited a black girl. Stella's skin is the hue of an ivory tusk, a maple leaf just turning from green in the fall; it is the soft yellow of a warm corn tortilla. But the child had probably seen my skin and pulled way back into centuries of racism to deny Stella access to the life she was enjoying. When Stella came home, tears of indignation streaked across her face, I held her in my arms and explained society's cultural ignorance, the centuries of racism living in people's blood and how, no matter what anyone else's perception of her could ever be, she is a beautiful creation of God, equal to everyone else. I sat back from her and looked into her eyes. "Today is an example of what lies ahead. You will have to work harder, fight to get where you want to be, and deny racism your whole life. Not just for you, but for all people who are different from what society pretends is America." Anger surged through me as I thought of every incident of racism I had ever endured or witnessed. It was painful to see the same prejudice I had experienced thirty years earlier inflicted on my child.

I have been given a gift in who I am. Each person is a repository of identities, ancestral blood, beliefs, revelations, and grace. We are our skin, but so much more.

2

King of the Blues

San Francisco, California, 1962

When I was twelve, our family moved over the hill from Majestic Avenue to Harold Avenue. My best friend, Karmen, and her family lived on Harold, too, and she and I walked to James Denman Junior High together every morning. Our friends were Chinese, Filipina, Latina, Greek, black, and white. We mixed because of our similarities, not our differences. I adjusted to a color-conscious world that rejected dark skin; I knew that I would have to fight for anything I wanted. At night we watched the news and followed the civil rights movement led by Dr. Martin Luther King, Jr. We knew the future of people of color was at the heart of striving for our legal stake in America's society.

In spite of the social turmoil, my immediate concerns were with my father and boys. When I came home from school, Dad would be in the yellow chair by the living room window, bent over his guitar, tapping a 4/4 rhythm with his foot while he strummed mellow blues chords. He watched Kitsaun and me closely, not wanting as much as a feather to touch us if it could undermine our strength.

One day, I came home an hour late. I waved hello to Dad, who widened his eyes in greeting as he sang with gentle vibrato, "What's your story, morning glory, what makes you feel so blue?" His black hair, pressed into wavy curls, topped his round face, perfect eyebrows, and bushy mustache. I closed the door, hung my coat on the hall closet doorknob, dumped my schoolbooks on the dinette table, and set my viola case on the floor.

"You're late, Deb," he called.

"We had cheerleading practice," I answered, sticking my head inside the refrigerator.

Dad grunted. Really I was late because I had waited to catch a glimpse of Arnzy, hoping the eighth grader would talk to me again——me, a seventh-grade cheerleader with skinny legs who was "first chair" viola in orchestra. He had smiled at me after fourth period and walked me to gym class the week before. I took a cold chicken thigh and a slice of corn bread to my room and flopped onto my bed.

Arnzy must have left before I reached my locker. I missed the shiver that rolled through my stomach when he smiled at me. His skin was like mine, his hair kinky and dark. Kitsaun——always correcting me with her ninth-grade smarts——told me he was a punk with a pretty face. But it didn't matter, I was smitten.

Dad's tunes serenaded me as I ate my chicken. I wished Arnzy would hold my hand. Dad would never let me date him. He glared if I talked to our neighbor Danny up the street. It was as though, with boys, Kitsaun and I had to keep moving or they would do something bad to us. Dad would never understand my being in love, so I hid it from him. I could talk to Mom about anything, but Dad was not easily approachable. Wary of anything outside our front door, Dad did not trust all of our friends or their motives, and he watched carefully any boy who came over. He did not tell us why; and as a teenager, I sometimes thought he was mean and too gruff.

If I said I was going up the street to Danny's or Johnny's, Dad said, "You don't need to go to his house. He can come over here."

"He won't let us do anything!" Kitsaun and I wailed to Mom.

"Your father wasn't raised to be at other people's houses. They were a church family who stuck close together and had strict rules," she explained.

Kitsaun and I fought with Mom and Dad to let us go places with our friends. Their response was always, "If all of your friends jump off a cliff, are you going to follow them? Think for yourselves, girls."

There was not much trouble I could get into, anyway. Hawkeyed Dad was home every afternoon before late-night gigs with his trio at a nightclub in Sunnyvale. We did not have friends over because we had homework. I practiced my viola, and Kitsaun went to dance lessons. Kitsaun and I began ballet and tap when I was five and she was seven. We wore black Danskin leotards with soft pink leather ballet slippers and changed to shiny black patent-leather tap shoes to make noise. Kitsaun's steps were fluid and her long arms graceful, and I tried to mimic her grace. We started piano a few years later; it was easier for me to reach my fingers across the keys than move my feet, so I stopped dancing. Kitsaun stopped piano, and we flew after different dreams.

Even at thirteen, I hoped Arnzy and I would date when I was older. I imagined him driving me to dances and kissing me in the front seat of his car. My heart stirred with longings.

I picked up my Nancy Drew mystery, knowing that I should get my schoolbooks off the dinette table and start my homework before Mom got home. Mom worked downtown at her government job until five o'clock, but she always called to check in by four. Dad's voice sang from the living room, "What a life, trying to live without you."

I listened to his beautiful tone, so soothing to my life. Dad's music drifted through every room of our house; his love of jazz became a living expression of our emotions and spilled from baseboards and light fixtures every moment we were awake. Mom sang, too—soft gospel tunes when she cooked and while we fell asleep; hymns that told us "everything would be all right by and by." Art Tatum, Louie, Miles, and Billie serenaded us from our Motorola record player. I loved to take the twelve-inch black plastic discs from their waxed-paper shells, hold them by their edges until they were around the steel pin on the turntable, and then gently drop the stylus between the grooves. When I was home alone I would sing along with Morgana King and Nina Simone, standing in front of our picture window—the living room my stage, our view to San Francisco Bay my audience. I belted out ballads, hitting high notes with outstretched arms and grinding out low ones with a swing of my hips. I ended every song with a bow, as though imaginary fans were wildly applauding.

One of Dad's most famous songs, "SK Blues," was written before I was born. We had it on a 78 rpm record along with Dad's other recordings. Dad sang, "Give me back that wig I bought you; let your head go bald." The song had become a hit, and Dad had traveled with his sextet, playing in nightclubs and supper clubs. Mom told Kitsaun and me that Dad stopped touring when we were born—to be at home with us. She said that when Dad's music was popular in the 1940s, he left hundred-dollar bills on top of their dresser. Now, Mom supported the family with her job at Social Security as a claims adjuster. I had never seen a hundred-dollar bill.

Many Friday nights Mom took us to the Emporium in Stonestown, where she charged dinner for us in the cafeteria. She said she put things on credit until her check from work would come. She was stretching our money so that Kitsaun and I could take lessons in the arts.

My first piano lessons were with Ms. Gaynor. I walked over the hill to her house with a small transistor radio in my hand, a white plastic earphone plugged into my ear as I listened to Aretha Franklin, Jerry Butler, and the Temptations on the R & B station, KDIA. Gold stars collected on my sheet music, even when I did not practice during the week. I did not know whether I was a natural talent or Ms. Gaynor was hard of hearing.

I progressed to classes at the Conservatory of Music, on Nineteenth Avenue, which required more practice and discipline. I studied music theory along with classical piano in halls that smelled of old sheet music and resin. Behind classroom doors, muffled notes of concertos, minuets, and scales were repeated over and over until perfection was touched for one moment. My teacher wound the metronome on top of the Steinway, willing me to play in time. Practice became a requirement for my keeping up; and Mom sat and listened to my songs in the evening after dinner.

Dad's minor chords and red-hot rhythms were a continuous backdrop to our lives—touching our thoughts, coloring our perspectives. He played his blond, hollow-body guitar for hours, running his wide hands up and down the steel strings, practicing scales or strumming along with Wes Montgomery and Kenny Burrell. While the news on TV showed civil rights demonstrators mowed down by fire hoses, he played his "box," minor chords and slow dirges rising from his fingers. My teenage body shook in anger and terror as Bull Connor and George Wallace shouted brutal orders against innocent people with brown skin like mine. Dad's fingers kept moving on his guitar strings. His tunes created a safe shelter I could hide within. I slept in the cradle of his notes in the midst of a harsh world.

3

A Teen in the Sixties

1963

✳

*T*he front door slammed, reverberating throughout the house. Kitsaun's voice mingled with Dad's, and I heard her drop her books on the table in the kitchen. "I am so mad!" she growled.

I jumped off my bed and ran to the hall. "What happened?"

"We're graduating in four weeks. And now, I'm the only one in my whole class going to Lowell. Carol was going, but now she's thinking of going to Balboa." Balboa was right next to our junior high, James Denman, which was next to San Miguel Elementary. They were the local schools everyone attended, on the edge of the Mission District and our Ingleside neighborhood. Lowell was an academic high school where only the best students went, and you had to have a 3.5 GPA to get in.

"Mom says you'll love Lowell," I said. "The teachers are better, and the campus is prettier than Bal."

Kitsaun shrugged and went downstairs to her room. After a few minutes I heard the whir of her sewing machine. A flawless seamstress, she had made my cheerleading outfit and my orchestra uniform, and she'd helped me finish my apron for homemaking class so that I would not get an F. It took me longer to hand-sew the turquoise rickrack edging around the hem than it took Kitsaun to make the whole apron.

Kitsaun graduated junior high on February 1, 1963. She bravely left her friends to attend Lowell and eased into new friendships. She began dating a fullback on the junior varsity football team, and never regretted that she didn't go to Bal. Two years later, I graduated junior high and followed her to Lowell because she loved it so much. I wore my hair rolled into a flip like Marlo Thomas on *That Girl*. Every morning, Kitsaun and I took the bus together, getting off at Stonestown, and walked to the campus down a street lined with eucalyptus trees. Karmen went to Balboa, so I plied fresh waters while holding on to Kitsaun and her friends. Karmen and I spent Saturdays walking from our street to West Portal to buy ice-cream cones at Baskin-Robbins. We sat on the giant sundial on Entrada Court, licking our cones and sharing high school stories. We could never figure out how the shadow hitting the Roman numerals on the concrete circle could tell us what the time was. We would stop at Saint Emydius to pray, Karmen laying a lace hanky on her head as we entered the dark Catholic church. Before entering the pew, I knelt as Karmen did, and savored the silence and vanilla smell of candles burning in rows along the sidewall. The cool, quiet sanctuary gave me a sense of God's presence and a feeling of completeness. In prayer and silence, I felt whole and strong from within.

In my sophomore year I put away my viola to sing in Lowell's choir, maybe because Karmen no longer was next to me as first chair, second violin. Our class was at 7:30 A.M. and Kit-saun and I both sang tenor, a low part for some girls but just right for our vocal register. The sound of Dad's pure, clear voice reverberated in my head as I sang. Sometimes I felt as though his voice were coming from inside me. I heard his distinct enunci-ation of vowels, the way his mouth closed around every sound. Mr. Blackburn taught choir like a dictator, yelling at us if we sang a wrong note. But when harmonies wafted from our rounded mouths, my heart opened wide, carrying pieces of me out into the world. At the end of our concerts, we held candles and stood around the perimeter of the auditorium, singing, "The Lord Bless You and Keep You." We stood—soprano, alto, tenor, and bass—having to hold on to our intonation and part with great effort, our notes hanging in the air right before us. Sometimes I cried: the feeling of God stirring inside my body, too immense to hold. I could feel a celestial joining of who I was with what I learned about God's Spirit in church; and I knew that there was blessing possible through praying and grace. It spun as an ache in my chest, but a good ache that made me long to be full of the vibrating warmth.

My crush on Arnzy turned into a crush on our sophomore class president, Jimmy, and then Calvin, a star halfback on the football team of a rival school. Calvin's father was a minister, and Calvin's Sundays, like mine, were spent in church. He read the Bible and studied scriptures. At his church, the congrega-tion prayed out loud as we did in our Oakland church. I ob-served a great difference between our Pentecostal church and the other black churches in my neighborhood and the Catholic and Lutheran worship services. Karmen's church listened to the priest and repeated his words. We did that at the Lutheran service, too. But most of my childhood had been spent at Christ Holy Sanctified, where we spoke out and praised God from what we felt inside. People testified out loud, during the service, about the manifestation of God's work in their lives. When I kneeled at night to pray before sleep, I thought of all that had troubled me or touched me, and I spoke out loud to God, never doubting He listened. Karmen had a little book that she read from, and she said a Hail Mary prayer from memory. I saw nothing wrong with either of the methods, but I'm glad I learned to be spontaneous with Spirit. There's nothing as comforting as being able to pray when I'm not sure of what's lurking around my soul, or when I'm thankful for a benevolent gesture from life.

Jimmy and Calvin—both sweet and polite—shook Dad's hand when they met him, and did not look shocked when they met Mom. Their bodies were electromagnetic fields drawing me to theirs. Dad scared boys when they would call; he answered the phone, "Yeah"—his tone impatient and cold, daring them to speak. If they were courageous enough to ask for me, we would talk on the phone until Mom told me to hang up and finish my homework. Dad allowed me to go out on dates when I was sixteen, my junior year of high school.

Gloria Averbuch and Luci Li were my best friends. We were song girls together, which was the sophisticated name for cheerleaders, and we spent Friday nights after football games at Luci's house in Forest Hills. Finally, Dad trusted another family and allowed me to spend the night. Luci's father was a doctor, she had three siblings, and her house smelled of crisp greens her mother fried with chicken in a wok. During our sleepovers, we talked about girls we knew who were getting birth control pills from Planned Parenthood and were sleeping with their boyfriends. My Pentecostal upbringing instructed us to wait until marriage to have sex, and these teachings put the fear of God's retribution in me, so I didn't consider sex a possibility. But I was curious to know how it would feel and what really happened when you took your clothes off and lay with a boy. The girls we knew and talked with in the school hallways who were having sex had so much more confidence in their bodies than I had. Sex practically crawled off the bodies of boys in their football uniforms, girls in shorter and shorter skirts, and teens just like us locked in embraces right on the street.

Gloria, Luci, and I lay on the U-shaped couch in Luci's living room, waiting for her brothers to go to bed, and clutched pillows to our chests, whispering about getting in trouble at school and everything that affected our lives. Gloria cried, telling us about her mother's mental breakdown, her anger rappelling off the walls, our hearts openly heaving with hers in pain. Gloria lived with her dad, a journalist with the *San Francisco Chronicle,* while her mom moved in and out of institutions. I told Luci and Gloria about Chris Anderson, the tall blond girl who had been my friend until she took me to her house on the edge of exclusive Saint Francis Woods. Mrs. Anderson came into the kitchen where Chris and I had our heads in the refrigerator. Chris introduced us, and her mother looked tersely from her daughter to me and then walked out of the room. I felt a chill of disdain and rejection and wanted to run from the house, but Chris took me to her room, where we played music.

I put her mother's rudeness out of my mind until my mom picked me up. The next morning at school, Chris's eyes were red as she told me her mom had forbade her to see me because I was not white. My heart was slashed with the familiar dagger of racism—its ignorant, tormenting recurrence in my life: being shut out, denied access because of my skin. "I thought Chris was my friend," I told Gloria and Luci, "but she didn't know how to stand up to her mother's racism or tell her how wrong she was." My method of coping was to withdraw from anyone who did not fight prejudice. It was too painful for me to endure alone. I never felt close to Chris after that. Mom told me that Grandmother King said to try your best to be a friend and to do what is right in life, but if people reject you, walk away.

After my story, Gloria stopped crying for herself and got mad. She was a loyal friend who could fight because she grew up being rejected, too—for her mother's lack of lucidity, for being Jewish. She lived in the Haight, a mixed neighborhood where she had played with kids of different ethnicities all her life. Gloria was warm, intense, and filled with daring. Her outrage made me feel loved. It had never occurred to me to exclude another person for their ethnicity or religion—not ever.

Luci turned on the radio and began dancing to lift our mood. Soon we were doing the Pony to the Young Rascals and the Swim to Bobby Freeman, laughing as we made faces in the sliding-glass door that reflected our forms. Our friendship encompassed a world of differences. We studied hard, but hung out, too. Sometimes Gloria and I hitchhiked from Lowell to her house in Upper Haight, unafraid of strangers and maybe to prove we were not just pom-pom-toting song girls. We listened to Joni Mitchell records and walked to Haight and Cole, where hippies sat cross-legged on the sidewalk, smoking weed and burning incense to cover the smell. We bought long, flowing skirts at a secondhand store and wore them on weekends, without shoes. We were never "flower children," but we were searching for who we wanted to become, and a part of us admired hippies, who were rebellious and free.

San Francisco, April 4, 1968

I rode the "Route 28 19th Avenue" bus home from school. Two women in front of me talked in low voices, and I heard the words "murdered" and "it's a shame." Sidewalks were empty, and I wondered what was causing the tension I felt in the air. I pulled the rubber cord to buzz the driver before my stop, gathered my books, jumped off the bus, and ran up the street to our house.

Dad stood in the living room, looking down at the TV. A newscaster said Martin Luther King, Jr., had been shot and killed on a motel balcony in Memphis, Tennessee. I looked at Dad. He stared at the screen, his hands rolled into fists at his sides. I slid my books onto the coffee table. Dad turned to me, shaking his head from side to side. "He should never have gotten involved in that garbage strike."

I ran to my room, the TV image of Dr. King lying on the ground scorched in my eyes. I had never suffered the torturous racism of the South, never had to ride in the back of the bus unless I wanted to; but I had seen the sneers and stares of hatred because of our family's mixed color. Dad had told a story of

Grandmother being shot in the stomach by white ranchers in Oroville, California. After moving from Louisiana, she and Grandfather had built a church in the small mountain town; they hoped to be free of the segregation and oppression of the South. White ranchers burned down the first church, trying to run them out; then the ranchers fired shotguns into the second building during Sunday morning worship. Grandmother was struck while she played her tambourine, the hate-filled ranchers riding off as she lay on the floor bleeding. She survived, and the family moved to Oakland, constructing a new church on Seventh Street where the black community welcomed all races to worship a colorless God.

When Mom and Dad married, interracial marriage was illegal in California. They drove to Seattle to marry, where anti-miscegenation laws had been abolished. Mom was spit on by a cab driver when she and Dad were together in Chicago. She was followed by San Francisco police officers on her way to work when she was pregnant with me because they were watching for Dad's participation in smoking weed at after-hours jam sessions. More than once Dad fought when someone "called him out of his name," as he would politely mask the word "nigger" to Kitsaun and me.

Frustrated and furious, I kicked my desk chair. I grabbed my stuffed dog and buried my face in his matted fur, crying, "Why? Why?" My body jerked and twisted, overtaken with anguish and despair. When would we win the struggle for equality? With Dr. King's death, integration seemed a faraway dream.

Kitsaun and I began attending rallies around the city, listening to Stokely Carmichael, a leader of SNCC (Student Nonviolent Coordinating Committee) who described the power of sit-ins and passive resistance. Members of the Black Panther Party shouted out that racism could not be conquered with passive nonviolence. We listened to Kathleen Cleaver, seeing ourselves in her light brown skin and wanting her bush-like Afro. She preached against the institutional racism that was killing black men and women. Winds of change rumbled through me, jostling my old beliefs in nonviolence. The Oakland and Los Angeles police departments declared war on Huey Newton and his army of revolutionaries. Maybe we would not be able to overcome four hundred years of slavery and hatred by turning the other cheek.

Kitsaun graduated from Lowell and attended San Francisco City College. In her second semester, she met Jake, an actor who was leader of the on-campus Black Panther Party. He was a beautiful, dark-skinned black man with a wide Afro, and a mustache curling over his full lips, which he moistened often with his tongue. Jake and his friends invited us to a meeting in the East Bay where Black Panthers would demonstrate how to use guns. I found an excuse not to go, my rhetoric stronger than my nerves, and Kitsaun accompanied her new friends, absorbing the revolutionary vernacular but never brandishing violence as a solution to racism.

I visited Kitsaun at Jake's house a few blocks from ours. The front room and kitchen were filled with people talking and eating, Afro to Afro, and smoking fat joints of marijuana. I did not want to sit around discussing the revolution with people stoned out of their minds, so I left. Drugs were of no interest to me. I had no desire to alter the way I saw reality.

In my senior year at Lowell, I applied to Cal State in San Francisco and also to Dominguez Hills in Southern California. It was 1968, and students at colleges around the nation were staging demonstrations against the Vietnam War and against good-old-boy politics that kept women and people of color down. The San Francisco State campus was a few blocks from Lowell, and we witnessed students closing it down to demand a school of ethnic studies and expanded black studies and Asian studies departments. College president S. I. Hayakawa was locked in his administrative office until riot police arrested the demonstrators. This forceful move by students shook up the establishment and made a huge impression on me. I realized the impact my generation could have on our country's outdated politics. The rebellion was successful, and the courses were added to the university's curriculum.

My plan was to study black history, as well as major in English. Maybe I would be a teacher as I had pretended so many times as a child when my stuffed animals were my students. I was accepted at San Francisco State and at Cal State Dominguez Hills outside Los Angeles. I chose Dominguez Hills because my uncle Joe had helped develop the creative writing department there.

Calvin and I double-dated with Luci and her boyfriend for the senior prom. Luci confided in me that she and her date were having sex. I felt like a dolt, inexperienced and prudish, but I did not really want to sleep with Calvin. I liked him, but I knew our romance would end with high school. After the prom, Calvin and I made out against the wall in my living room. He was barely taller than I was, so I scooted down to lift my face to his, as they did in the movies. He pressed his body against mine and I felt hardness in his pants, but I never let my guard down. At any moment Dad could have walked in and caught us. I knew that if he had yelled at me for merely talking with a boy from up the street, he'd kill a boy whose lips and body were glued to mine. Besides, I was waiting to make love when I would be swept off my feet. I no longer felt I had to wait until marriage. It was 1969, and free love was born in San Francisco. I did not even think about marriage. The world was out there for my discovery without boundaries or limits.

Graduation day, I lined up with my class in the vestibule of the Masonic Auditorium, the orchestra tuning their instruments in the pit. As "Pomp and Circumstance" began, sadness, like a tincture in my heart, mixed with my excitement to be moving on. After the ceremony, I stood with Luci and Gloria as our parents snapped photographs, the three of us wiping tears from our cheeks.

4

Fringe and Fur

I found summer work at Pacific Bell Telephone Company as a long-distance operator and prepared for my coming independence. I loved plugging the cords into the outlets and placing calls around the United States and internationally, connecting people I did not know and could not see to faraway voices as I reached out to the unknown, like I was reaching into my own unknown future by leaving home to attend college. Wanting to grow up and meet new people, I talked to the adults working my shift and pretended I was responsible and independent, too. My voice sounded capable and mature as I connected faceless people together through thick, black wires. People called my supervisors and praised my efficiency, and I won commendations for my service. Kitsaun thought that was pretty funny; I always tried so hard to please—but she was proud of me and showed my awards to anyone who came over to visit.

One afternoon, on my walk up Harold Avenue after work, absorbed in thoughts about living on my own and going to college, a loud honk beside me made me jump. In the middle of the street, a two-toned beige camper lurched to a halt and a tall, cinnamon brown man with dark, curly hair and a wide, impish grin jumped out.

Leaving the engine running and the door wide open, he swaggered toward me, like a pirate caught on dry land. His berry-black eyes scanned my body from head to toe. He wore butter-yellow leather knickers with two-inch fringe hanging down the sides. Furry brown boots came up to his knees. The fringe on his black leather jacket swung as he walked. He looked completely out of place, his clothes a colorful plume against the cement and asphalt of Harold Avenue.

As he came closer, my heart boomed in my chest. It was Sly Stone. I had just seen him on *The Ed Sullivan Show* with his band, Sly and the Family Stone, a few Sundays ago. Now he stood in my path and stretched his arms up to the sky, as if to pounce on me like a wild cat. His clothing was a little bit Haight-Ashbury, with Fillmore Street mixed in—the black neighborhood where soul food and holiness churches shared space with Black Muslims baking bean pies and saying *Ah Salaam Alakaam* (peace be unto you) and pimps sending women out to work.

"Who are you?" he asked in a deep baritone. He walked around me in a circle, looking me over with a smile and glimmering eyes. "Do you live around here? You've gotta go out with me."

Moisture beaded on my upper lip; a warm blush rose from my neck to my cheeks. I could not find a voice to answer him. He was standing too close. I leaned my body back to get some distance from his strong and overpowering energy. "I don't think so," I said.

"Let me drive you home," he drawled.

"That's okay. I just live up the hill." I wished my voice wouldn't shake so much.

"Then, at least give me your phone number. Please—" Sly moaned.

His eyes bore through me. I was accustomed to men making passes at me, even stopping their cars to tell me how "fine" I was. But I had never given anyone I had met on the street my phone number. I debated silently: *This is crazy! But it's Sly Stone. He's from San Francisco. You've seen him on TV. He's practically a neighbor.*

I stood there as he ran back to his camper, returning with a pen and paper, which he pushed into my hands. I wrote down my name and phone number. Our hands brushed, and I shivered at his touch. Beaming, he jumped back inside his camper, slammed the door, gave me a quick wave, and took off with a roar.

I turned and began walking up the hill, dazed. I worried I had done the wrong thing. What if he did call? What could I possibly say to someone famous?

In junior high, Kitsaun and I had gone with Karmen and her sister Johnette to see Johnny Mathis in concert. We loved his voice so much that we found his home out in the Avenues. We had spied on the house one evening until we saw lights. Holding hands and giggling, we rang the doorbell, squealing with delight when the door opened. Mr. Mathis answered and told us his son was out. That was the only musician I had been in love with. Earl Fatha Hines had lived in our neighborhood, but he was old, and Dad never brought his musician-friends home. He kept his music world separate from us. Mom said because the musicians depended on Dad, calling to borrow money, often drunk, Dad didn't want drummers and trumpet players, bassists or piano men around his daughters or wife.

When I walked in our front door, the phone was ringing.

Kitsaun called, "Deb, it's for you." When she handed me the phone, her wide-open eyes and pursed lips formed a question mark.

"Hello?"

"This is Sly. Let's go out tonight." His voice was like a DJ on the radio, smooth and sure.

"I can't believe you called. But, I can't go out tonight. I have to work tomorrow."

"Okay. When?"

"Maybe Friday."

"Good. What's the number of your house? I'll pick you up at seven."

I told him. He hung up. Had I said yes? He was coming here Friday. I put the receiver back and leaned against the wall.

Kitsaun stood outside the kitchen door. "Who was that?" she asked.

I started talking as we walked to my room.

"Whoa. Slow down."

We sat on my bed, and I recounted every second from the horn honk. It seemed like a dream. Sly Stone had asked me out. Kitsaun and I tried to think of all the songs we knew by his band, Sly and the Family Stone. Laughing and screaming, we danced around the room. "Different strokes for different folks. So on and so on . . . Shoobey, doobey doo bah . . . I-I-I am everyday people."

Kitsaun flopped into the chair by my desk. She patted the edges of her rounded hair, now puffed out into an Afro like Kathleen Cleaver's. "Dad will never allow you to see him! How old is he?"

"I don't know. I won't tell Dad who I'm going out with until he gets here," I said, planning. "I'm eighteen, you know."

Kitsaun rolled her eyes toward the ceiling. "Good luck," she called, shaking her butt and swinging her arms over her head as she danced out of my bedroom.

I swung the door closed and lay back on my pillow. Sly's eyes had sparkled, almost teasing me. I rolled every word he had said over my tongue. They tingled through my body and made me want to laugh out loud.

All day Friday, I was nervous. Had I been crazy to say yes to a date with a man who seemed so different from me? My heart jumped each time I thought of seeing him again. I plugged my headset into the switchboard and answered, "Operator. May I help you?" But I couldn't wait for my shift to end.

At home, I tried on outfit after outfit, my wardrobe in a pile on the floor in front of my closet. I didn't know what to wear to go out with Sly Stone. My clothes were fine for high school dances, but I was going out with an adult—and one whose sense of style obviously outshone mine. My dressy clothes were fine for church, but even my fancy graduation dress was a prim, high-neck number. I finally decided on a gold gauzy top over brown bell-bottom cords, not daring, but at least hip. My hair, tied back with a purple scarf, fell in smooth waves down my back.

Dad asked, "Who did you say you were going out with?"

"Sly Stone, Dad."

"You mean that character with big hair and fur boots? Looks like a clown?"

"Dad!" At least he hadn't said I couldn't go.

By 6:45 P.M., I was pacing the living room. A loud engine rumbled outside. I peeked out the front window. The longest, shiniest car I had ever seen was in the street by our driveway. It looked like the cars in gangster movies. Low and sleek, it was pale yellow with four chrome pipes hooked from the side fenders to the vented hood. The black canvas convertible top had an opaque plastic window in the back. The driver's door opened. I jumped back from the window. Sly rang the bell. *Will he hear my heart pounding?* I opened the door.

"Hi," I said, motioning for him to come in.

He smiled at me and bounced and bobbed like a boxer. He wore skintight brown leather pants, a silky, purple, V-necked shirt, and sunglasses that covered half his face. "Let's go," he said.

"I'm going," I yelled back into the house. I heard footsteps heading toward us and shrugged my shoulders: He would have to meet my parents.

Mom still wore her dress from work, knowing I was going out. She stood next to me and looked Sly over from bushy head to leather boots. "Mom, this is Sly."

"Hello," she said, folding her thin arms across her stomach.

Sly added, "Sylvester Stewart, Mrs. King. Nice to make your acquaintance."

Dad came up from behind Mom. His cheekbones were sharp; his lips closed. Not a hint of a smile. "Dad, this is Sly. This is my father, Saunders King."

Dad pumped Sly's hand, glared into his eyes, grunted, and walked to the living room. Dad stared out the window as he spoke: "Where do your folks live?"

"On Urbano, sir, about half a mile away."

"Have her home by midnight."

Sly grabbed my hand, pulled me through the threshold, and we ran down the stairs to the roadster. He opened my door, and I sank into the deep leather seat as he ran around the back of the car, opened his door, and jumped in. I looked up and saw Dad's face in the window, grim, without the pretense of a smile. Disapproval and wariness were in his eyes, but I put my parents out of my mind when I turned to my date.

Sly tipped his head and smiled wide. He turned the key in the ignition. The engine growled, and we took off in a leap, my head jerking back on the headrest. My heart idled as high as the motor. Sly maneuvered the car onto Ocean Avenue, turning right toward the freeway. I felt the chill from the fog out on Ocean Beach. I felt small, out of place in the luxury car, next to Sly in his expensive clothing.

"Where would you like to go?" His voice was deep, his words articulate. He cocked his head and peered at me from above his shades.

"I don't care." I tried to keep my eyes on the road, but I kept staring at him. His skin was dark and moist, like clay before you mold it. His hair was two different textures: tight black spirals at the root, rising into loopy curls that sat loosely all over his head.

"What kind of car is this?" I asked.

"A Cord Duesenberg—it's made of Fiberglas. There are only a few in America."

"Where are you from? You sound like you have a Southern accent."

He laughed, a big, boisterous laugh. When I looked at him, he pointed his finger at me, lowered his sunglasses, and winked. I noticed his teeth were very square. "You ask a lot of questions," he said. "My people are from Texas. Are you hungry?"

"Not really."

"Then we'll just drive," he said in that dreamy voice.

I sat back as he wound the car through city streets. I peeked at him as he drove, fidgeting with cassettes, looking for one he wanted to hear. On his left pinkie he wore a thick gold ring with a diamond set in the center. I looked down at my own light brown hands, fingers long and slim, perfect for playing piano, my parents always said.

San Francisco sparkled with a luminescence that came from the sun touching the bay and bouncing back to caress windows and faces. We drove to Coit Tower, which looks out over the pastel buildings that curve up and down Telegraph Hill. Sly parked and came around to open my door. We walked to the stone wall surrounding the parking lot and looked out at the city.

Sly asked, "What do you do? You're so beautiful. Are you a model?" He took my hand and looked in my eyes.

"No." I laughed. "I modeled once for a friend who designs clothes. Now I work at the phone company, but I'm going to college in September—Cal State Dominguez Hills, outside Los

Angeles. And you?" I pulled my hand from his and covered my face. "Oh, God! That was so stupid. I know what you do."

"Well, I'm a musician, a songwriter. I play piano, guitar, and drums. I used to be a DJ at KFRC. My sister Rose and my brother, Freddy, are in my band. I have a little sister, 'Vet,' and an older sister, Loretta."

"I have an older sister, Kitsaun. My dad's a musician. My mom works for Social Security."

"Your dad looks pretty tough." Sly put his arm around my shoulder. "My dad, KC, is our road manager." He pushed his leg against mine, his leather pants straining at the seams. Every cell in my body was awake.

Sly took my hand and led me back to the car. As I stood beside the Cord, he leaned against me, pressing his lips on mine in a long, wet kiss. He stood back, grinning, and I collapsed into my seat. He jumped into his seat like an elf, pulled up his pants leg, and removed a small cigarette from his boot. He lit the joint and passed it to me.

"No, thanks. I don't smoke." So many people had tried to get me to smoke pot. I hated the smell, the choking fumes, and the spacey way people talked after they did it. He shook his head, laughed, took a few puffs, and snuffed it out before returning it to its hiding place. "You're something. Different . . . different." He turned on the engine. "Now I'm hungry." He chuckled. "I want to take you to this oyster place on Polk Street. It's a gas."

We roared down the hill, drove to Polk Street, and parked. Sly held my arm tightly as we strode down the sidewalk. We sat at the counter, and he ordered a dozen raw oysters in shells with hot sauce. I ordered soup. I had never even seen a raw oyster up close, much less thought of eating one, but Sly was determined I try. The waiter set a silver tray on a pedestal with opened gray shells piled on rocks of ice. Prying my lips apart, Sly slipped a cold, slimy mollusk onto my tongue. As it wiggled down my throat, I tried not to gag.

Sly was on, joking with the waiters and me. They knew him by name and came over every few minutes. Sly bantered with the men, making rhymes of their names. "Jim, you're so slim. Harry, please don't tarry." They laughed together, and I ordered root beer to burn away the oyster taste.

Sly picked up the bill. He reached inside his boot, pulled out a roll of cash, and slapped down a fifty.

We drove noisily up my street a few minutes before midnight. "Thank you for taking me out. It was fun." Sly leaned over me, looking up at our living room window. He kissed my cheek, then put both of his hands on my face and turned me full into his lips. "Good night," he said. "I'll call you."

I stepped out of the car, stood back, and watched Sly Stone turn his Cord around and blast off down the street. I sat on the steps outside our simple house. What a night. Sly had so much power. I felt like a doll in his hands—like he was playing with me, too.

I opened the front door. "Deb?" Dad was awake.

"Yes, Dad, I'm home," I answered, floating into my room. My mind buzzed with Sly's big face, his words. He had a way of holding my eyes in his gaze for a moment, then looking away with a chuckle. Maybe that was the weed. Too thrilled to sleep, I lay on top of my bed, a smile across my face.

Sly called again, and we went out. He was different from

anyone I had ever known—twenty-five years old and traveled, he played his newest songs for me. I was overcome by his world. He whispered in my ear, and held me close to him when we walked, possessive of me in a way that made me feel special, beautiful. When he called, I dropped whatever I was doing to wait for him to pick me up. My plan was to work through summer, then pack for Cal State Dominguez Hills, where I would move on campus to begin classes at the end of September. Being with Sly took over my life, and I didn't make time to be with my friends or family. He took me to his house on Urbano Drive, where he lived with his parents, Mama and KC. Sly had the whole bottom floor of the house. His Great Dane, Stoner, liked me right away, and I would sit on the couch and pet him while Sly played the piano, writing lyrics on yellow tablets and setting notes and chords onto staff paper. His sister Rose and his brother Freddy would come by and hang out with us, then we would go upstairs to see Mama and KC.

Greg Errico, the drummer, would also hang out. The downstairs had a drum set and amplifiers, guitars, bass, and Hammond B3 organ. Mama made the group play softly because of the neighbors. Mama was usually in the kitchen cooking, or sitting at the table in the window, reading her Bible. She was sweet, with a twinkle in her eyes. Her heavy body moved slowly, and Sly danced around her, running back downstairs, where she never went. I would sit with her and answer her questions about my family and church.

Most evenings, Sly and I ended up kissing on his bed, me submerged under his wiry body. I made it clear that I wasn't ready to sleep with him, but his charm was ravishing my heart;

and each time we lay together, I knew my resolve would eventually melt. Lying with him was like being rolled up in a web of heat and feelings, and when he touched me, I wanted more. But I always pulled away as he began moving my blouse up my waist or putting his hands too far down my pants. He would laugh, but sit back, and we would talk. I didn't ask him if he had a girlfriend. Back then I was so innocent, it never occurred to me he would spend so much time with me and be involved with other women. I wonder if Sly knew how unsuspicious and naive I was. I told him I had broken up with Calvin, who was at the University of Washington on a football scholarship, in his own cloud of celebrity. Mom told me Calvin called sometimes, but I was never home.

I spent time with Karmen, who was also working downtown, and talked to Luci and Gloria, who were missing me because I was spending so much time with Sly and who wanted to know what he was like. We met at Luci's as we always had, perched on stools in her kitchen, and I told them about Sly's house, his camper, the music he composed. They listened as if caught in the same spell I was in.

Driving up Market Street one afternoon in late July, Sly said, "The band is going to New York next week. Why don't you come with me?"

"New York?" I had been to New York two weeks in June, when Kitsaun had been there to visit her friend Frank. Would Mom and Dad let me go with Sly? I would die to go. "I don't know," I said. "I'm still working."

"Come on, baby." Sly looked over at me and took a hand off the steering wheel to touch my neck. "We're going to play a show in Upstate New York on a farm—some big festival." Sly put on his puppy dog look, the one he'd worn when he first had jumped out of his camper.

"I'll try," I said, acting casual, as though I were asked to go to New York every day. "When are you leaving?"

I imagined being in New York with Sly twenty-four hours a day and thought of what that meant for our relationship. I would have to get birth control pills. There was no way Sly was only going to keep making out with me, and I *wanted* to sleep with him.

All night I practiced telling Mom and Dad that Sly had asked me to go to New York. I made up ways to ask them if it was all right. In the end, I was too afraid they would forbid me to go, so I didn't bring it up, much less ask their permission. I confided in Kitsaun. She listened to my reasons for wanting to go, a wistful look on her face.

"Oh, God. New York is wonderful. You have to go! Just don't tell them," she said. "It's only for a few days. I'll think of something to say after you're gone."

The next afternoon, I left work early and took the bus to Fillmore and Clay to Planned Parenthood. I went home with pamphlets on birth control and a plastic disc with pills.

Sly bought me a prepaid ticket. He told me he would be waiting at the gate. He wouldn't let me say I wasn't coming. Clearly he expected me to work everything out and be there.

I packed a small suitcase with clothes for four days. The morning of the flight I got ready for work as usual. Mom and I had the habit of riding the streetcar downtown together. This morning I dragged out the process of getting dressed and putting on my mascara. Mom called from the kitchen, "Deb, it's time to go. Are you ready?"

My hands were sweating. "Almost, Mom."

I sat in the bathroom on the end of the tub, willing her to leave without me. Dad was still in bed. I knew he was awake but that he wouldn't get up for another hour. He read the morning paper or "rested his eyes" until we all left.

Finally, Mom said, "I'm going to be late. I'll see you tonight."

"Okay, Mom. Sorry."

When the door closed, I went into the kitchen, pulled out the phone book, and dialed Yellow Cab.

"Pick me up on the corner of Harold and Grafton," I whispered to the dispatcher, afraid to wait inside and have Dad see that I wasn't going to work after all.

On the drive to the airport, I reasoned with myself: *I'm eighteen, almost leaving home for college. I'm old enough to do this without asking.* But deep down inside I knew my actions were outrageous. I had never gone completely against my parents' wishes. Karmen and I had walked around the city barefoot after Dad forbade me to do it, but that was light compared to sneaking off to New York. I knew Mom and Dad would never have given me their blessing to go away with Sly. Dad said he had heard about Sly in the street. He called him a pimp. I loved my parents and knew they would always be there for me, but I had never felt like this about a man before. My desire to be with Sly fueled a passion that recklessly propelled me where it wished. I risked shattering my parents' trust to follow this man.

At the airport I paid the cab driver, grabbed my bag, and

got in line at the American Airlines ticket counter. I walked to the gate, clutching my ticket and my purse, and I stopped at a pay phone to call work and tell them I wasn't feeling well. Nervous, I approached the gate. There he was. Sly was sitting in the middle of the band members: a carousel of tight pants, pink-and-blue geometric shirts, and a sea of sunglasses. Greg wore a leopard-skin vest; Rose, a blond wig, too bright against her brown face. Next to the business travelers in their dark suits, Sly and the Family Stone looked like a circus. Sly was talking to Freddy, who looked just like him, but with a baby face. When Sly saw me, he stood and walked to me. "I knew you'd make it, baby," he said, pulling me into his arms.

5

Hallucinating

ꝼly introduced me to the band members I hadn't met: Jerry Martini, the saxophone player, his long, reddish hair hanging over his eyes; Larry Graham, the bass player, six feet five inches, dressed in a white suit and a tie, thin as a yardstick. Cynthia Robinson, the trumpet player—fair skin and soft Afro highlighting guarded amber eyes—reached her hand out to me. Rose, a familiar face, hugged me, making me feel like her sister, as she popped her gum. KC stood at the counter with everyone's tickets. I walked to him and said hello.

On board, we sat scattered through first class. Sly swayed down the aisle of the airplane and sat on the arm of Larry's seat, leaning over his conked hair. Larry handed Sly a large book; I could see the title: *The World of Dogs*.

I pushed the round silver button to recline my seat and breathed deeply. I had made it. A flight attendant leaned over. "Champagne, mimosa, or orange juice?"

"Orange juice, thank you." I couldn't believe she was offering me alcohol. She didn't know I was only eighteen, but I was not about to get drunk on a plane.

Close to the thrill I felt in getting away without Mom and Dad knowing sat a gnawing worry about how they would react when I did not come home from work. Would Kitsaun be able to appease Mom and Dad, or would they call the police to bring me back? The flight attendant offered me a magazine, and I buried my concerns in *Glamour*. Sly's voice carried loudly through the first-class cabin. When I looked up, his eyes were on me. I thought about what a puzzle he was. He was obviously smart, but acted like a thug rather than intelligent in front of others. Since we had met, I had come to respect his poetry, his view of the world through his songs. Like Bob Dylan, a spokesman for social change for our generation, Sly's lyrics cleverly touted racial harmony, acceptance of those different from the mainstream, and standing up for one's beliefs even when the whole world tried to tell you that you were wrong. He was charismatic and sparkled with energy. When he spoke, his voice hummed, animated with laughter. I loved being near him when he captured melodies on the piano, singing new lyrics.

He sat in the seat beside me with the book in his hands and bent his head close to mine. My skin grew hot. "You're like music," he breathed, "new melodies I've got to play. We're going to have fun. 'Hot Fun in the Summertime,' " he said, quoting the title of the single the band had just released. He threw his head back, laughed, and opened the dog book. "What do you think of a bulldog?"

I looked at the photo of a short, stocky dog, swaybacked

with loose jowls. "Hmm. Pretty ugly. We always had German shepherds. Don't bulldogs get lockjaw?"

"Only if they get in a fight—I like that they lock onto the other dog," Sly said. "Stoner's getting old. I wanna get some new dogs. I'm thinking about a pit bull or a bulldog. Maybe both." He turned the pages, and I looked at the photos and read the descriptions with him.

We flew over Manhattan before landing, the Empire State Building's silver art deco spire glimmering in the distance. I followed Sly from the plane onto the Jetway. A thin wave of blistering air seeped through the rubber molding and scorched my arms and legs. I was glad I had worn my white knit sleeveless dress. It was perfect for the August heat. Outside the terminal, Sly guided me to a waiting limousine. I had never been in a limousine, and I looked around to see whether the other band members would get in first. The driver opened the door of the long black car, and Sly put his arm on my back, gently pushing me in. I saw Freddy, Rose, Larry, Jerry, Cynthia, and Greg— the rest of the band—climb into a long van. *Sly sets himself apart from his musicians.* I wondered how that made everyone else feel. I felt awkward—ostentatious—sitting in the back of a car that could hold six people. "Should I get my bag?" I asked.

Sly ducked into the limo and yelled to his father, "Dad, don't forget Debbie's suitcase!" The driver closed our door and climbed into the front seat. Sly said, "Let's go to Forty-second Street. I want to get a new tape deck." He raised the smoke-tinted window.

I had gone to Forty-second Street when I was in New York in June with Kitsaun. The shops with electronics piled high in windows, signs with "slashed prices" dangling, and dark-haired men hanging in doorways had intimidated me. Sly knocked on the glass. "Stop here."

He pulled me along from shop to shop, where he haggled with salespeople. I felt like a rag doll behind him, the limo cruising slowly along the curb beside us. In front of me, a tall, shapely black woman switched her hips from side to side as she walked in a skintight miniskirt, her hair curled in lustrous ringlets. Her arm was extended, holding a leash. "What a cute dog," I said, looking at the bundle of white fur she followed.

"Every working lady in New York has a dog," Sly said, his voice gruff. It took me a minute to realize what kind of work he meant. He pulled me closer to his side and tipped his head toward the woman. She smiled at him.

At the next store, Sly made his purchase. We were driven to the Hilton, Sly clutching his new tape deck and grinning. KC was waiting for us in the lobby. He stuttered, "I-I wish you had c-come on with the band. I-I was worried."

"Thanks, Dad." Sly patted him on the back, took the room key and my hand, and led me toward the elevator.

"Y-You have a press c-conference tomorrow, Sly," KC called after us. Sly raised his hand in the air as a response and pushed the button for the elevator. He turned to me and put his face nose-to-nose with mine. When the elevator doors opened, he almost carried me inside, not noticing other people or moving to let them on. At our floor, he put his arm around my shoulders, glanced at the key, and steered me down the hall.

Now that we were alone, my confidence waned. I wanted to leave my "good girl" lifestyle to be with Sly physically, but I was also scared. He opened the door to our room, waved his arm through the threshold, and bowed as I entered. I tried to drift easily into the room like a woman, but I felt awkward, like the inexperienced girl I was. The suite was large, grand. An overstuffed couch covered in bright yellow flowers sat between dark mahogany armchairs. Our suitcases were leaned against the wall. I scanned the room: A door led to a bathroom; the bed sat in front of a window; curtains were open; and New York City skyscrapers towered outside.

Sly set his tape deck on the coffee table and pulled up his pant leg.

Oh no, I thought. *Not the weed already.* I had been so preoccupied with thoughts about making love with Sly that I had forgotten about how he liked to get high. He reached into his sock and extracted a square piece of foil. Carefully unwrapping it, he took out two flat orange pills that looked like children's aspirin.

"Honey," he said, walking me to the couch, "you look like a scared rabbit." He held my hand open and put one of the pills on my palm. "This will relax you. I've taken it before. It's 'orange sunshine'—very mild."

"You mean acid?" I asked, my back stiffening. *What have I gotten myself into?* Sly's eyes were slits as he watched my reaction.

"Come on," he coaxed. "We'll take it together. It'll be fun. I won't let anything happen to you." I wanted to do what he asked, but I had heard nightmarish stories of people having bad trips on LSD, even dying.

Sly threw one pill in his mouth, swallowing it without water; then he ran to the bathroom and returned with a glass of water for me. I didn't have time to weigh the pros and cons of ingesting a drug I had never considered taking before this moment. *Will he really take care of me?* I believed he cared for me and wouldn't give me anything that would hurt me. I had resisted all offers of drugs, which began in high school. *I guess I can loosen up now.* Sly lifted my palm to my mouth. I set the pill on my tongue and swallowed the orange sunshine with a gulp of water, wondering what I was going to feel like and how long it would last.

"You said you write poetry. Did you bring any with you?"

I laughed, trying to cover my nervousness.

"What's so funny?"

"You know just what to say," I said.

"Your eyes are like sunsets," Sly said, moving toward me.

When our lips met, I was already inside his mind, his cologne, his arms. We lay together on the couch, kissing as we always had, but Sly's body pinned me. I tried to relax into the sheer pleasure of being alone with this man I had fallen in love with; I felt as though until now I had never before cared for anyone.

I knew the LSD was taking effect when the heavy, flowered drapes began waving back and forth against the pale yellow walls. The round-backed, Victorian chairs sat up straight. The ceiling vibrated as though there was an earthquake upstairs. Everywhere I looked, something moved. Sly's face had a green tint. I closed my eyes, fear gripping my stomach; but Sly caught me as I fell, his arms a net that encircled me.

The acid came on stronger, and my senses became more confused. Time was suspended above my head. Sly started to laugh; the sound seemed to come from my chest, then out of my mouth. We melted onto the couch, unable to stop giggling—tears running down our cheeks.

"Hey! Watch this," he said excitedly, and waved his hand in front of our faces, creating bright colors and golden light in a trail of mirrored hands that followed his. We sat for a long time just moving our hands back and forth.

"Let's go to bed," he drawled. Sly unbuttoned my dress as my head swirled round and round. I climbed under the covers, the smooth, soft sheets billowing and dancing on top of me as I settled on the pillow. Sly floated off toward the bathroom.

My senses were awake on the surface of my skin. The sheets became a landscape I was flying over. I felt as though I were hearing through my eyes and seeing with my touch; only my sense of smell seemed to be in the right place.

A tall, rectangular light shaft bled into the room when Sly opened the bathroom door. He spotted me gripping the covers up to my neck and smiled.

"What are you doing? Hiding?" His grin grew large, exaggerated, like an unfriendly cartoon character. The short laugh that burst from his gut held a sinister tone. *Is he laughing at me?* As he climbed into bed, the entire room began to undulate and vibrate over me. Holding me in his arms, Sly began to love me, rubbing my skin, rolling on top of me. The bed and room became a vista of tall mountaintops, my body riding the peaks, up and down, up and down. It was an exquisitely beautiful country: verdant, lush, tall grasses; sunny skies; snowcapped peaks. I thought I was in Austria, a place I had never been.

I could feel his body on mine, his legs around me, his pressure inside, but I was still flying. "Whew!" Sly cried out, holding me—landing. My legs shook. I kept my eyes shut, skimming down the mountaintops like a bird.

Sly rolled over and jumped up from the bed, pulled on his Jockeys, and walked to the phone. "We had better get something to eat."

Eat? I thought. I had just made love for the first time. It had felt heavenly, and my body was in a fluid form, open and alive. I looked around the room—the clock read 1:00 A.M. Five hours since we had taken the acid. I didn't think I could eat.

I watched Sly talk to room service. His thin, brown body was firm and taut. I could make out sinewy ripples of ligament and muscle beneath his skin. He hung up, put on his leather trousers, and bounced around the room like a toy with brand-new batteries.

A knock startled me. Sly jumped to open the door. A waiter rolled a table into the center of the room. I made sure every inch of my body was concealed. The silver domed plate covers looked like a miniature city. Sly signed the bill. As the man left the room, he looked back over his shoulder, leering at me.

"Come on," Sly beckoned. "You need to eat or that acid will tear up your stomach."

Obediently, I climbed out of my soft hiding place, the soles of my feet tickled by the carpet. I walked toward the bathroom, feeling exposed to the world, as though my veins and blood vessels were saying "hi" by reaching through my skin to wave. I closed the door behind me. My legs were wet with drops of blood trickling down my inner thigh. I had heard this could happen the first time you made love, but I felt like crying. My innocence ran from me. I mourned and rejoiced. I ran hot water on a washcloth and cleaned my body. A glance in the mirror showed a wild-eyed, bushy-haired animal looking back.

A robe lay folded on the counter. The terry cloth felt rough and nubby against my body as I wrapped it around me. I joined Sly at the table. Rainbow auras pulsated around him as I pulled out a chair. "You okay?" he asked.

I wanted to say, "I'm not sure. I'm not a virgin anymore." I wanted to cry and to celebrate. But I couldn't speak all that I felt. I answered, "Yes."

My senses continued to play in a dimension I had never experienced before. Every move of my hand still created flashes of colors. I picked up a fork, feeling its cold, steely hardness. The scrambled eggs Sly ate looked like lumpy puddles of plastic vomit. My stomach told me I couldn't possibly touch them. The bacon smelled delicious but seemed to be wiggling across the plate.

A wicker basket of toast, partially covered by a cloth napkin, looked like a baby in a blanket. Cautiously, I opened the white folds. Aaah. It looked just like bread, toasted. I gently took a piece, careful not to wave it too much. As I bit into it, the toast tasted like construction paper. I swallowed a gulp of orange juice and sat back in my chair.

Sly was happy tripping on his own. I thought of Mom and Dad, and tears sprang to my eyes. Sly, naked again except for his Jockey shorts, turned on his music, took out his guitar, and devoured the songs coming out of the small black speakers. I was alone to feel the waves of acid rise and fall on my mind. I wiped tears, but he didn't notice. My heart felt like an ocean in my chest, love and worry floating about.

Out of the corner of my eye, a Chinese vase began to levitate from the table. I looked at Sly and wondered whether he saw it, too. His eyes were shut, headphones covering his ears—he remained submerged in his sounds.

Shadows moved like clouds around the room, making large monster shapes that loomed above me. The bass guitar thumped from Sly's songs, echoing through his headphones, sounding like giant footsteps coming closer. I pushed the chair back and stumbled to the bed, sliding under the covers to hide from my LSD imagination. I shut my eyes hard. Rainbows and stars burst against my lids like bright fireworks. A thought passed through my mind to jump out a window to escape. I covered my head and recited the Lord's Prayer—over and over.

By five o'clock in the morning, Sly was asleep next to me. I kept my eyes closed, praying to follow him to dreamland.

The phone rang. I opened my eyes: Nothing was moving. The room was light. The clock said noon. Sly was by my side. I remembered the night before and smiled in the ecstatic knowledge that I had survived taking acid. I had also made love for the first time. The physical connection I felt with Sly was so different, as though my body were cabled to his with a silky desire. It felt glorious to not be afraid of making love.

Sly rolled toward the phone by the third ring. "Hello?" His voice was like tires over gravel. His eyes stayed closed. He put his arm around me and kissed my head.

I tensed. *Could it be Mom or Dad on the phone?* He said, "Okay," and hung up. "The press conference is moved to tomorrow. We have a free day."

We got up, dressed, and Sly said he wanted to take me to Greenwich Village. The doorman blew a silver whistle, summoning a taxi. My senses still were confused from the acid, and my vision was hazy, but Sly held me in his arms and I felt safe. The stores we passed reminded me of Haight Street, where Gloria and I traversed at home: records hanging in windows, psychedelic smoke shops, wild clothing. We were going to visit Jimi Hendrix at his Electric Lady studios on Eighth Street.

Jimi wasn't there. We walked through his dark, low-ceilinged recording world. A six-foot-long black console covered with knobs and buttons looked like a launch station for spacecraft. I watched the engineer slide back and forth in front of the soundboard, adjusting the music that wailed from the speakers. Sly raised his hand to the man, and we left. In high school Calvin had worshipped the guitarist and had danced in front of me, playing air guitar while he'd blasted "Wild Thing" on his record player.

We walked down Sixth Avenue, and Sly stopped in front of a shoe boutique. "Do you see any you like?" he asked.

I looked with desire—like a girl in front of an ice-cream store. A pair of ankle-strap platforms was calling out to me. *Should I say yes?* No man other than my father had ever bought me something to wear. "Those," I said, pointing.

We went inside, and I walked out wearing three-inch platforms the color of lime sherbet.

Our hotel room became a jam session. Jerry brought his sax, and Larry his bass; and Sly's creativity spilled from his hands onto his clavinet. The musicians jammed while I sat on the couch, listening. Jerry's reddish-brown hair, goatee, and freckles all lit up when he laughed. Cynthia came by with her trumpet; she wore a shirt with sleeves that hung to her knees, and when she raised her horn, her sleeves slid down her arms like limp pennants. She was soft-spoken but blew the trumpet powerfully. They played for hours.

All of the band members sat around the table, passing joint after joint. I still didn't like the smell, but I finally succumbed to taking the cigarette in my hand and inhaling. I coughed and coughed, choking on the smoke. The relaxed, loose feeling that tingled through my body made everything funny. Sly put the fire end of the joint in his mouth, inhaled the smoke, and then blew it into my mouth. He laid cocaine out on a mirror and snorted it through a short straw. I didn't want to try it. I had taken acid yesterday and smoked weed today. I had to hold on to some part of my previous conviction, didn't I? Sly wiped drips of white crystal from his nose, sniffing as though he had a cold. We stayed up until dawn.

My second day in New York, I called Mom and Dad to tell them I was fine. Mom's voice choked. Dad came to the phone. I swallowed hard and looked out the window at the lights coming on around Manhattan. "I'm really disappointed, Dobs. This isn't what I expected of you," he said. Dad was a man of few words—but in his voice I heard his acceptance of being unable to protect me from the streets he knew so well, from loving a man he didn't approve of. I heard his dashed hope that his child would get through life unscathed.

"I'll be home soon, Papa. Don't worry." I didn't want to think about hurting them. Sly lit a joint, and I smoked it with him to forget the call.

Early the next morning, I went to JFK by myself. Sly begged me to stay and drive with the band to Upstate New York, but I had to get home and back to work.

When I landed at San Francisco Airport, my hair fanned out behind me like a lion's mane as I stood outside baggage claim waiting for Kitsaun. My thick locks were usually tamed by setting them on two-inch plastic rollers, but I hadn't thought to take them with me when I packed.

I pulled my sweater tight over my white sleeveless dress. The blustery afternoon fog was cold. I already missed Sly. It seemed much longer than three days ago when I had flown to New York. I stood tall, my feet apart, cool air rippling my dress.

The Dodge Challenger wended toward me in the slow traffic. I waved and smiled. Kitsaun stopped the car in front of me and motioned for me to get in. "You look exhausted," she said dryly, her eyes surveying me from my hair to my shoes. "I like those platforms."

I hugged her with both arms, squeezing her neck. Kitsaun was the lining of me; we were like a reversible jacket that could be worn inside or out. We were closer than feathers on a bird, our words spliced together before we even spoke.

"How are Mom and Dad?"

"I think Mom's so happy you're back, she won't yell at you," she said, maneuvering the car through the airport back to the freeway. "But Dad is still furious. He hasn't said two words to me."

I bit my thumbnail, elation and self-assurance dissolving. My time with Sly in New York was worth whatever I had to go through at home. Mom and Dad wouldn't stay angry forever.

As Kitsaun drove, I rattled off each of my trip's events, my words running together breathlessly. We arrived at Harold Avenue much too quickly.

"Why didn't you stay for the concert?" she asked.

"They were going to a festival someplace in Upstate New York. It would have taken two or three more days to get there and back," I said, getting out of the car.

The front door opened before I got up the stairs. Mom stood in her housecoat, eyes blazing.

"I'm sorry, Mom."

"You must have lost your mind to run off like that without telling us! We don't know that man or his family. Kitsaun didn't even know what hotel you were in!"

"I'm leaving for college soon. You're going to have to trust me sometime."

"College isn't New York with Sly Stone."

I stared at the floor.

Dad came into the front hall. His eyebrows were furrowed. "Your mother was sick with worry. You had better think about what you're doing, Dobs. I know who he is. My buddies on the street are watching him. He's not worth the cement he stands on. He's nothin'."

6

Lost in His Sounds

August 1969

✳

*S*ly called me when he got back to San Francisco. It was late—eleven o'clock. I lay in bed listening to him tell me how I should have stayed for the concert in Upstate New York.

"We drove into this small town, Woodstock, with cows on the hills and red barns and shit. Backstage was a bunch of trailers with musicians everywhere. We went onstage, and all I could see was bodies for miles. You should have been there when we hit 'Higher'—people started jumping up and down, thousands of them."

It sounded like the pinnacle of concerts, an unexpected three days of musical bliss—and I had come home. But Mom and Dad never would have forgiven me if I had been gone one second longer. I could not really envision what I had missed. I hadn't been to many rock or R & B concerts before: I had seen Johnny Mathis, acoustic guitarist Bola Sete, and a free show in Golden Gate Park with Richie Havens and War. Woodstock had 500,000 wet, muddy people listening to thirty-two bands for three days. Sly was high for weeks remembering the experience. By the time I read about it and saw the photographs in *Life* magazine, I was sorry I had not been there.

I worked my final two weeks at the phone company and spent most evenings with Sly. We slept together—made love— at his house. I was embarrassed around Mama, thinking her Baptist rule book was the same as that of Christ Holy Sanctified: No sex before marriage. Mama did not lecture me or treat me differently than before my New York trip with her son. Sly would drive me home by midnight, and I would softly close the front door and tiptoe to my room. Mom and Dad frowned when Sly picked me up, but they did not fight or argue with me or forbid me to be with him. It would not have changed my path. I would have lied to be with him.

Sly had an office in Hollywood with a small staff that booked the band's tours and managed their recording. Stone Flower Productions was on Vine Street, and Sly's manager, David Kapralik, lived in Los Angeles. I packed my suitcase for Cal State Dominguez Hills, and Sly decided it was time for him to move to Los Angeles, too. He suggested I live in an apartment rather than in the dorms. "That way, when I'm in L.A., we can be together," he said.

I could not afford to rent a place. I would not even risk the scene of discussing it with Mom and Dad. Sly had his secretary, Stevie Swanigan, find a one-bedroom apartment, and Sly promised to pay the rent. He told me I could drive his purple 1957 Thunderbird with a paisley convertible top to L.A. and use it for school. I could not believe it. The car was flashy and expensive—quite a contrast to my parents' drab Dodge Dart I'd been allowed to drive at home. Sly treated me as though I was integral to his life, the girlfriend he did not want to be without. He couldn't drive to L.A. with me because he was going on the road; and he warned me that the engine had just been rebuilt, so I would have to drive fifty-five miles per hour the whole way. Kitsaun made the trip with me—my suitcase and a box of books stuffed into the small trunk.

Our apartment was on Fountain Avenue, one block below Sunset Boulevard, near La Cienega, an upscale area of Hollywood. The two-story building I was moving into was modest and run-down compared with the elegant, 1930s stucco buildings a few blocks south that had wrought-iron gated entrances with enormous fan palms and rows of bright impatiens. Stevie met Kitsaun and me out front with the key. She was about five feet three inches tall, with green eyes that glowed brightly against her skin, which was the color of beach sand. Her smile was wide and welcoming as she showed us around the tiny apartment. She had worked for Sly two years and was also originally from the Bay Area.

The front door of the apartment opened onto a long driveway with parking spaces squeezed into the back. Across the drive was another apartment complex. It was as though we were living in a miniature city with everyone close together.

The morning of registration, Kitsaun and I drove the hour and a half to the college. Dominguez Hills had been built on farmland south of Los Angeles. There was nothing for miles around. I stood in lines for classes in creative writing, math, and

Afro-American studies. We toured the campus and drove back to Hollywood, the T-Bird sputtering and heating up because I had forgotten to keep the speedometer at fifty-five.

Kitsaun flew back to San Francisco. I was alone for the first time, car horns on Sunset waking me just after I had fallen asleep; people walking by at all hours of the night howling and talking so loudly, it sounded as though they were right outside my door. I slept with lights on in the kitchen, bathroom, and by my bed. The daily drive to school took me through some neighborhoods with mansions and others with tiny houses. Palm trees swayed above them all. I did not remember apartment houses at home having names like "Cahuenga Gardens," "Sunset Arms," or "Los Feliz Casitas," but every housing complex in L.A. had a name.

I made my first friend in my Afro-American studies class. He was the president of the Black Student Union and lived in South Central L.A. We ate lunch together a few times a week, and he taught me what it was like to be black in Los Angeles— where police drove through South Central stopping young black men just for being out on the street.

"That's why I have an American flag sticker on my bumper," he said. "Now, the pigs think I'm patriotic and don't pull me over just because I'm black."

One day he saw me drive off, and caught up with me in his Volkswagen Beetle. "That is a *bad* car," he said. "Is it yours?"

"No. It's my boyfriend's." He began interrogating me about who my boyfriend could be, and when I told him, he nearly fell out of his car. His bowled-over response was similar to the reactions I had witnessed just walking down the street with Sly. People were overly impressed with him because they knew his songs, had seen him on TV. I guess it wasn't that different from how I'd felt the first time I met him, but I learned to keep my mouth shut about Sly so other students wouldn't look at me as a star's girlfriend, or try to get to know Sly through me.

Sly came home and stayed with me two nights. He wanted me to go on the road with him; so, six weeks into my first semester, I flew with the band to Cleveland to see Sly and the Family Stone in concert for my first time. Sly hung his arm around my neck, dragging me around backstage while he and the other band members chose clothing from an array of satin shirts, leather, and gold lamé on a garment rack. Cynthia blew her trumpet in the hallway; Larry thumbed his bass. Sly pawed my body. "I can't make it out here without you."

KC called for the band to go on, and Sly darted into a bathroom. KC paced the floor, shaking his head and mumbling. I knew Sly was snorting coke. He swung open the door, pranced out, and threw a kiss in my direction—his furry boots shaking. His pupils were dark and dilated. As he twirled, the fringe on his Western-style satin shirt caught the glare of the spotlight.

In a fleeting, intuitive moment, I saw his false bravado, his vulnerability. *He's nervous.* I had assumed he got off on performing with his band and getting the adulation of the fans.

I walked out front to the audience and climbed stairs to the balcony. Cynthia and Jerry moved side to side as they played their horn riffs. Larry slapped and thumped his bass, his knees bending deep as he marched across the stage. He wore a hat over his hair, cocked down over his forehead. Greg played the drums as though he were multijointed, a massive swing popping his beat. Rose stood center, her straight, blond wig flapping against her cheeks as she sang "Everyday People." Freddy was stage right, his wah-wah pedal distorting his guitar chords.

Sly sang the intro to "Stand," raised his right arm high, and leaped straight up in the air behind his keyboard. People jumped up from their seats and sang along. A funnel of music poured from the speakers, overtaking us all in exhilaration. When the chords to "Hot Fun in the Summertime" started, I dipped and danced to the memories of New York and my first time making love with Sly.

The day after the show, we all waited at the airport for a flight to the next city on the tour. Sly and I left the group to grab something to eat. He joked and riddled and teased the waitress, and we laughed, our eyes locked on each other. We heard the last call for our flight and ran to the gate just as the plane was lifting off with the rest of the band on board. I stood still, afraid we had done something terrible.

Sly put his arm around my waist and said, "We'll fly out later. Let's go to the zoo!" He hailed a taxi, and we spent the afternoon watching monkeys swing through trees, hippopotamuses wade in water, and lions sleep in the sun. One moment Sly's fingers traced the outline of my face as we sat on a bench, the next he grabbed my hand and pulled me down a path where we fell on the lawn rolling in laughter. We took a taxi back to the airport and flew to Kansas City immersed in our love.

By finals, I was struggling to study and spend time with Sly. He was recording in L.A. and staying with me when he wasn't in the studio all night. One night I was falling asleep on a couch in the control room. It was three o'clock in the morning, and I had to be at school by eight. Sly handed me a rolled-up dollar bill and said, "Just do a line, Debbie. It will wake you up." I took the dollar and put it against the mirror at the edge of the white crystals. I didn't think it would kill me to try cocaine once, and I did need to leave for school soon. I leaned forward and inhaled the coke through my left nostril. It shot through my nose like a miniature cannon and exploded in my brain directly behind my eyebrow. I looked up, squeezed my eyes closed, and sniffed the crystals down my throat. I bent over again, inhaling through the other nostril, even though the burning pain made my eyes water and my head pound. It took a while for the stimulant to recharge me, but when it did, a needle-sharp energy flung open the door of my careful control and I stayed awake through school and made it home, where I fell asleep on our couch by five at night. It became impossible to complete my schoolwork, drive the hour and a half to school, and be with Sly in the studio at night. Unaware of the sacrifice I was making to be with a man, I chose the studio over attending my classes and I dropped out of Cal State Dominguez Hills in March of 1970.

When I told her, Mom screamed on the phone, "You're throwing your life away." She put her hand over the mouthpiece and said something to Dad, and he came to the phone.

"Watch what you're doing, Dobs. You're heading for a brick wall," Dad said stiffly.

"I'll go back to school, Dad." My words were a promise to myself rather than to my father, whose heart held my dreams. Cal State L.A. had a campus much closer to our apartment.

"I certainly hope so, Dobs."

Sly told me he wanted to live full-time in L.A., but that the apartment was too small. Stevie rented a house in the Hollywood hills near Mulholland Drive.

"Tell the landlady you're moving out," Sly said. I gave notice to the sweet little grandmother who had checked on me when I was alone and interrogated me about the cars when Sly brought the Cord down. I had packed and finished cleaning the apartment when Sly and Stevie came to pick me up and load the cars. After putting my suitcase inside the T-Bird, I ran back inside for my books. I walked in to see Sly kicking through the broom closet in the kitchen, broken pieces of wood scattered across the floor.

"Why did you do that?" I screamed, feeling the strike of his violence in my chest.

"That bitch shouldn't have kept the deposit," he said, "or told me to turn down my music."

"She kept the deposit because we broke the lease, Sly. She didn't do anything wrong." His anger permeated the apartment, and I was shocked and scared at him lashing out and destroying property that way. It was a mean-spirited and flagrant use of force.

"It doesn't matter. She shouldn't have done it." He turned and walked out, kicking the front door against the wall. I stood in the apartment, trying to grasp what had happened and where I was going. I had not doubted moving in with Sly until this moment. It was too late to turn back. I closed the door gently and walked to where the cars were parked.

Sly was behind the wheel of the Cord Duesenberg. I followed him around the curving road in the T-Bird, my arms holding the steering wheel tightly as the pile of clothes in the backseat shifted from side to side. Stevie followed in Sly's camper. She brought his musical equipment, clothes, Stoner the Great Dane, and two new dogs—Max, a bulldog, and Gunn, a pit bull.

At the top of a hill, Sly turned on his left blinker. I steered the T-Bird into the circular drive of 2622 Coldwater Canyon.

The house was a mansion that looked out over palm tree–dotted hills winding to Laurel Canyon. The front door opened into a curved hallway, and stairs ascended to the master suite. An archway opened to the white country-style kitchen. In the sunken living room, a grand piano sat near French doors leading to an expanse of lawn and a swimming pool. I walked through the furnished rooms, awestruck.

Stevie dutifully carried in Sly's clothes, the dog food, and guitars. She looked like a tiny version of Sly, with knee-high leather boots and tight jeans tucked inside them. Her dimpled cheeks strained as she struggled with the load of clothes. Sly brought the amp and my box of books, trying to catch my cheek with his lips. He had gotten over his anger quickly—I was still reeling.

The three sniffing pooches pulled on their leashes, Gunn snapping at Max's stout leg. Stevie put Gunn in the study and the other two dogs on the patio behind the kitchen.

Sly took me in his arms and danced me through the living room. "Do you like it?"

"Of course," I said. But my mood was somber.

Stevie finished and called a taxi to return her to the office. Sly pulled out a vial of coke and gave Stevie and me a hit. Hugging me, he apologized for his actions and held me until I said I forgave him. We sat outside on the patio by the pool. Hibiscus bloomed in front of columns, thick ferns were wet with drops from the sprinkler, and hot pink bougainvillea with long, spiky thorns climbed up the trellis. I had seen Sly's desire for power when we were around his friends. I could tell that everyone was afraid to disagree with him. He had actually asked them to "cosign his shit," meaning, "tell me what I want to hear." I thought it was crude and narcissistic. In the studio, everyone applauded his solos. Yet, when we were alone, Sly was not a show-off. He asked me my opinion and said I was like a wise Indian maiden. He called me Princess Running Water. Today had been the first time I had seen his "other" side.

Sly interrupted my thoughts. "You want to go eat?"

"Sure," I said. We walked through the garden to the driveway, Sly's arm around my shoulder. He put the top down on the Cord, and we zoomed over the hill to the Good Earth in Westwood. He played his music, holding my hand when we stopped in traffic, and he parked the roadster a few meters from the restaurant. He leaped over the door without opening it. Hugging me and kissing my neck, he linked his arm through mine. Heads turned as we walked. Sly's looks and swagger created an aura of drama everywhere he went. Sitting face-to-face in the soft light of the restaurant, we ordered Belgian waffles with strawberries and whipped cream and went home to our new house happy as before.

1971

In early summer, Sly's aunt died. He wanted to attend the service, so we flew to the Bay Area. A limo took us to his hometown of Vallejo for the funeral. Afterward, I went to Mom and Dad's for dinner. I was glad to see them, but I wanted to get back to Sly so we could return to L.A. on the midnight flight. Kitsaun drove me to meet Sly and Freddy at Wally Heider Studios. When we walked into the music-filled control room, Sly was snorting coke from a small mirror on the side of the soundboard. The engineer and Freddy were pushing knobs on the board, adjusting the bass levels.

Sly looked up. "Hi, honey," he drawled. I leaned over to hug him. His eyelids drooped, and his body was stiff. "How's it sound?"

"Great, but you look tired." I looked at Freddy. "Have you two eaten?" He shook his head to say no.

"We had better get some food."

Sly leaned on the console to stand up, but fell back in the chair, his eyes rolling up in his head, his back arching. "Sly!" I screamed. "Freddy, something's wrong!"

Sly's legs were sticking straight out. He looked unconscious. Freddy's eyes bugged out in his face. He began crying, shaking Sly. The engineer said, "I'll call an ambulance."

"No! We'll take him to the hospital. Debbie, go get the car! Get the car!" Freddy screamed at me.

I ran outside and around the corner to McAllister, where we had parked. When I sped back to the studio, Freddy was standing outside, cradling Sly. Kitsaun was in the street, wildly waving her arms. They climbed in. Sly's mouth hung open. His eyes were closed. I sped up Leavenworth to Geary and swung right onto Scott to Mount Zion Hospital, pulling into the emergency driveway for ambulances. Freddy ran, Sly in his arms, through the automatic glass doors. I screeched into a parking place. I had never been so afraid in my life. What if he died? I loved him and couldn't believe something so horrible was happening. Kitsaun's face was ashen. She held my hand as we ran through the emergency room doors to the nurses' desk. "Where did they take him?" I asked. A nurse looked up, her face calm.

"Sly Stone," I said. "Where did they take him?"

"Are you relatives?"

"Yes!" I shrieked. Kitsaun squeezed my hand. The nurse led us down the hallway and pointed to a room. I peeked through the window. A doctor looked up as he adjusted the flow of fluid from a glass jar hanging over the bed. Thank God, he was alive. I pushed open the door.

Sly sat propped up against two pillows, Freddy at his side. The doctor looked at me. "Mr. Stewart had cocaine poisoning. He's told me what he ingested today. If you had not gotten him in here, he could have died." Tears slid down my face. Sly looked over at me, slurring his words: "I'm okay now, baby."

"I'm giving him tranquilizers to neutralize the stimulant that was paralyzing his nervous system," the doctor continued. "Cocaine is not only illegal and highly addictive, it can cause seizures and heart attacks."

"I just need some food," Sly droned. I lifted his hand to my cheek. It was cold. He looked haggard; his hair was pushed up in a cone shape. His smile was weak. "Give me my boots, Debbie. We're going home."

The doctor looked at Sly and shook his head from side to side. He took the needle out of Sly's arm.

Kitsaun and Freddy walked into the hall with the doctor.

"Are you sure?" I asked. "Maybe you should rest here longer."

"Shiiiit. I'm as strong as ever." He stood up, chucked my chin lightly, and laughed as he wobbled.

I watched him closely, ready to catch him if he fell. He sat down on the bed and scratched his head. "Where's my hat?"

I handed him the knit beanie. "Sly, I wish you would stop cocaine."

"I will, baby, I will."

But he couldn't do it. We went back to L.A., and instead Sly found a doctor who wrote him a prescription for Seconal. He reasoned that if tranquilizers had saved him from cocaine poisoning, he should take them all the time.

I tracked Sly like a young nocturnal animal following her mate. We slept days and roamed at night, my stomach raw from infrequent meals and from staying up in the studio snorting coke—a world of drugs and music I had never before known. Sly recorded Bobby Womack and Joe Hicks, two talented singers he wrote songs for; he also produced their tracks. I hung out, watching his musical genius, squandering my own goals and purpose. I stayed just tired enough and high enough to be unable to reason with myself that I needed to extract myself from the wayward life I was living. As Sly got higher and higher on drugs, anguish crept into my heart, tearing a hole in it. Feeling guilty about the innocent and pure young woman I thought God had intended me to be and the way I was living, I used Sly's Seconal to hide. The barbiturate let me slide comfortably into the emptiness; the hazy numbness helped me forget how disappointed I was in myself. Loving Sly was a deadly grip around my life, strangling me in a menacing noose.

One evening, I stood looking over the canyon, the sun reflecting orange against the veil of smog. I turned on outside lights leading to the pool.

The doorbell rang. David, the band's manager, strode quickly into the living room. He wore a silky red ascot in his white shirt, his brown hair slicked back like a movie producer's, neatly pressed slacks over his sandals. David's eyes darted around the room. He hugged me and kissed my cheek before sitting down across from Sly. "After the exposure from Woodstock, you've got to have a strong record to continue the momentum," David said.

Sly leaned over the coffee table and tapped a few long lines of coke out onto a mirror. He rolled up a dollar bill, looked David in the eye, laughed eerily, and snorted the powder into his nostrils. "I've got the music, man," he said.

He danced over to the tape player and hit the play button. Music jumped from the speakers, filling the living room with booming bass, horns, and B-3 organ. David stood up and began dancing, jerking his hips and arms.

It was amazing to hear the music, Sly's great talent rushing from the speakers. David sat down on the piano bench. He brought a brightly wrapped square out of his briefcase and handed it to me. "I thought you would enjoy this."

"Thank you." I slipped my fingers under the seams of the wrapping paper. It was a book with a deep indigo cover, silver words spiraling in a circle, *Be Here Now*. I had leafed through a copy of it at David's house. Ram Dass's words eased inside me, reminding me of my childhood faith, reviving an essence of God that had been escaping from my heart like sand in an hourglass.

I leaned over to David and hugged him, excited to start reading.

Sly sat down at the piano, crunching his hands along the keyboard following his new songs on the tape player with acoustic brilliance.

After a few hours, David went home and Sly went upstairs. I stayed in the living room coherent and alive, reading Ram Dass's words. When I climbed the stairs, Sly was passed out on the bed, fully clothed. I pulled the bedroom drapes closed so that the sunlight would not awaken us before early afternoon, and I began to undress him. The fur boots stuck to his sockless feet. His stomach fell inward as I unzipped the leather pants, peeling them down his legs. His frame was skeleton-like beneath his satin shirt. White powder was caked dry and hard around the edges of his nostrils. I lifted the covers over him. Climbing into the soft bed next to Sly, my body was tired and ready to sleep soundly, but my head was spinning.

I puffed up my pillow to read a few more pages of *Be Here Now*. Would we live like this always? I hoped not. I still dreamed we would be as we were when we'd first met, laughing all the time.

Sly snored loudly, and I did not want him sleeping on his back, so I leaned into him with my shoulder and pushed him onto his side. Hendrix had died on his back, asleep in a drug-induced stupor, choking on vomit he'd thrown up. Such a pitiful way to die. For a few minutes longer, I listened to Sly's breathing. I was listening for life.

7

Tarnished

$\mathcal{O}$ur days and nights followed a topsy-turvy pattern. I forgot about returning to school, caught up in the cycle of Sly's recording and gigging. For the first time in my life, I traveled outside North America. Mom and Dad had taken Kitsaun and me to Vancouver, British Columbia—but with Sly, I went to London, Paris, and Berlin. In Paris we stayed in an ancient hotel, the pulleys and cables exposed above lifts that creaked and strained, carrying us to our rooms. One night the power went out, and Sly lit candles to illuminate the bedroom and bath. It was romantic and spooky, and I giggled in the hallways as we found our way to the restaurant in the courtyard where the gas stove was working. Sly and I ate steak and *pommes frites,* drank water from bottles that looked like vases, and watched shadows grow into skyscrapers on the walls. I was mesmerized by the French language, which danced in my ears as we walked on streets with Africans and Arabs who wore their countries' dress. Even Sly did not look out of place beside them.

I met Lynn on the airplane to London. She had flown over to meet Jerry, the saxophone player she'd just started dating. "Jerry's told me so much about you," she said, and offered me her thin hand.

I clasped it. "It's nice to meet you." She had heart-shaped lips and creamy almond skin.

We ate together at the hotel café, and I asked her about the novel sticking up from her bag, *The Driver's Seat*. We shared a mutual love of reading and writing. Lynn had been enrolled in college like me, and had dropped out to travel with Jerry.

When we returned to America, Sly asked the band to come to L.A. for a few months to record the new album. Lynn and I met again beside the pool at Coldwater. A fragrant honeysuckle vine climbed over the fence and mixed with her powdery lilac scent. Lynn was three years older than me. She told me about her family, which sounded like mine: old-fashioned values, deep spirituality, and sisters who were very close and involved in one another's lives. Late at night, we wrote poetry by firelight. Often we chose to read our poems to each other rather than smoke dope with Sly and Jerry. We talked about entering poetry contests and going back to college. Lynn's friendship brought me wisdom and laughter, and she encouraged me to write.

Sly had composed a thumpin' tune, "Thank You (Falettinme Be Mice Elf Agin)" that was climbing the charts. The last lines were "Dyin' young is hard to take, sellin' out is harder." I watched him ingest coke, barbiturates, and weed, and I wondered whether selling out might not be better—at least he would be alive. He got so stoned at night that his pencil would roll from his hand to the floor, and his head would nod forward. Once bright-eyed and feisty, Sly slumped over a lot, and I would have to kneel down in front of him to look in his eyes. Love became a mystery to me. I had fallen hard for Sly: charmed and bewitched by his robust energy, the twinkle in his eyes, and his commanding care for me; his manhood so much more powerful and attractive than the boys I had dated. I belonged to him, and wanted to believe he would come alive again. Rhymes and lyrics twirled out of him before his head hit his chest, and he would smile at me, reminding me of the man he was beneath the veil of drugs and demons.

Mom and Dad drove down to check on me because I did not write and call as often as I once had. I cleaned the house and tried to smooth the lines of concern on my face, but when I opened the door and let them inside Coldwater, their eyes darted quickly from me to Sly, sensing that our lives were out of kilter. I was so glad to see them, to feel their arms squeezing unconditional love into my body. We sat in the living room talking, Dad on the edge of his chair, his jaw tense, his hands on his thighs in fists as Sly tried to keep up conversation. Mom kept asking, "Who takes care of all these dogs?" I think she was afraid that was one of my jobs. "I sure wish you would go back to school, honey," she said when they stood to leave. Closing the door as they walked down the stairs to their car, I sighed in relief and anguish. Although I was happy being on my own, their loving presence far outshone what I felt from Sly.

In late spring, Sly began making excuses for why he couldn't take me out with him at night. As independent as I was, I hated being alone in the five-bedroom house, with the dogs howling in the yard. I would call Lynn and keep her on the phone for an hour. These talks were what allowed me to hear myself admit that my commitment to my own life was eroding and that my role with Sly was changing from girlfriend to care-taker. I was merely twenty, unable to see that he was in a down-ward spiral that he did not want to come out of. He bought drugs from a freaky doctor with bushy white hair and a square jaw that barely moved when he talked. Lumbering along in the camper, we sometimes drove to the secluded road in the Holly-wood Hills where the doctor lived, and we would sit in his hill-side home cluttered with books and magazines covered in dust while he counted out the barbiturates, one by one. At home, Sly locked the jars of downers in the safe and sat in the living room playing piano until the drugs took effect. He'd say, "Baby, take down these lyrics," and I waited beside him, holding my pen, eager for his muse to arrive.

The band played a gig in Fresno, and we stayed up all night. In the afternoon, Sly and I packed our clothes in silence to drive back to L.A. There was a loud knock on our motel room door.

Sly growled, "Who is it?"

"Hey, man. It's me, Bubba."

Sly jumped up, his chest bare, and he opened the door wide to embrace a caramel-skinned man who stood about five feet eight inches, with hair so short, it looked like a shadow on his skull. "We're running buddies from way back," Sly said to me. "My sister Rose's husband, Hamp da Bubba da Banks." He made a song of his name. "This is Debbie."

I shook his hand, thinking he was cute in a little-boy way. His light brown eyes sparkled deviously when he said, "Nice to meet you."

Our room was dark, even though it was afternoon. The drapes were pulled shut, making the brown furniture and shag carpet look drab and dirty. A hanging light over the table cast a sallow glow.

Hamp and Sly sat on the bed, talking in low voices. I combed my hair in the tiny bathroom, took my book from the nightstand, and sat in a chair to read. Hamp picked up his black bag and unzipped it. Sly said, "We'll be right back." They walked into the bathroom, closing the door. After a few minutes the door opened a crack, and a voice called out, "Bring me my bag, bitch."

I froze. Was that Sly? What had he said? I didn't move. I couldn't move. He called louder, "I said, bring me my bag, bitch!"

My face flushed. I put my book down and sat up straight. What should I do? I wanted to run, but my purse was across the room in the small alcove next to the bathroom. Panic shot through me.

While I sat half in and half out of the chair, Sly threw open the bathroom door, flooding the bed with light. I stood up as he rushed toward me, his legs skinny but quick. He grabbed my blouse with both hands and jerked my body in the air. Letting go with his right hand, he backhanded me across the cheek, his diamond pinkie ring catching my lip. I screamed as my head snapped back over my shoulder. My neck made a cracking sound.

"When I tell you to do something, you do it, woman," Sly sneered. "Hamp Banks has seen me do worse to a woman for much less. Do you understand?"

"All I understand is that you'd better not touch me again," I said through clenched teeth.

I pried his hand from my blouse, shoved past him, and grabbed my purse. Hamp sat in the bathroom on the counter, a vial of white powder swinging between his fingers, a smile across his lips. I pushed past Sly, opened the door, and stepped out into the bright sunlight. Walking and running toward the lobby, I could hear Sly laughing and I shuddered.

I stumbled, and a sob hiccuped from my throat. I could still feel Sly's hand on my cheek—like a branding mark. I clutched my purse to my chest. This was not the Sly I had gone out with in San Francisco. This was the person I had seen kick in the broom closet door at the apartment on Fountain. The glass doors to the lobby opened automatically, and I hurried to the ladies' room across the carpeted foyer.

I ran the cold water and leaned into the mirror. My lip was split open where Sly's ring had made contact. My eyes were red and swollen. With shaking hands, I splashed icy water on my face and gently dabbed my cheeks with a paper towel from the silver canister on the wall. My heart ricocheted through my chest, wounded as though from a bullet. I gulped back tears as I remembered Dad's words: "You're headed for a brick wall, Dobs." I had had no idea what he'd meant when he said it, but I knew I had just hit the wall head-on. Where could I go? Should I call Kitsaun to come get me?

The bathroom door opened. I jerked my body around, a

scream waiting to spring from my throat. Without raising her eyes, a gray-haired woman entered the room and walked into a stall. My heartbeat slowed, and I fumbled through my purse for lipstick. Hands shaking, I rubbed color to my lips, careful to avoid the cut. I couldn't stay in the bathroom all day. I had ten dollars in my purse, so I cautiously stepped back out into the lobby and headed for the coffee shop.

"Table, honey?" The waitress smiled.

I nodded yes. She led me to a small booth and handed me a menu. I felt lost, like a bubble floating above my own life, not knowing where to land, or whether I could without bursting. A fat tear splashed onto the salad section of the menu. I squeezed my eyes closed and dabbed my cheeks with the paper napkin. If Kitsaun picked me up, it would be a three-hour drive. Where would I wait for her?

"Do you know what you want?"

The waitress's question startled me. "Uh, I'll have a tuna sandwich," I stammered. *Tuna? I hardly ever eat tuna. Well, at least I'll have a reason to sit here.*

"Something to drink?"

"Iced tea, please."

I could see the glass doors to the outside in the mirror over the counter. The waitress set down my tea. As I tore open a sugar packet, I saw Sly push the door open. He wore a bright yellow shirt and a cowboy hat. Shades covered his eyes. I slipped down in the booth, hoping he hadn't seen me. I thought about kneeling under the table, but the waitress's eyes were on me. *Oh, God,* I thought, sitting up. *He can't hit me in public.*

I poured the sugar into my glass and stirred frantically. I kept my eyes on the swirling ice cubes as Sly slipped into the booth. He put his arm around my shoulder and pulled me into his chest. His shirt was soft against my bare arm. "I'm sorry, baby," he whispered, kissing my neck. I tried to pull away, but his grip on me was tight, forceful.

When I opened my mouth to speak, a gurgling sound came out. I closed my mouth. When the waitress came back with my sandwich, she asked Sly, "Would you like to see a menu, sir?"

"No. I'll have what she's having. She's really healthy."

I knew he was teasing me, and I glared at him.

When the waitress turned away, Sly pulled me closer, turning my face to his. He lightly fingered my lip. "I love you. I didn't want to hurt you. I love those beauty marks on your neck." He was twisting compliments and apologies together. It was confusing, but his whole way of living bewildered me. One minute his charm and passion drew me in; the next minute his selfish need for power attacked me. "You want some coke?" he asked.

"No." I slid two inches away and looked Sly straight in the eyes. "Don't you ever hit me again," I sneered.

His jaw tightened, but he said nothing. I was not afraid of him. I was sad that our love was turning into misery, and I would fight to the end to be who I was and not a slave to his indiscriminate moods. Even though I was in love with the charming Sly, my father's and mother's courage and bravery were in my DNA. I was a fighter, even in my confused state of love.

While we ate, Sly clowned to entertain me. He smiled and tried to move close again, touching my arm. He reached behind me, rubbing my back. I watched him warily. He dropped two Seconals into my palm after I finished my sandwich. I drank them down with the last of my iced tea, knowing that in minutes I would feel mellowed by the drug.

"It will never happen again. I promise," Sly said. "Ready to drive back home?"

His face was serious, his voice gentle. I wanted to believe him. I felt desperate by myself in Fresno. If I did not go with him, where would I go?

I nodded.

He paid the bill and wrapped his arm around me as we walked back to the room. Hamp had vanished. I never wanted to see him again. I finished packing, wrestling with my thoughts, which were muddled now that the "red devils" had taken affect.

Back at Coldwater, Sly tried very hard to be charming, and he begged me to go to the studio with him for inspiration. He could be so close, pull me into a kiss, under the roof of his power. He made the act of getting high—whether it was sharing a smoke or having me bend into his hands to snort coke from his tiny mother-of-pearl spoon—an intimate exchange of love. Sly made me feel as though he needed me. Stevie told me I was different from other girlfriends Sly had had. "You're sincere," she said.

Sly asked Stevie to find a bigger house with a studio so that the band could record day and night. She quickly found a house to rent in Bel Air in which John and Michelle Phillips of the Mamas and Papas were living—they would be moving out in a month. More grandiose than Coldwater, the Spanish mission–style house was in the center of circular footpaths beneath hundreds of fragrant blossoms. The living room led to a balcony overlooking a sunken garden with rounded hedges and a stone-edged pool next to a pool house. The master bedroom had a window seat hiding cupboards beneath plush cushions, a marble bathroom, and pink carpeting. There was a recording studio on the third floor and a suite over the garage, with peacocks living in the dense pine trees surrounding the drive.

Just before the move, Wendy, a young blonde from the San Fernando Valley, began hanging out at Coldwater. I suspected Wendy was trouble when she staggered drunkenly out of her baby-blue convertible Mercedes. Not knowing where she had met Sly, I assumed she was around because she had drugs. She brought a dark cloud with her. Wendy liked to sniff a white crystal powder called PCP, which was a horse tranquilizer that could cause seizures. I begged Sly not to snort it. He pushed me away as Wendy sprinkled the PCP onto a mirror. My grandmother's sweet brown face appeared before me for an instant, and I knew—without a doubt—the drug was evil. I stood up and left the room, my grandmother's image a strong warning. But Sly tried it. He was incoherent and immobile for hours. His mood was unreasonable and paranoid. I hated Wendy.

The week we were packing to move to Bel Air, Kitsaun came down to visit. I was happy to see her and hear about home. Her Afro had grown out, and her hair curled around her brown, angular face. She was completing her second year at City College, and she and Jake had broken up. "I'm working with Frank as a showroom model to make money. I want to go to Europe this summer," she told me.

Kitsaun looked in our refrigerator and asked why there was no food. "How do you guys survive?" she asked. My consumption of drugs made eating a once-a-day event. Coke squelched my appetite completely.

"We order a lot of Pioneer Chicken and Chinese food," I said. She shook her head in dismay, and we ordered dinner by phone and went upstairs, where everyone was hanging out in our bedroom. I sat down on the bed near Sly. Jerry, Lynn, Kitsaun, and Freddy all sat on the rug around us, talking. Sly had given me a Seconal and a Placidyl. He talked about new songs, his words beginning to sound like a tape on slow speed. I looked at Kitsaun, and her face became fuzzy and began losing its shape. My head felt heavy.

The next thing I knew, water was filling my nose. I sputtered and coughed, opening my eyes. Sly was holding me up in the shower, my clothes plastered to my body under the stream of water pouring over me. I looked at Sly. He was fully dressed, too. What were we doing in the shower? "She's awake!" Sly called out. He turned the water off.

Kitsaun stood at the door, gulping back tears. "Are you all right?" she asked, handing Sly a towel. He dried my face.

"What happened?" I asked.

Sly walked me out of the stall.

Kitsaun cried, "You were sitting there, and then you fell straight back. Your eyes were half-opened. I thought you were dead."

"She's okay now," Sly said, trying to calm Kitsaun. "Let me get her undressed and in bed. I'll be downstairs in a few minutes."

Sly took off my clothes, rubbed the terry towel gently over

me, and laid me on the bed. I was still groggy. He covered me with blankets and the comforter. He kissed my forehead, brushed my hair back, and stepped into the walk-in closet to change his wet clothes. I wondered if I had passed out because I was trying to escape from my dead-end life. Kitsaun said I had looked dead, and I definitely felt as though I was traveling on an unstable road of harm. I drifted to sleep listening to Sly's deep voice through the floor as he sat in the living room talking with everyone else.

Late the next morning, Kitsaun and I sat outside on the stone terrace facing the line of mulberries and madrones bordering the property. "I don't know why you faded out last night, but it really scared me. You're so thin, Deb."

Kitsaun had always been the closest person in my life. We had not talked as much lately—but there was no schism in our honesty and love. "I love Sly, but he's changed into a different person—not the man I met. I should leave and go back to San Francisco, but it's like I'm addicted to him."

"He's doing more drugs," Kitsaun said. "I can see that."

"Yes," I whispered. "And so am I—"

"Remember when you were little and Damon gave you a rope burn across your face?"

"Yes." I laughed. "You beat him up during recess."

"Well, I'm twenty-one now and I'm still your big sister. I can be down here in a couple of hours if you need me. If you want to come home, come. And please eat more than fried chicken."

I drove her to Burbank Airport in the Thunderbird, coming back over Highland Boulevard in the summer sunshine. Marvin Gaye was on the radio, "Oh, mercy, mercy me. Things ain't what they used to be . . ." I sang along with his gentle, plaintive voice. Mercy—yes, the world was full of suffering, and my life was far from what it had been. I was not cultivating a fertile life of promise or purpose. My body knew this. I realized that I had faded out due to the excruciating pain of physically knowing the truth but not making a change.

Sly began recording in the studio the first night we moved into Bel Air. Stevie helped me unpack. Lynn and Jerry moved into the pool house. I had made a vow to write poetry every afternoon, to try to get my mind motivated. Cal State L.A. was going to mail me their schedule of classes. I thought my life might be getting back on track—until I missed a menstrual period. I waited three weeks and then made an appointment at a women's clinic on La Cienega. The nurse confirmed what I feared: I was pregnant. She asked me to step onto a scale and measured my weight and height.

"You are underweight, young lady. At 5 feet 6 inches and 104 pounds, you're no more than skin and bones."

I looked in the mirror. I was flat front and back. Even my butt was gone.

"What are you going to do?" she asked. I stepped off the scale and looked down at the floor. She repeated her question.

"I don't know."

"Get dressed. I'll be back."

She gave me pamphlets about birth control, pregnancy, and abortion. "If you need someone to talk to, call us. We have counselors."

When I left the clinic, I drove down Fountain Avenue, where I had lived when I moved to L.A. Then I drove west, out Sunset Boulevard to the beach. *I cannot have a baby—I have taken too many drugs. The baby will not be healthy or normal. I don't want a baby. I need to turn my own life around—start work or go back to school. I will have to get an abortion. It isn't legal, but I have heard of women finding doctors who perform them.*

I drove back to Bel Air.

Sly was alone in the control room, his music turned up to ten. His hat was pushed back on his head; his shirt, unbuttoned to his waist, was hanging over black leather pants. "Where were you?"

"Driving."

"Why didn't you tell me where you were going?" His dark eyes looked through me.

"I had an appointment."

Sly pushed the knobs on the console down. The music softened.

"I'm pregnant."

He dropped his forehead on the board. His hands were above him, still holding the knobs.

"I don't think I'm going to have it."

He looked up at me and smiled, like the old Sly. "Phew. I mean, whatever you want, but phew. Look, my cousin's a nurse." He stood up and put his arms around me. "I'll call her. Maybe she can help."

It was a lonely walk to the bedroom. On the bed, I spread out the pamphlets and leafed through them, staring at the titles: *Pregnancy. Birth Control. Abortion.* I tried to remember when I had last refilled my birth control prescription. God—what irresponsibility. I really had only one choice. I was not healthy with all the drugs I had taken. I wanted to go back to school and not have a child.

Sly brought his cousin to the house a week later. "This is

Toni," he said. He pushed two Seconals in my hand and bolted up the stairs while Toni and I stood facing each other in the living room. She looked about thirty. Her square, mocha-colored face opened into a smile.

"Hi," she said.

"Hello. Thanks for coming."

I led the way to the bedroom. "Sly said you're a nurse."

"Well, an aide."

My legs felt wobbly. I poured a glass of water and swallowed the pills.

"If it helps, I've done this before," she said. She opened a shopping bag and took out a sheet and a stack of dark towels. "Take off your underwear and lay on the towels on the bed," she said. I did as she instructed. "When did you have your last period?"

I silently counted. "Seven weeks ago."

She walked to the closet and lifted a hanger off the wooden rod. Twisting the neck counterclockwise, she glanced at me while she unbent the wire into a straight line.

"What are you going to use that for?" I asked.

She looked down at me, hesitating for an instant. "This is what I'm going to scrape you out with," she said.

Nausea tightened my throat. My stomach turned over, and a sour taste coated my mouth. I closed my eyes when she told me to open my legs. They were trembling uncontrollably. She inserted something inside me and said, "We have to wait a few minutes for you to dilate."

I heard the peacocks jump onto the roof and imagined their bluish-green tails swaying in the breeze, their heads turning side to side. "Okay," she said.

The metal was cold as it climbed up my vagina. "Ow!" I screamed as it poked into the tender tissue below my stomach. Opening my eyes, I saw her on her knees, peering into my womanhood.

"I know this hurts," she said, "but there's no other way right now. I'll be finished soon."

I grabbed fistfuls of the bedspread. She scraped the pointy metal around my uterus. It took forever and hurt so badly that I wondered if she had punctured an organ. Tears poured out of my eyes.

"There," she said, pulling the bloody weapon out. "You'll probably cramp up, but that's a good sign. Drink lots of liquids tonight."

Sweat beaded on her forehead. She pulled the towels out from under me and handed me a sanitary napkin to put on. Then she walked into the bathroom and shut the door. I could hear the water running in the sink.

I wrapped my arms around my stomach and stared at the ceiling. I hadn't known how painful it would be to end my pregnancy. My stomach was already cramping in circles of spasm.

She came out of the bathroom and sat down next to me. "You should go get yourself some birth control pills, honey. Take care of yourself."

I did not know what else to say, so I said, "Thank you."

She walked out the door. I heard her talking to Sly for a minute, and then a car engine started up.

I walked into the bathroom, poured a glass of water, and gingerly sat down on the floor. So much had happened to me in the past few months: Sly hitting me; moving; an abortion. I felt as though I were in a pitch-black tunnel without light at either end to guide me out.

The marble floor was cool. I put a towel under my head and lay down with my eyes closed.

"Debbie?" Sly's voice called softly through the door.

"Yes?"

"What are you doing?"

"Resting."

"Let me in."

I stood up slowly and wiped my legs with a wet washcloth, as I did that first time I had made love with the man on the other side of the wall. Breathing deeply, I opened the door.

"Are you okay?" he asked.

"I'm in a bit of pain," I said, trying not to cry.

"I'll bring you a Placydil." He handed me an envelope, "This came for you today." He ran to the safe, got the pill, and put it in my hand. He helped me to the bed and, with his hands on my shoulders, sat me down. He ran to the bathroom for my glass of water. I leaned into his chest while I looked at the letter and swallowed the pill. I recognized Mom's slanted handwriting.

"I'll be downstairs," Sly said. "You rest. I'll leave the door open. If you need me, just holler."

I crawled under the covers and opened the envelope. Mom wrote that Grandmother King was visiting Aunt Daisy and that Kitsaun was going to Europe with her friend. A second page read:

When I think of you in Los Angeles, I worry. Every day I pray you'll come home. I wrote this poem for you:

He said, "Come, do this."
I said yes.
He said, "Come, do that."
I said yes.
He said, "Give me your youth,
your innocence,
your precious time.
In return, I'll give you things.
I'm nice,
I'm a sheep—see my wool."
Now the priceless gifts I gave
are gone.
The things he gave
are dung.
Now I see
I should say NO
to wolves in sheep's clothing.

Love, Mom

I read it again and again. She knew what I had never said. I had given Sly everything I had, and it meant nothing to him. I turned onto my side, clutching Mom's letter, feeling her intuitive connection with me. I grabbed my pillow in my arms, hugging it for comfort—and prayed to God to give me the strength to leave.

8

The Holy Ghost

I felt stronger after a couple of days, but not strong enough to leave Sly and take care of myself. I was emotionally trapped in needing Sly's attention because I could pretend it was love, the movement I felt in my heart for him. I imagined I saw signs that he cared for me; and I resumed taking care of his health and the house, as well as imagining our love whole once again. I hid Mom's letter in the bottom of a drawer. Kitsaun cancelled her trip to Europe and came back down to L.A. to stay with me awhile, watching over me, and she hung out with Stevie at the Stone Flower Productions office.

Sly left on tour early one Saturday morning, after we had been up in the studio all night. Harvette, Sly's caretaker for the Bel Air house, asked me to go with him on an errand. His wife, Peachy, was very pregnant and stayed home sleeping. I was tired, but awake enough, and fidgety from the cocaine we had snorted.

Harvette always drove his Corvair as though he were in a

racecar. He made a wide left turn onto Santa Monica Boulevard, brakes screeching onto the four-lane street. I put my hand on the dashboard to brace myself. Then I heard sirens. Over my shoulder, I saw the LAPD behind our car, lights twirling, siren wailing. Harvette pulled over, and one officer appeared at his window, another at mine. The cop standing over me said, "What's your name, miss?" He had a red face, twitching fingers, and a drawn mouth beneath his crew cut. I panicked and gave a false name. The LAPD had a reputation for harassment, brutality, and racism.

The officers said that Harvette fit the description of a man who had robbed a store, so they had reason to search the car. *What could they have seen of Harvette when we passed, other than his skin color?* We stood outside the shimmery blue Corvair. Harvette wasn't shaved. He wore a sweatshirt with ragged sleeves above his elbows, khaki trousers, and tennis shoes. His hair was cut very close to his head. I looked down at my black bell-bottom jeans and white-and-navy-striped shirt, and I did not think my outfit was menacing. My hair was pulled back in a ponytail, and the only makeup I wore was lip gloss. One of the officers raised himself from the car with a long grin and held up a pistol. "This was under the driver's seat," he said.

I stood, mouth agape, cutting Harvette a blistering glare. Why did he have a gun? I wasn't street-smart, but after more than a year in Sly's wild world of drugs and dealers, I was accustomed to being out of my element and in alarming situations.

The police radio cracked and hummed as one of the officers called for backup. It was early enough that few people were on the streets. I thought nervously of jail—*God, what would Mom and Dad do if they found out?*

When the backup squad car arrived, a female officer pushed me into one vehicle, and Harvette was slammed into the other. Two women drove me over the L.A. highways. My arms were painfully cinched immobile behind my back, so I could not even slide down in the seat to avoid the eyes of drivers on the freeway who casually glanced over at the young criminal. I remembered the Seconal and Tuinal pills inside my boot and wondered what would happen to me if the police found those drugs. Inside the jail, they sat me in a metal chair with a cold Naugahyde seat and took off my cuffs. A desk sergeant pulled out paperwork. He wore a button-down shirt with the collar open, an easy attitude, and greasy hair. My eyes darted around the office, looking for someplace to dunk the drugs. The desk sarge was called away; and I reached into my boot, took out all the pills, swallowed two, and quickly dropped the rest in the gray metal wastebasket in front of me, breathing in relief. When he came back, I was pushing the pills down my throat by gathering saliva in a pool in my mouth and swallowing hard. I gave him my real name— Deborah King—and was booked.

The officer asked me what I was doing with Harvette. *Where had he gotten the gun? Had he robbed the liquor store? Was I his girl?* I answered that we had been on an errand; I had not known he had a gun; we had not gone to a liquor store; and Harvette had a wife who was at home waiting for us. I wasn't scared, now that the pills were gone—we had not committed a crime. While I sat in the police station, I reflected on my repugnant universe of drug-taking and all-nighters, Sly's friends who weren't friends, the women who slept with anyone, and the men who demanded it.

"You get one phone call," the officer barked at me. I called Kitsaun. "What happened?" she screamed. I explained Harvette's driving and the gun. "Oh, my God," Kitsaun said. "Okay. Don't worry. I'll get you out."

I was taken to an industrial bathroom and told to undress so I could be searched. It was a greenish room with mirrors, and I was thinking that I was in a movie, a bad, scary movie. The female officer who searched me walked me to a cell with bars, and I entered a dark, cement room. By then, the barbiturates were taking effect. A small-faced Caucasian woman sat on the bunk on the other wall. I sat down on the thin, hard bed across from her, feeling confident I would not be there long. I knew that Kitsaun could get money from Sly's house and bail me out. In a small voice, the girl asked what had happened.

"My friend and I were pulled over for an illegal turn." My tongue felt thick, and the room was looking fuzzy. The familiar warmth of drunkenness was overtaking me.

"I was arrested at a house where my friends and I were at a party," the mousy woman said. "I was stoned, and I think something really bad happened."

She kept talking, but I fell into a deep, drugged sleep. I awoke to a female voice calling my name. I stood, stiff and cold, and followed the jailer into an outer room. Kitsaun ran over to me, her eyes overflowing, and hugged me tight. Stevie stood skinny as a stick and smiled at me with her dimple folding into her light brown, freckled face. Sunlight poured in through the window. I could not believe it was morning again.

"Sly wouldn't bail you out, because you were with Harvette," Stevie said. "It took us all night to borrow the money from our friends."

I could not believe Sly wanted to punish me for being with short, stocky, married Harvette—especially since we were running an errand for Sly. "What an asshole!" I yelled. Rage flew through every pore in my body. I refused to go to Bel Air.

Kitsaun and Stevie took me to Leora's. She was one of our friends who was not involved with Sly. When he called from the road, I wouldn't speak with him; I was so angry that he hadn't helped me. He came back to L.A. and had the limo driver immediately take him to Leora's. He explained that he had only been trying to teach me a lesson when he didn't bail me out.

"And what lesson was that?" I asked, my teeth clenched. "That I should not do things for you, or that I should have known Harvette had a gun?" I stared him down, hands on my skinny hips, daring him to prove he was right.

"Listen, baby," he said. "I'm sorry. Please move back home." He told me that I would need his lawyer, Peter Knecht, and that he could get my charges dropped. I did not understand how I could have charges, but I agreed to see him. Sly kissed and cooed, and I got into the limo with him and went back to Bel Air. When he took me to his lawyer, Mr. Knecht informed me that the woman who had shared my cell was Lynette "Squeaky" Fromme, one of Charles Manson's girlfriends who was on trial for the murder of an actress named Sharon Tate. It was frightening to think I had slept across from an accused murderer.

The house at Bel Air was filled with a circus of people coming and going: Jimmy Ford, with his twangy Southern accent and funny jokes; two Italian drug dealers from New York; and a doped-up Wendy—types my dad would have called hangers-on. Harvette and his wife, Peachy, moved out so that their baby could have a normal life. Kitsaun went home to San Francisco. And Sly and I spent time in the master suite talking before people would arrive in the evenings to play music and share drugs.

One night, Sly was getting ready to go out. "I won't be gone long, baby," he said, and leaned over me with a long, wet kiss. "I want you to stay in the bedroom. Some of the guys might be going in and out of the house."

"I'll be fine," I said, even though my heart was not. I had been examining my weaknesses and looking for a way out of the self-destruction I was living. Just the night before I'd remembered the habit I'd had since I was a small child of saying my prayers every night before I would fall asleep. Now it must have been months since I had prayed.

He pulled on his black nylon striped "pimp" socks and slid two joints inside, along his shinbone. He pushed his feet into fur boots and twirled in the mirror, the fringe on his suede knickers dancing. Sly walked to the safe. He opened the door and lifted out the jar of tranquilizers. "Here, have a Placidyl." He dropped two into my upturned palm.

I listened to his steps down the stairs. My heart sank with disappointment in myself. *Oh, well, I'll call Lynn. Maybe we'll write for an hour or so.* I walked downstairs to the kitchen. The house was quiet. There was some sort of lunch meat in the refrigerator, but it had a pink tint. I looked in the pantry and saw crackers and peanut butter. A bowl on the counter had apples in it. I set the crackers on a plate. The front door creaked open, and footsteps climbed the stairs.

"Debbie!" I heard Sly yell gruffly.

"I'm in the kitchen," I answered, closing the cabinet.

Like a savage storm, he was next to me, leering into my face. "Why aren't you in the bedroom?"

"I wanted something to eat," I answered, moving back against the wall.

"I told you to stay in the bedroom!" he screamed. His eyes were cold and dark, his body tense, fists balled at his sides. "You do what I tell you, woman," he shouted, and grabbed my right arm, lifting me off the ground. I tried to wrestle my arm from his grasp. The plate of crackers spun across the counter and crashed on the floor. Sly dragged me up the stairs and shoved me into the bedroom. I tried to catch myself, but fell back on the bed, the heat of his fingers twisted into my arm. He straddled me and raised his arm. I reached out to stop his hand, but he pulled it free and slapped me.

"You're crazy!" I wailed, covering my face with both hands, trying to roll away from him.

"Maybe," he snarled, hopping off the bed. I kept my face hidden as he walked out, slamming the door. The sound of his footsteps grew softer as he descended the staircase.

I rocked back and forth on the bed, moaning. My cheeks burned from his dry hands. *I'm going home tomorrow. Then he'll miss me. Maybe he'll even beg me to come back, but I won't.* I went to the bathroom and filled a glass with water. The Placydils went down my throat like the medicine they were.

A soft rap came at the door. "Who is it?" I asked, knowing such a gentle knock could not be Sly.

"It's Lynn. Are you okay?"

I slid off the bed and dizzily stumbled to the door, peering through a slit at Lynn's bird-like face.

"I heard shouting. Is Sly here?"

The concern in her voice brought tears to my eyes. "No," I whispered. Lynn came inside and looked at my face. "Oh, God," she gasped. "You're hurt." She gently slid her hand over my cheek. The skin throbbed. She guided me to the bed.

"This is the second time he's hit me," I said.

"That's not right, Debbie."

"I never dreamed I would be with a man who would hit me. I've never seen anything like this. I'm no match for him. We've been together a year and a half." I looked at the ceiling. "I don't know what set him off tonight. Maybe he is going insane."

"He cares for you. But the whole band is going crazy now," Lynn said. "What about going back to college?"

I laid my head in her lap. "I'm going to leave," I said. "I'll go home for a while."

"Maybe that would be good." Lynn rubbed her fingers in circles on my temples.

When I opened my eyes, hazy sunlight filtered through the windows. I was curled up at the edge of the bed. Sharp pains pulsed in my face. Sly was snoring loudly, lying fully clothed on the other side of the bed. I must have fallen asleep while Lynn and I were talking. I had not heard her leave or Sly come in. Quietly, I slid off the bed and crawled into the dressing room. Standing woozily, I pulled a soft satchel down from the closet shelf. From the drawers I pulled T-shirts, bell bottoms, and undies, my childhood Bible with my name embossed in gold, and Mom's letter. I stuffed everything in the bag and snapped it closed. In the bathroom, I leaned into the mirror. A purplish-red bruise curved like a quarter-moon beneath my left eye. I ran my tongue over the inside of my lip, swollen and cut, where a tooth had jabbed when Sly's hand slammed into my face. It was raw and metallic tasting. I squeezed my eyes shut. What had happened to my dreams? I believed nothing could stop this man from seriously hurting me. Looking at him lying on the bed, skinny, drugged, and unconscious, I could not find anything attractive about him, or one soul-stirring reason to stay. He was mentally gone; his soul dying.

I gently brushed my teeth and combed my hair back into a ponytail. I pulled on pants and a turtleneck. Sly's pouch was on the table. I slid my hand in, watching his still body on the bed, ready to run if he moved, and pulled out a hundred-dollar bill. That should be enough to get me home.

My head throbbed as I unlocked the bedroom door and tip-toed down the stairs. I called a taxi from the study. I wanted to go down to the pool house to say good-bye to Lynn, but I was afraid Sly would wake up and find me. What would he do to me if he saw me leaving? *Be Here Now* was on the desk, and I picked it up and cradled it in my arms.

A sense of relief washed over me as I walked out to the flag-stone stairs along the driveway to wait for the cab. Everything that had happened since I had been at this house seemed to be an end for Sly and me. I was glad to flee the darkness of Bel Air. A fan-shaped palm hid me from its view. The sound of a door slamming sent me scrambling up the hillside to the lawn along the street. Thank God, the cream-colored taxi was turning into the drive.

In the cab, my thoughts turned to my family. My heart hung defeated in my chest. What if Mom and Dad were angry with me? I had run off with Sly, dropped out of college, and had been terrible communicating with them. Now, I was crawling back.

I could not go home with this bruise on my face. At LAX, I ran into the sundry shop, bought makeup, and smeared the watery foundation onto my face. I purchased a standby ticket to San Francisco on PSA.

Staring out the plane window, I watched L.A. grow small as we ascended through the clouds. Tears smeared my makeup, but I could not stop crying. I let my sadness tenderly flow out and I prayed for strength not to return to Sly.

I reapplied the foundation at SFO. My stomach was caved in with hunger; my navy sailor pants hung on me like a kite in the wind. I bought an orange juice and drank it on the taxi ride to Harold Avenue as I rehearsed my lines for Mom and Dad.

I climbed the stairs to my home. "Hi, Mom. Hi, Dad." I mocked cheerfulness when I opened the front door.

"Debbie!" Mom exclaimed. She set her knitting on the coffee table, smiling as she walked quickly toward me. Dad set his guitar down and stood up. Surprise lit both of their faces. Mom hugged me. "You're skin and bones!" she exclaimed. "What's that on your cheek?"

I tried to pull back from her arms. "Where?" I asked. "I don't know. Oh! Maybe I got a bruise when Gunn reached up to lick my face last night. His snout is hard as a rock."

Mom did not look convinced, but she played along. "I didn't trust that dog when I saw him."

My eyes took in our small living room, the oval mirror hanging crooked on the wall, the marble end tables, and the yellow-flowered couch. I remembered the afternoon when Kitsaun and I had tried to rearrange the living room and dropped the long coffee table. The marble cracked, and we wrote Mom and Dad a note saying we had run away because we knew it couldn't be repaired. Then we hid in the garden. They were not even angry, because they were so glad we had not run off. Now we have two tables instead of one.

Dad watched as Mom and I chattered. "Are you home for good?" he asked, eyes clouded.

My heart felt squeezed like a wet sponge when I answered, "Yes." There. I had admitted that I'd left Sly.

Dad's face shone like stars blinking in a dark sky. "Well, we've missed you."

"And been worried sick," Mom added. "Oh well, you're home now. You must be hungry." She hugged me again.

"Where's Kitsaun?"

"She didn't tell you?" Mom's lips pulled tight. "She moved into a small apartment in the Haight with her friend Rosita."

"Oh," I said, missing my sister more than ever and grateful beyond words to be home.

I did not call Sly that night. I moved into Kitsaun's bedroom downstairs, feeling safe but shaken that my life was blown apart. Sleep would not come, and I turned the events of the past months over and over in my mind.

I called Sly the following day.

"Why did you leave without telling me?" he asked, his voice edging through the phone in a slow, drunken drawl.

"Because I wanted to get out before you would hurt me again. I'm staying with my parents, getting a job, and returning to college."

"Anytime you want to come back, you can," Sly said.

How I wished I could. My heart yearned to be with the Sly I had first met. But the fantasy was over. We talked a few more times, and Sly's life sounded unimaginably crazier than before I had left. Sly said promoters were "messing" with him. He bought a baboon that lived in a cage outside the Bel Air house. He was a lost soul, as I had been with him.

At night, I dreamed of Sly looming over me, a giant seething with anger, shaking and slapping me. I winced and cowered in the safety of Kitsaun's bed, scarred in places no one could see.

Mom hovered close, fussing over me, cooking brown rice and vegetables, baked chicken and corn bread, giving me more love in a week than I had felt in many months. Dad stood close, hands in his pockets, nervously jingling his change. Kitsaun and I met at the movies, ate at the Hot House at Ocean Beach, and bought It's-It ice-cream sandwiches for dessert.

My family tended to my broken body, and my spirit cried out for healing. When Mom invited me to our family's Pentecostal church in Oakland the next Sunday, I accompanied her and Dad. My stomach jumped nervously as Dad put the car into park. I had not been in church in two years, not since I wore my purple satin hot-pant suit. Grandmother had put her long, thin arm around my waist and said, "Baby, you forgot your skirt," in her soft, crackly voice.

I felt I owed this day to God, because the desire for drugs left me when I came home. It seemed like a miracle. After a year of burying my pain in drugs, I sensed it was my mother's prayers here in this church with the other believers that had raised me from the depths of my stupor.

We walked toward the bright red stairs leading to the front doors of the stucco building. I took a deep breath entering the foyer, my eyes squinting in the sunlight that streamed delicately through the stained-glass windows.

In the sanctuary, it seemed that I had entered a forest. Arms were raised, waving from side to side, like tree branches in a gentle wind. A few voices called out "Jesus!" in a plaintive cry. Other voices moaned low and guttural. Some sang "Oooooooo" in a rising and falling pitch, like sleepy dogs on a moonlit night.

Dad, regal in his gray sharkskin suit, carried his guitar to the amplifier next to the piano. Mom and I slipped into a mahogany pew. Ten rows up, in the pulpit, high above the congregation, stood my uncle U.S. wearing a full-length black wool robe with thick folds; an embroidered golden cross lay over his heart.

"The Lord is good," he proclaimed, wiping his forehead with a white handkerchief.

The congregation responded, "Amen. Praise the Lord. Thank you, Jesus"—incantations to the God I had forgotten.

Aunt Bitsy sat at the piano, her hands rising and falling over the keyboard like a school of dolphins at play. Dad fingered his guitar next to her, and my cousin Calvin thumbed the bass. Bitsy's eyes were closed; her head was tilted back; a heavenly countenance shone from her face. She began to sing "How Great Thou Art," never glancing at the hymnal. Goose bumps stood the hair up on my arms, and a shiver of faith ran down my back.

Sister Fields sat in front of me, to the left, crowned in her little straw brim with the polyester rose on top. Her light brown hair, streaked with gray, was pulled back in a soft bun. Her white missionary dress hung starched above the tops of her hard oxford shoes. Now that she was in her eighties, it was hard to imagine her the way I had heard she was when she was young: striding by the old church on Seventh Street in high heels and a tight dress, smoking a cigarette on her way to work at the house of prostitution. I'd heard her testimony many times over the years. "Once the Holy Spirit got ahold of me," she had said, "I left that house of sin and ran home to look in the mirror, because I knew I looked different!"

I smiled as she clapped her thin, brown hands together, singing in a soft, confident voice. *God had forgiven Sister Fields her past. Wouldn't a merciful God forgive me, too? Can I stay away from Sly's world and the people who have forsaken their souls to flirt with fame and fortune?* I glanced around at the sweet faces. *Why had I ever left this safe haven?*

Sister Hogg ushered. In her uniform white blouse, black skirt, and white, wrist-length gloves, she smiled as she passed me a fan. I was not warm enough to use it, but as I held it in my hand, I remembered hot summer revivals when members of the Texas churches had come to Oakland. The Holy Ghost had moved through the church, laying believers out in a sanctified faint. I had been afraid to be slain in the Spirit because I did not understand how its invisible power made people dance, speak in tongues, and fall over. I still did not comprehend how, but I believed Spirit could change lives. I had felt it in my own since I returned from L.A.

Thank you, God, I prayed, *for bringing me out of the fiery furnace.* I had heard saints pray about the fires of hell when I was young, but I had no idea what they had meant until now.

The singsong cadence of Uncle U.S.'s sermon bathed me in peace. His words washed over me like healing waters—a baptism. Perhaps I could start anew, the sins of my L.A. life forgiven.

9

The Water Fountain

Spring/Summer 1972

Whenever I thought of Sly, I would wrap my arms around our German shepherd, Nureyev, and stare out the living room window, wondering whether the pain of sorrow would make me perish. Day after day, Nina Simone sang lazily from the stereo, "The Other Woman," her voice vibrating.

For a couple of weeks, I drove past Mama and KC's house on Urbano to see whether Sly might be visiting his parents. I looked for the camper and the Cord, any sign of his presence, even though I would not have gone to the door. I had not talked with Sly since my first week home, and wondered whether our love had been a hallucination. The memory of his hands slapping hard against my face made me confident that I was better off without him. I told myself to put one foot in front of the other, and I willed myself not to abandon what I knew was necessary—"Save yourself!" I screamed to my insides, the weak part of me still cared about Sly.

Lynn and Jerry left L.A. and moved back to their Bay Area home in Forest Knolls. They invited me to stay with them for a few days, and I welcomed time away from Mom's and Dad's protective arms. Lynn picked me up, and we drove over the Golden Gate Bridge through winding, tree-lined roads, to a country town an hour away. We sat on their deck beneath spruce and cedar trees, butterflies languidly gliding by. Lynn offered me lemongrass tea with honey in a china mug. Los Angeles had not changed her at all: She was bright and loving, and her house was quiet and commodious, a haven from the tumultuous past months. I was curious about Sly, but Lynn steered our conversation far away from him. It was just as well; I needed to let my heart dry out, to allow my friendship with Lynn to change its orbit. Jerry rolled cigar-like joints, but I vehemently declined sharing the smoke. Fresh air, the beauty of the Bay Area, and being free of fear was enough of a high for me.

Kitsaun and Lynn held my fragmented life together with loving talks. My solitude allowed me time to plan for my future, rather than mull over memories of the past. I applied to San Francisco State for the fall 1972 Creative Writing Program and was accepted. I started taking hatha yoga on Dolores Street, letting quiet soothe my body and the gentle exercises rebalance my spirit.

Goodness came back into my life in surprising ways. Sly's secretary, Stevie, called me in early June, saying, "I've left L.A. Those people have completely flipped. Sly is too stoned to work, and he's not showing up for gigs. Hamp is living at Bel Air, and they're carrying guns."

Terror shot through my body. Hamp da Bubba da Banks in L.A.? I remembered his cold eyes after Sly hit me. "God, Stevie." My head felt light.

"Hamp and Sly are against Larry. Something crazy is going to happen soon." She paused.

"It must have been unbearable for you," I said. I never thought she would leave.

"It was horrible watching Sly totally lose it. I called because I'm working in the city at Black Expo. It's a temporary job in an office on Oak Street. I need a receptionist. Are you interested?"

I was stunned and didn't answer at first.

"Debbie?"

"Yes! I'm interested, just shocked," I whispered. "I would love to work with you. How long will the job last?"

"Just this summer. It will be great. We're putting on a conference of speakers and music for the community," she said, and gave me directions to the office. "Debbie, I always liked you and thought of you as a sister. It was such a combative atmosphere for me. I wanted to tell you the truth about Sly, but I was drowning, too." I was touched by her kindness to call me and offer me work, as well as tell me she had cared about me.

Her news had stunned me—now that I heard her story, I felt lucky to have escaped with my life.

How had I lost my identity and purpose in Sly's life of duplicity? I had been drawn in by his smooth, slick words that complimented the way I looked. How very stupid of me. He had never known me or wanted to know me, had he? Now that I knew his reckless character—the lack of respect he had for women, the lies he told as easily as he swallowed his pills or inhaled a cigarette—I felt cheap and disillusioned with love. But I was wiser, too.

The Black Expo staff was organizing a weeklong summit of nationally known black entertainers in August. Ray Taliaferro, local radio announcer and talk show host, was the director of the project. Stevie managed the office staff and production co-ordination of the conference; she was experienced from having been Sly's personal secretary and from planning his tours, studio schedule, and travel details. She was a hard worker who accomplished every job given to her. As receptionist, I directed calls to staff, took messages, and spoke with artists' managers. We worked with eight other people, and I loved being busy and using my mind. My life had its own significance again.

In July, Lynn and Jerry invited Kitsaun and me to a Tower of Power concert at the Marin Civic Center. We rode the ferry from San Francisco to Sausalito, the wind briskly churning the water gray as the boat plied through the bay. It felt strange being near San Quentin, the prison where George Jackson had been shot to death barely a year earlier. I had recently read about the legendary political prisoner and leader of the Black Panther Party—his book *Soledad Brother* had just been published. Imprisoned ten years for allegedly robbing seventy dollars from a gas station, George Jackson was forced to spend seven of those years in solitary. His murder was a tragedy of the war between the Black Panther Party, the government, and the police. His legacy would live on in his writings and in the thousands of freedom seekers, like me, who refused to believe that blacks were inferior or that we should accept a lesser system of civil rights. Now that my mind was clear from drugs, the old fire of social justice was stoked in me again, and I wanted to regain my purpose to work toward eradicating ignorance and injustice.

Lynn and Jerry picked us up two blocks from the ferry launch at the Trident Restaurant. Lynn squeezed me tight. "You've put on some weight, Deb. You look great."

"Thanks. Mom's been stuffing me with macaroni and cheese, meat loaf, fresh orange juice with brewer's yeast—I'm eating three meals a day." I actually had bulges in my eyelet sweater, and my hips were round again.

Jerry sped up Highway 101, bringing the Jeep to a bucking halt in the Marin Civic Center theater parking lot. Donning dark glasses, we hopped onto the pavement and sauntered to the round box-office window where tickets and backstage passes were waiting in Jerry's name. The sun, just beginning to slide behind Mount Tamalpais, cast a peach-hued glow over the hills around us. Ripples of heat shimmied skyward from the turquoise-tiled dome of the crouching buildings. Jerry led the way through corridors, stopping to slap hands with musicians he knew. Kitsaun saw someone she knew and bid us farewell. Lynn and I walked through dressing rooms, where musicians and their lady friends looked up from conversations, and trumpeters and sax men were running their fingers up scales. We sat together on a couch and talked about our idea to compile a book of poetry written by the girlfriends and wives of musicians. We were going to ask women to submit poetry written while their boyfriends or husbands were on the road. I had written at least twenty poems while Sly was gone and I was waiting for him.

Lynn raised her hands, excited by her thoughts. "We could call the book *Road Widows*. I'll get a list of people to call from Jerry's phone book."

"I'll ask Stevie to help me get names and phone numbers. She knows everybody."

A man's voice, muffled from below, announced Tower of Power. The music blared through the floor, and the bass vibrated the cushions in the couch. We strained to hear each other over Tower of Power's horn section. "Let's go listen to the band from the stage," I shouted.

I trailed Lynn downstairs, weaving between men and women who were swaying to the music on the side of the stage. We passed a man with dark hair curling down the back of his off-white suit, standing with a black guitar case against his leg. Long-waisted and skinny, he was a head taller than the two blondes who stood next to him. His shoulders curved forward, and his head bent shyly. I stared, caught by a bewitching energy. He returned my glance, cocking his head inquisitively at me, his dark eyes claiming the distance between us.

Lynn and I walked closer to the stage. He followed, standing right behind us. Tower hit the opening notes to "You're Still a Young Man," and I got lost in the keyboard solos and the vocals of the song. The band started "You've Got to Funkifize," with the bass amplified to ten. The long-haired guitarist walked out, lifted his guitar strap over his head, and played a blistering solo. The audience roared. I asked Lynn, "Who is that?"

She turned to Jerry and asked him. "Carlos Santana," he said.

The music stopped, and the house lights were raised. Lynn and I were pushing through the crowd toward the dressing rooms. I stopped at a water fountain near the stairs for a drink. When I lifted my head, Carlos stood next to me, his gaze washing over me slowly, gently.

I turned and walked back to Lynn. We went upstairs, my heart pounding. His handsome, mysterious face stayed in my mind. Without speaking a word, Carlos had imprinted a desire inside me to know him. On the drive back to Lynn and Jerry's, my mind lurched and my stomach rolled. *How can I be attracted to another famous musician?* Santana's songs "Black Magic Woman" and "Oye Como Va" were constantly on the radio.

When we reached their cabin, Jerry went outside to smoke on the deck.

Kitsaun, Lynn, and I stretched sheets across the daybed where we would sleep. "I saw Carlos staring at you," Lynn said. We tucked in the blanket. "Jerry says he's a real gentleman."

"I noticed him, too. But musicians are off my radar screen."

"Well, we could call him and ask if his girlfriend writes poetry."

"Fine. You can do that. After I'm gone."

The next day, after Kitsaun and I left, Lynn called Carlos. She then called to tell me that he'd asked for my phone number—and she'd given it to him.

"Lynn! I'm hardly over Sly! Oh well, I'm sure he won't call."

A few weeks went by. I called women on my list who had been involved with musicians or were dating them at the time, asking for a literary submission. I was so busy working, I forgot all about Carlos Santana. Then one night, Mom called me to the phone.

"Hello?"

"Hi," he said. "I saw you in Marin a few weeks ago. I'm Carlos. Carlos Santana. I would like to meet you." His voice was soft. His words sounded moist as though each one rested awhile on his lips before coming out.

"Oh, I remember." I saw his mustache above his full lips, his dark eyes piercing mine.

"Would you like to meet me next Friday at the Carousel Ballroom? Azteca's playing."

"I don't know." I liked Azteca's music, but I didn't know whether I wanted to take a chance on seeing Carlos.

What was it that pulled me to him?

Carlos said he would leave my name on the guest list, and hoped I would come. I hung up and lay against the pillow in my room. It had been merely three months since I had left L.A. I was starting college again. I had definitely moved beyond believing Sly and I would ever be together again, or even that we should have been together in the first place. He was never seriously in love with me, but he had been my first real love.

I wrestled with myself all week. Between phone calls at Black Expo, I felt excited to see Carlos, and fearful, all mixed together. Wanting to see Carlos again and talk with him overrode my trepidation about his being a musician. On the drive downtown to the Carousel, I was nervous. I got my pass and found my way backstage. The cramped dressing room was smoky. Carlos stood surrounded by a circle of men and women in front of an old red velvet couch. I recognized a few people from my days with Sly and nodded hello, making my way to a chair across the room, my eyes on Carlos's face, waiting for him to notice me. He looked handsome, his eyes black, his mustache rising and falling on his full, pink lips. When he looked my way, I curved my index finger, beckoning him to leave the crowd and come to me. He excused himself and walked toward me with a smile. He took my hand and bent forward to kiss my cheek. We moved into a corner.

"How are you?" he asked. "When I saw you, I couldn't forget you."

His dark mustache was bushy like Dad's. "Thank you. I'm fine."

"Do you live in the city?"

"Yes. I live out by City College." His eyes were smoky lanterns in his pale skin.

"What are you doing now?" I asked. "Are you touring?"

Carlos rubbed his thumb and index finger down his mustache. "My band just broke up. I'm starting to rehearse with some new musicians. Two of the original band members stayed with me."

"Why did you break up?"

"People change." He looked from my eyes to his hands. "I want something different in my music. I want to play Miles and Coltrane. Some of the guys were into drugs more than music."

Don Weir, the owner of Don Weir's Music City, approached us, begging Carlos to go out and jam. Carlos shook his head. "Maybe later, man. I'm busy right now." His mouth was a waterfall of words and tenderness. I watched it move, wanting to swallow every word. "Let's go listen on the stage," he said.

I recognized too many musicians who eyed me with a methodical scan. I could feel them thinking, "If Sly's not around, why not spend a night with me?" I had no intention of sleeping with any of those men or lingering in the lust-filled environment. Carlos asked me to stay until he played, but I had work in the morning and was still questioning the sanity of being attracted to another musician.

"Can I walk you to your car?" Carlos held my arm.

"Sure."

He stood close enough to melt all the fears I had had, then kissed my lips like a brush of fire.

I drove home without remembering what streets I had taken and called Lynn to give her every detail of my time with Carlos.

"Jerry said Carlos is the nicest man in the music business," she said.

Carlos called the next evening and invited me out.

I sat in the living room looking across housetops to the bay. Telephone lines disappeared in the large sky that covered San Francisco, Berkeley, and beyond. Was I rushing by saying I would go out with him again? Nureyev looked up at me and wagged his tail. *Yes,* I told him silently, *it's nice to feel a thrill again, but my heart is not strong enough to be hurt another time.* I petted his smooth fur.

Friday, Carlos picked me up from work. He seemed taller than I'd remembered, stepping out of his low, hatchback Volvo, casting a smile to me as I waved from the doorway of the Black Expo office. He wore snakeskin boots under jeans, and a tattered T-shirt. He wrapped his arm around me as we left the Oak

Street Victorian. We ate veggie burgers and drank fruit smoothies at Shandygaff, a dimly lit health food restaurant on Polk Street.

"Would you like to drive over to Mill Valley with me to see where I live?"

I wiped my mouth with my napkin and thought for a few moments. *If I go, what will I find? Does he do drugs? I can't be around them anymore. It's only a drive.* He watched me as I thought. My inner knowing told me to go slowly. I had been home only three months. Peace and patience with myself were just beginning to surface again.

"I don't do drugs, if you're worried about that. I'd like to get to know you," Carlos said.

I smiled. "I'm on a search for myself, Carlos. It's important that I think my actions through. God has to be in my life."

"Mine, too. My band broke up because I started meditating."

"Then I would love to see where you live." I was impressed that Carlos was not afraid to talk about God.

Carlos drove north across the Golden Gate Bridge. The sound of Coltrane's sax slid smoothly from the car speakers. His Volvo moved easily around the curves of Mount Tam. Dense thickets of trees crowded the roadside, parting now and then for driveways leading to secluded homes. I had been here only once before when Kitsaun and I went to Stinson Beach.

Carlos's profile was soft in the dusk. His long hair was topped by a bright rainbow-knit cap. The creamy skin on his face was stark beneath his thick, black mustache and spiky goatee. His nose was broad, his eyes hooded with heavy lids.

When he turned to me, he said, "I moved up here about a year ago. It was so quiet, I couldn't sleep when I first left the city."

"It's beautiful here," I said.

He turned off Shoreline Highway onto a gravel driveway. The car bumped along, past small, wooden houses. Carlos turned into a parking spot in front of a tower-like house. We had not spoken much. I was absorbed in imagining living so far away from the city—there weren't even streetlights. He turned off the car engine, pulled the key from the ignition, and turned to face me. In the moonless night, I could barely make out his features. "Welcome to my home," he said.

Three small spotlights lit the house. Shutters framed the windows, and the house was painted like a Bavarian chalet rising in the treetops. "It looks like a castle in a fairy tale," I said.

"Let's go in." He opened his car door and walked around the front of the car.

I swung my door open and stepped up, right into his arms. He pulled me close. I felt the light of a million stars. "You're like an angel with a broken wing," he whispered.

A soundless cry caught in my throat. I burrowed deep in his embrace, spiraling in the scent of the soft leather jacket on his long, lean frame. His arms around me eclipsed the pain that had overwrought me and clothed me in tender hope that my heart would heal. Not today or tomorrow, but sometime soon.

We walked across the driveway, beneath a trellis covered with climbing roses. Crickets trilled ceaselessly; moths flitted beneath the lights along the path to his front door. He turned the key and walked in quickly. "Hold on—I have to turn off the alarm." When he came back, he turned on a lamp. The living room came alive: wood-paneled walls, a tiled fireplace with 1936 painted in gold beneath the mantel, and red tulips hand-drawn on ceiling beams. There was nothing in the room except a rust-colored couch.

"Come on," he said. "I want to show you the meditation room. It's outside. Keep your coat on."

He led me through the living room to a steep staircase in the hall near the dark kitchen, where cat eyes peered from the shadows. "That's Gingi," he said. "I have two cats." At the top of the stairs, we walked through a small bedroom with windows on three walls. I could make out the shapes of trees, their dark outlines swaying in the light wind.

Carlos opened a glass-paned door, and we were outside on a deck. My eyes adjusted to the dark, and I could see the velvety mountain sweep into San Francisco Bay. The Richmond–San Rafael Bridge, draped in hanging lights, sparkled over the water.

One more flight of stairs led to the tower room I had seen from the car. Carlos opened the door—and silence engulfed us. "Would you like to meditate?" He held my eyes and my hands in his grasp.

At the end of each yoga class Mom and I took, the instructor led us in silent meditation. I enjoyed sitting still and calming my mind. "Sure," I said, glad for a chance to slow my heart.

"We leave our shoes outside," he said.

We sat down, folding our legs beneath us. Carlos struck a match, lighting a candle and a long stick of incense. We faced a small table covered with a white cloth, a painted likeness of Christ centered in a gold frame. The simple room had nothing else in it.

Carlos bowed his head to his hands, so I did the same. Then he rested both hands in his lap and stared straight ahead. I closed my eyes, the sweet incense becoming a part of me. I struggled to feel light coming in through my heart, but my awareness of Carlos's body made my senses yearn to close the space between us.

When I opened my eyes, the candle flame shivered. Shadows of our bodies flickered on the wall nearest me.

Carlos bowed, and I followed. He stood and then reached down for my hands and lifted me. His touch tripped off all my alarms. He blew out the candle and we started our descent, carrying our shoes in our arms.

"How long have you been meditating?" I asked. We walked down the steep stairs to the hallway.

"Almost six months." He put his arm around me, leading me through tiny halls into his bedroom. Slipping my coat off my shoulders, he motioned for me to sit down on the bed.

I hesitated. "Maybe we could talk in the kitchen?"

"There's no music in the kitchen." He turned on a brass lamp on the nightstand. There were no chairs, just a stool by his amplifier and stacks and stacks of record albums—and the bed. I walked around the room, looking at his albums and the tall stacks of cassettes. In the corner, three guitars rested on metal stands: a turquoise guitar, a bright red one, and a walnut-stained one. I had grown up with the sound of Dad's fat, round Gibson guitars; their melodies were my universe. Dad's tunes were my nursery rhymes, a second language in our home. Carlos's guitars were skinny and tall, as he was. I turned and saw him watching me.

"My dad plays guitar," I said.

"I know. He's Saunders King, right?"

I nodded.

"Jerry told me. I've read about him, but never really listened to his music. B. B. King worships your dad."

"You're kidding. I didn't know that." I walked to the only resting place and sat down on the bed. "So what are you doing with your new band?"

"We're rehearsing. When the old band broke up," he said, leaning back against the headboard, "I wanted that. After Woodstock, our egos got inflated. My life became more and more synthetic: I felt like a fake. All I care about is music, but I got pulled into the drugs, the parties. It was painful to lose my friends. I started meditating, seeking a new way, new music—a new life."

I crossed my ankles and leaned back against a pillow; very interested in this man and the direction he was taking his life.

"I've been fasting and praying for a teacher to help me," he said.

I nodded, not wanting to talk about how false and sad my life had been. The lamp cast a soft glow across our outstretched bodies. "I've been praying a lot, too. I want Truth in my life. I feel like hope is out there, even though I got lost for a while." I watched John Coltrane's record spin on the turntable beside the bed. An electric keyboard stood in front of two conga drums.

"Have you meditated before?" he asked.

"My Mom and I took hatha yoga when I was in high school. I just started classes again at Integral Yoga on Dolores Street."

Carlos slid his palm along my arm as I talked. "I love the quiet of spirit touching my soul."

He scooted closer to me on the bed, sliding his arm behind me. I lifted my head and sank back in the cradle of his shoulder, our faces an inch apart. The heat from his body pulled mine closer. We kissed, our lips a noon blaze, our tongues moist.

"You feel so strong," Carlos told me. "But I know you've been through hell. I saw you once in L.A."

"You did!" I sat back from him. "When? Where?" Any reminder of L.A. was a reminder of me on downers, out of control, with no connection to beauty or goodness. It was me at my lowest ebb. I was embarrassed.

"I was sitting on the fence outside Sly's house on Coldwater, waiting for the guys in the band. They went in to see Sly. I didn't want any part of him." He pulled me back into his arms. "You drove up in a car with another lady. I noticed you immediately. I even thought about going in when I saw you."

I laughed. So, he knew about Sly. He knew, so I didn't have to tell. And he remembered me. I thought about destiny's touch in my life. Were Carlos and I connected in some special way? "Thank you for noticing me again," I murmured softly. "That wasn't the best time in my life."

"Nor mine," he agreed. "But now we can start over together."

I lay in Carlos's arms, "After the Rain" playing on the stereo. "This is my favorite Coltrane song right now," Carlos murmured. I drifted on the notes gently blowing from the speakers and awoke later in quiet darkness. I remembered where I was as Carlos's hands skimmed my shoulders. His fingertips lifted my sweater, and my senses flamed. We sought each other's bodies, peeling our clothing off, kicking them onto the floor. His skin was soft, especially his hands. My broken places opened.

In the morning, I awoke in Carlos's arms, amazed that I could begin over again. My body felt revived; I perceived an extraordinary possibility that love was not a phantom. I wanted to walk out onto Carlos's deck and scream to the trees, "I'm alive!" But I lay in his embrace, savoring the promise of our friendship, no matter what it became. We drove down the mountain into Mill Valley and ate breakfast at a corner café. Carlos held my hand, and we walked to Old Mill Park and sat above a creek twisting through the redwoods.

"Where did you go to high school?" I asked.

"Mission. I was a blues guitarist and a stone hippie. I didn't want to come to the United States when my family immigrated to San Francisco. I was playing in a band in strip joints in Tijuana, making my own money. I was twelve. They had to leave without me because I hid out and they had a special day and time to leave."

I looked at Carlos's thin face, imagining his scrawny determination when he was younger. I was a Girl Scout when I was twelve, still reading novels about Freddy the pig. My memory of my own face was captured in a photograph of Karmen and me, before our orchestra performance, smiling proudly in our matching uniforms.

"My brother Tonio came back to get me. By the time I got to Mission High School I was playing blues with local guys, cutting school, and getting stoned. I moved out of my parents' house. And when the band first got together, I lived on Hartford Street in the Castro with the bass player, David Brown; our manager, Stan Marcum; and the road manager, Ron. Ron's girlfriend, Diane, would come over and cook. We were always hungry." Carlos laid his hand on his flat stomach. I trembled, remembering touching him in the night. "So when we got money from playing in the Panhandle in Golden Gate Park or at a wedding, Diane made big pots of spaghetti. One night we had enough money to buy a steak. We were sitting at the kitchen table salivating, waiting for the meat to be done. She opened the oven and turned away. Her dog, Troy, grabbed the steak from the hot pan and ran." Carlos and I laughed.

"We took off after him, a trail of mad musicians, but he was out the front door in two seconds. As much as I loved that dog, that night I wanted to kill him." Carlos shook his head.

"We were just kids out of high school trying to play music. We didn't have any guidance. Everybody smoked weed and hung out, even our manager." Carlos laughed dryly. "Actually, he was the most stoned of everybody. When our music took off and we started getting gigs and touring, we were still street punks with no manners. The guys in the band would show up late, and I would be furious. We'd start fighting—real fistfights sometimes."

A sports car zoomed down the park road, shifting gears and spouting exhaust.

"I remember bands playing in the Panhandle," I said. "In high school my girlfriend Gloria and I wanted to be hippies. I wanted a Volkswagen bus so badly. When I went away to college in L.A., I forgot about that."

"Where'd you go to high school?"

"Lowell."

"Oh, the smart school."

"Well, I was pretty social."

I looked up at the redwoods—magnificent, giant creatures. I felt as though the branches were reaching for God, carrying me up with them.

"I'm reading Paramahansa Yogananda right now," Carlos said. "He says the essence of everything is light, divine light. I can feel it here, in these trees."

The sun's rays touched every treetop. "Me, too," I said. "Since I've been practicing yoga again, my thoughts of where God lives have opened up. When I was little I thought God was just in heaven. But I have felt His presence inside me more and more." We threw stones into the creek, Carlos picking flat ones that skimmed along the top of the water.

"I had better get home," I said.

He stood up and dusted off the seat of his pants; he took my hand, and we walked through the park to his car. I was infatuated with this man and wanted Mom and Dad to meet him. Carlos was quiet as we climbed the stairs to my house. When we walked inside, Dad did not smile, but he shook Carlos's hand and invited him to sit down in our living room. Carlos's eyes were glued to Dad's blond Gibson guitar.

Mom said hello and turned the radio down. She began asking questions, as she always did with our friends. "Where does your family live?" she asked.

"We're all here in San Francisco," Carlos said. "I have four sisters and two brothers. My parents live in Noe Valley."

"Are you the oldest?" Mom pried.

"No. I'm right in the middle."

Dad picked up his guitar and began playing scales. Carlos leaned forward, watching Dad's hands. When Dad looked up, he said, "What kind of guitar do you play?" The mood in the room lightened, and Carlos and Dad talked instruments and musicians. Mom interjected opinions and asked questions, too.

I walked Carlos to the door and stepped outside on the porch with him. "Your dad is the cat," he said.

"He's a great musician." I smiled. We kissed good-bye, and I waved as he drove away.

"He seems like a nice young man," Mom said, walking toward the bedrooms.

Dad grunted. I didn't fault Dad's lack of enthusiasm, and knew he was remembering Sly as my boyfriend.

But Carlos was nothing like Sly. He was seeking God. His world was not drugs and deception. Carlos was filled with passion for music, especially the blues, which Dad had heard tonight. And I was different, too. If this unburned patch of my heart continued to pulse with love, I would not abandon the light within me. Dad's soft-spoken love for Kitsaun and me was unconditional. Grumpy and stiff sometimes, but always there. I walked to my father and put my arms around his waist. "I love you, Daddy." He squeezed me back.

10

Winterland

$\mathcal{C}$arlos called every night, and we talked for hours as I lay in the dark in my bedroom. I wanted to know what gave him the courage to leave the Santana Band at the peak of their success; he said spiritual progress was more important than gold records.

I explained how I had been betrayed by Sly, by his violence, and that I suspected he had been going out with other women when he left me home alone. I confessed how naive I had been and that I was trying to forgive myself because I had been only twenty. Carlos and I told each other our hopes and dreams. Carlos was one-pointed, determined to play music and only that.

Carlos picked me up from work, and we drove to Sausalito to eat and watch boats sail calmly on the bay. We meditated together and leaned on the railing of his mountaintop deck, watching birds swoop through the trees.

"What are you going to study in college?" he asked.

"I want to be a teacher—I love kids and learning."

Carlos sighed. "I can't imagine being anything but a musician. Even when I played violin in my father's mariachi band, I thought about having my own band. When I started playing guitar, I joined a rock band as soon as I could.

"In high school, I worked with my brother Tonio at Tick Tock's on Third Street. That's how I bought my first amplifier. We kept the kitchen clean and cooked French fries and burgers. I hated the smell of the bleach we used to mop the floors. I'll never forget it." He paused. "You'd make a great teacher. I've never met a woman who has goals like you." I smiled at his compliment.

"I thought I was going to write poetry," I said. "Remember the book Lynn and I were writing? We didn't receive enough interest from women, so we put it on hold. I sent one of my poems to a Sonoma magazine, but it was rejected." Carlos looked disappointed for me. "The first time I read Rainer Maria Rilke's *Letters to a Young Poet,* I fell in love with poetry. I bought a long, flowered dress at a secondhand store and combed out my braid, letting my hair spread wildly in the air. But it's very difficult to compose something great."

Some nights after work, I met Carlos on upper Fillmore Street, where he practiced with his new band. I waited outside until the band finished. I didn't want to intrude or distract the musicians. Michael Shrieve, the drummer, and Chepitó Areas, the timbales player, were from the original band. Michael grew up in the Bay Area and had introduced Carlos to the music of John Coltrane and Miles Davis. Chepitó was a jokester from Nicaragua. Sensitive about his height, he always wore high heels, and he panted strangely when he talked to women. Carlos said Chepitó was talented and played flügelhorn and trumpet as well as percussion. Together, they had hired local musicians to expand the band's repertoire to an open, free-flowing jam of jazz and rock, at the edge of an undefined genre of music. Carlos did not want to perform the band's hits when they began touring. He created a three-hour set of music without "Black Magic Woman," "Evil Ways," or "Oye Como Va." I admired his daring.

My identity was important to me. I felt that I was Carlos's girlfriend—someone to respect. It was imperative to me that I not be viewed as a groupie: I knew musicians used women around a band as disposable, or as something to share, a "thing" to assuage their hunger. I had seen Sly's band members, as well as guys in acts that opened for them, licking their lips while looking at women backstage. They would choose one, or sometimes more, to spend the night. In the morning, we would gather in the lobby to leave; and the women, in their concert garb, faces smeared with mascara, stood proudly as they waved good-bye. It was the guys' low voices and snickers that taught me that the women were not valued but rather were pieces in a board game to be touched, played with, and thrown back in the box—forgotten. I despised the groupie culture, with sympathy and pity mixed together in my heart.

Atop Carlos's TV was a photo of a smiling woman with hair below her shoulders and her arms around a young girl and boy. I asked Carlos who she was.

"That's my friend Linda and her kids. We broke up before I met you. She lives down in Mill Valley. When I met Linda, some guy had tossed her in a garbage can behind a club."

I wondered why he kept her photo out, and I recognized that I, too, had been treated like rubbish before I met Carlos. He said they were friends, but my suspicious, hurt part wondered if that was all they were.

"I love her kids," he said. "We used to eat bowls of cereal in bed Saturday mornings and watch cartoons together. It gave me a chance to have the childhood I was never given."

On Sunday afternoons we started a ritual of lying on the deck above the canyon, slathered with coconut oil, basking unclothed in the sun. At six o'clock, we would dash downstairs and jump on the bed to watch Carlos's favorite TV show, *Wild Kingdom*.

"Look at that," Carlos would exclaim, watching the antics of a lion cub or a gorilla. I was surprised he adored animals, and I was charmed by his innocent display of joy. We laughed from our bellies.

My job at Black Expo ended with a concert at the Civic Auditorium in downtown San Francisco. Because I was on the production side of the show, I was there from early morning, checking in musicians and equipment and monitoring ticket sales in the box office. I worked beside Stevie, who knew the entire process. A manager of one of the groups talked to me as though I were there for his ego and captivated by his charms. When I rebuffed his come-on and tended to the business, he said, "Oh, I see. It's like that," implying I preferred women to men because I was next to Stevie. I thought about defending myself, but decided *who cares what he thinks?* and ignored him, which felt powerful. I never wanted to have to explain myself to a man again.

San Francisco State was about a mile from my parents' house. Classes began in early September, and I used the money from my last paycheck to buy my books for school. Most nights I was with Carlos at his mountaintop chalet. He let me drive his Volvo to school after I dropped him at rehearsal. I wrapped my mind around creative writing and Spanish, excited to be in college again.

Santana's fourth album, *Caravanserai,* was soon to be released. I played "Song of the Wind" over and over, trying to decipher which guitar was Carlos's and which was Neal Schon's. I felt as though I were flying when they traded solos; the band's music soared with layers of rhythm and melody unlike any I had heard before.

Carlos was focused on rehearsing for the upcoming Santana shows with the new lineup. Three concerts in three nights were booked for October at Winterland in San Francisco. The shows would be a warm-up to a European tour in November.

The day of the first concert, we drove to Winterland in Carlos's Volvo. No limos, no fringe, no sparkly sequined shirts, no drugs. We arrived in the early afternoon for the band to have sound check. Carlos wore blue jeans, boots, and his faded, ripped Jesus T-shirt.

Winterland held 5,400 people. Fans were already lined up outside, even though the doors would not open for three hours. Carlos grabbed my hand as we walked inside the dark, cavernous hall, his guitar case swinging at his side. I felt as small as a mouse moving through narrow hallways to the hospitality suite.

"I'll see you later," Carlos said. I hugged his neck, holding on to his embrace, afraid to let go. My insides were shaking as I remembered almost two years earlier when I had been here. I reluctantly put my arms down and watched him walk to his tuning room. My eyes took in the dressing room.

I recalled the night perfectly: Mom and Dad let me borrow their Dodge Dart to meet Sly at Winterland. I parked a few blocks from the Steiner Street entrance, zipped my keys into my purse, and strode confidently to the "will call" window inside the lobby. "Hi," I said to the woman behind the glass, "my name is Deborah King. There should be a ticket here for me."

Her ring-clad fingers shuffled through the box holding tickets with names handwritten on green envelopes. "I don't see anything for you," she said, flipping her dishwater-blond hair off her face. She looked over my head at the man standing behind, dismissing me.

"Well, Sly was supposed to leave my name," I explained, holding my ground. "Could you check with someone in back?"

"I can't leave the box office. Stand over there and I'll try to find someone who can go backstage," she said, waving her hand toward the street in a show of irritation.

My shoulder blades tightened. I moved about ten inches from her window—just enough to let the hundred other people in line step up closer to the front.

I thought about what I would do if she didn't find someone to go backstage. *I should have come earlier with Sly,* I scolded myself. Well, I would wait a little longer before I would ask her again.

Pretty soon, a man burst through one of the doors leading inside. He wore a white shirt with rolled-up sleeves and blue jeans. He walked fast, a scowl spread darkly across his face. "Get in line!" he screamed at me as he buzzed by, slicing his hand past my face toward the other ticket buyers.

"I'm waiting for my ticket." My voice rose in anger.

He stopped, shoulders hunched, and turned around, his face dark. "Well, wait outside!" he bellowed, his bushy black eyebrows furrowed in a diabolic frown.

I looked hopefully at the lady in the ticket booth. She would not look at me. I would not move.

A husky security man approached me. "Bill says you have to wait outside."

I tried explaining my dilemma to him, but Bill Graham yelled from across the vestibule, "Put her outside!" His deep voice echoed wildly across the tile floor.

The man picked me up, threw me over his shoulder, my stomach squeezed by his muscular arms. The line of people parted for the guard to sit me down on the sidewalk. Some people close by screamed at him for his roughness, and a man in a tie-dyed shirt kneeled next to me. "Are you okay?" he asked, reaching out his hand to help me up.

"Yeah. Thanks." I looked into his kind eyes and brushed off Sly's shaggy goat-hair coat that I was wearing. More embarrassed than hurt, I stormed down the street, tears pushing at my eyelids. I was too angry to let them fall. My feet kept moving until I was near the stage door entrance. Sly's dad, KC, stood outside, talking with a security guard. He waved, and I ran to him. Words and tears gushed out together. He put his arm around my shoulders and hustled me inside, telling the door guard that I was "okay."

In Sly's dressing room, KC explained to him what had happened. Sly's expression was grim, and his shiny red ruffled shirt cast an eerie glow in his eyes. He told KC, "Tell Bill Graham I'm not going on until he apologizes." KC rushed out of the room.

I said, "Just forget it." Sly had not bothered to answer. He sat on the Formica counter in front of a wall of mirrors and bright makeup lights. I moved to the couch across from him. When Bill Graham entered the dressing room, Sly said, "I hear you threw my lady out in the street."

"I didn't know who she was," Bill brashly answered. "She didn't have a ticket." I could not take my eyes off the big mole over his bushy left eyebrow. His hair was parted just above that, and his forehead had a deep crevice, probably from screaming and frowning, I thought.

"Well, you owe her an apology, man, or I don't play." Sly slowly raised his head and glared into Bill's eyes, Sly's voice shaking on the last three words.

"I'm sorry, miss," Bill said as he turned to me, feigning remorse.

Not opening my mouth, I nodded slightly, shaking with the same anger that electrified the entire room. The weight of the goat coat was making me hot and light-headed.

Bill Graham turned and walked out of the room. I had met the great promoter.

Tonight, my fear was that I would see him again, when everything was perfect with Carlos, and that he would still be angry.

"Would you like something to drink?" a voice broke through my thoughts.

I looked toward the doorway and saw a bushy-haired man, wearing round glasses on the tip of his nose, smiling at me.

"Hi," he said. "I'm Killer, Santana's stage manager. Carlos wants me to make sure you have a place to watch the show."

"Thank you. It's nice to meet you."

"The band's almost ready to go on. Would you like me to take you onstage?" he asked.

"Thanks, but I think I'll go out in the audience. Could you get me a backstage pass so I can get back after?"

Killer smiled. "Sure," he said. "I'll be right back."

I stood looking at my face in the mirrors across from the couch. My hair was brushed over my forehead and wisped onto my cheeks. My tight, cropped sweater hugged my waist. I had gained seven pounds since my move home and no longer hated looking at my reflection. My features weren't lined now with painful twists of despair from trying to break away from Sly.

Killer came back with the pass. I pulled off the waxed backing and stuck the adhesive side to my top. Walking down the narrow corridor, I felt a little jumpy, wondering whether Bill Graham might be around the next turn.

Killer led me to the velvet curtains opening to the concert hall. The house lights were turned up, the lighting tech waiting for the signal that the band was ready. Technicians tuned the congas and set Carlos's guitars next to his amplifiers. As men moved into the shadows of the stage, the arena went black, and a cheer went up from the audience. Blood pumped through my body anticipating seeing Carlos onstage. I had never seen Santana in concert.

A lone spotlight turned on Tom Coster, the new keyboardist,

who struck a brass gong. Carlos stood, his back to the audience—long curly hair angling down his T-shirt. The music began as a prayer, with soft, minor chords; then notes sang from Carlos's guitar. The drums crescendoed, church chords shimmied from the keyboard, and music rolled off the stage like a ship on the ocean, wave after wave of rhythms and melodies, the guitar sailing on the crest of it all. I followed each musician's solos for the two-and-a-half-hour show. "Incident at Neshabur" was the finale. Carlos bowed and thanked the audience. The crowd stood clapping, whistling, and waving their arms for more.

Music echoed in my ears. Notes that had danced from Carlos's fingers clutched my heart. I shouldered through the crowd and the backstage curtains.

The audience would not stop screaming, whistling, and stomping on the floor. "More! Encore! Encore!"

Killer found me in the hallway to the dressing rooms and led me up wooden steps to the side of the stage where the musicians huddled together. Carlos looked up, his eyes brimming with light. His mouth was wide open, laughing jubilantly.

Someone bumped my arm. There, as close as my breath, was Bill Graham. He charged past me. I stepped back in the shadow, hiding behind the raised lid of a road case. Bill was talking wildly nose-to-nose with Carlos. Carlos watched him, nodded his head, and then led the band back onstage.

The organ played a familiar opening that sent the audience into a shrieking frenzy: "Black Magic Woman." The percussive rhythms had the audience jumping to the beat like a tribe of Africans moving through a savanna. After the encore, Carlos danced into my arms, his T-shirt soaked with perspiration. Screams echoed from the arena as we walked to the dressing room.

Bill Graham slapped Carlos on the back, "See! You can't leave all the hits out of the set. Your audience would never forgive you."

Carlos smiled and raised his hands in surrender. "Bill, this is my friend, Debbie. You might know her father, Saunders King."

Bill looked me in the eyes and put his hand out. "Hello. Nice to meet you."

I shook his hand, relieved that either he did not remember me or did not let on that he did. "Hello, Bill." We were quickly swallowed in a crush of admirers surging into the dressing room.

Caterers laid trays of sandwiches on a long table. The sound of beer cans popping open mixed with laughter, and people pushed close to Carlos—voices rising to a clamorous high.

After the weekend of concerts, I went home and studied hard for my classes, trying to put out of my mind that Carlos would be leaving for a European tour in less than a month. I did not want to be without him for five weeks.

One afternoon at the Mill Valley house, Carlos pounced on the bed. "Guess what?" he said.

"What?"

He gripped my shoulders and exclaimed, "John McLaughlin wants me to record with him. He's a magnificent guitarist, a musical giant. He played with Miles."

"That's great," I said, although I had never heard John

Deborah Santana

McLaughlin's music. I knew anyone who had played with Miles
Davis was a god to Carlos. I remembered Carlos's face when I
told him Dad's story about Miles. Dad had taken Mom to hear
Miles at a club in San Francisco in the early 1950s. Miles spotted Dad and jumped from the bandstand, hugging Dad so tight
that he picked him right up off the floor. They had played in the
same clubs together years earlier. When Dad introduced Mom,
Miles said, "Man, what'd you do, rob the cradle?"

Now I was worried that if Carlos recorded with John, he
would be gone longer than I had thought. I swallowed my sadness and tried to look glad for him. "That's a great opportunity."

Carlos riffled through the stack of albums by the bed. "This
is John's last record, *Birds of Fire*. It's amazing." He put it on.
Strings poured out with electric guitar, keyboard, pounding
drums. We sat on the bed, covered by music. I picked up the
album. John's band was called the Mahavishnu Orchestra. The
back cover showed a poem called "Revelation" by Sri Chinmoy.
Carlos had mentioned that Larry Coryell, another guitarist he
knew, had a guru named Sri Chinmoy.

Carlos tucked my hands beneath his. "Why don't you come
to New York with me?"

I looked into his chiseled face, his deep-set black eyes, and
wrapped my arms around his waist, squeezing him tightly. "I'd
love to, but, school . . ." I did not know how I could take time
off. Plus, hadn't I just returned to college after having dropped
out to travel with another musician? Disappointed, I said,
"Thanks for asking me."

All week I thought about not going to New York with Carlos. I went to my professors to see whether it would be possible

* 144 *

to continue my work outside of school for a short time. All of them consented. I was thrilled.

Mom told me she wished I would not go to New York, but rather stay and concentrate on my studies. "You're twenty-one now, honey," she said. "You've got to think about your future."

As soon as she finished talking, I packed. I knew Mom was right; she cared about the practical, sensible responsibilities in life. But I was unreasonably in love, and there was no place I wanted to be except with Carlos. I did not have Mom's blessing, but at least this time she and Dad knew Carlos and I left them our hotel information.

New York's skies were streaked with lavender hues. The sun's last blaze backlit the haze above the horizon. Our jumbo 747 banked through the clouds and rumbled onto the tarmac. I touched the small oval window, looking at the sleek airport buildings. I glanced at Carlos, his droopy eyelids and Aztec nose looking out the window. He smiled a wide, mustached grin and grabbed my hand with his long, butterscotch fingers.

I shoved my book into my shoulder bag. Carlos slung his soft-case Gibson Les Paul over his shoulder, and we walked down the Jetway into the embrace of John McLaughlin. He was two inches taller than Carlos, his face was square, and his hair cut in a thick crew.

"This is my wife, Mahalakshmi," John said with a British accent.

"This is Debbie." Carlos pointed to me. We all shook hands.

Mahalakshmi reached my shoulder. Her blond hair was pulled back into a straight ponytail. Clear, blue eyes caught mine, and she smiled warmly.

We strolled to baggage claim, weaving in and out of hundreds of passengers who rushed in every direction. Skycaps yelled, "Need help?" A man in a navy chauffeur cap and wrinkled trench coat elbowed up to me and said in a quiet voice, "Only thirty dollars to Manhattan." I shook my head and moved closer to Carlos. Police whistles rang outside, while suitcases banged down baggage chutes.

Mahalakshmi turned to me. "Have you been to New York before?" She also spoke with a clipped British accent.

"Only twice. Very short trips," I replied. The summer I had met Sly flashed through my mind.

Carlos and I pulled our bags from the carousel. John took mine, and we headed for the automatic doors.

A brisk breeze snapped against my face. John led us to their Volvo sedan in the parking lot across from the terminal, and Carlos and I climbed into the backseat.

As we drove out of the airport, I saw stripped, broken-down cars lining the roadside, with windows shattered and tires gone. Their empty shells looked lost and harshly abandoned.

"We'll just stop by home if you want to clean up a bit before popping into our restaurant for supper," John said over his shoulder as he entered the Grand Central Parkway.

"That's fine," Carlos said. He squeezed my hand. I looked into his eyes and leaned over, kissing his lips. I was grateful not to feel lost or abandoned anymore.

Brownstone buildings with metal signs sat above us on the frontage road. "Mahavishnu and I would like you to meet our guru, Sri Chinmoy," Mahalakshmi said. "We've studied with him two years. He teaches us meditation and to serve the world through love, devotion, and surrender to God."

She calls John by the same name as his band. It must be related somehow to the guru.

Carlos scooted forward and rested his arms on the front seat. "Larry Coryell stayed at my house last year. He had a photo of Sri Chinmoy that he meditated on. Before I met Debbie, I fasted seven days, asking God to lead me to my spiritual teacher."

John and Mahalakshmi looked at each other and smiled.

"Our restaurant is one of the divine enterprises that disciples have here in Queens."

Jesus' closest followers had been called "disciples." I asked, "What are 'disciples'? And 'divine enterprises'?"

John laughed. " 'Disciples' are what we call ourselves when we follow Sri Chinmoy's teachings. We consider ourselves 'devotees' who tell others about guru."

" 'Divine enterprises' are businesses owned by disciples," Mahalakshmi said. "Our menu is vegetarian. I hope you like it. Guru says that meat is full of aggressive animal consciousness, which interferes with our meditation." I had eaten at the Source on Sunset Boulevard when I lived in L.A. It was vegetarian, and I had loved the salads and casseroles, drawn to the purity of the whole grains and organic produce, fresh-squeezed juices, and the luminescence in the eyes of the workers. My body felt more buoyant and agile eating less meat.

John parked on a street lined with two-story houses with small front yards. Leaves hung from trees in brilliant shades of red, amber, and gold-flecked green. We walked upstairs to their flat. The stark whiteness of the walls stood out in contrast to the dark Long Island skies. Mahalakshmi took off her coat and asked to hang ours. She wore a long, flowing drape around her body that I had seen on women from India. She saw me staring. "Guru asks that we wear saris for meditation and work."

"Oh," I said. "It's pretty."

Carlos and I sat in the living room, looking at books by Sri Chinmoy on the coffee table. There were photos of the guru on the walls, too.

In a few minutes, we tumbled back inside the car and drove to their restaurant, Annam Brahma, a few blocks away.

"Mahavishnu and I own the restaurant," Mahalakshmi said as she opened her car door. "I manage the day-to-day operations, with five disciples to help me."

The women who waited the tables wore saris as well as sandals with sockless feet, as though it were summer rather than fall. Their blouses exposed a few inches of midriff. The men were dressed in white from head to toe. Every wall in the restaurant was brightly painted in reds and golds with images of Indian gods and Sanskrit symbols. My eyes kept returning to a print of an Indian woman in red, standing above a circle formed by the heads of twenty men. A wreath of arms framed her body. A huge photo of Sri Chinmoy, similar to the one in his books, hung in a recessed alcove. Vases of flowers sat beneath the photo, and incense burned in a small brass holder. Disciple waiters floated around our table, bringing plates of spicy Indian curries.

Mahalakshmi pointed. "That yellowish stew is *dahl*. The flat bread is *chapati*."

"What is this delicious drink?" I asked, gulping a delicate, white liquid.

"Ah," John smiled. "My favorite. It is a sweet *lhasi*—yogurt blended with honey, ice, and rose water."

Carlos's eyes flashed. "Remember when I saw you at Slugs with Tony Williams? I asked you what it was like to record with Wayne on Supernova."

"Yeah. I told you how wonderful that session was," John answered.

"Where's Slugs?" I asked.

"Here in New York City," John said. "Tony's a great drummer."

"Your drummer Billy Cobham is a powerhouse," Carlos said. "I can't wait to play with him."

The restaurant bustled with customers and workers. "Do you work here every day, Mahalakshmi? Am I pronouncing it right—Ma-ha-'lock-shmee?"

"Yes, that's right. I work five days. I also travel to Europe to give talks about meditation." She tore a piece of *puri* and scooped *dahl* into her mouth.

"Life was rather bleak until we found Guru," she said. "Now Mahavishnu and I have a purpose deeper than we had ever known before."

"What is that?" I asked, looking into her serious blue eyes.

She spooned chutney onto my plate. "We've accepted that God-consciousness can be attained in this lifetime. That's why we have the restaurant—so we can meditate even while we work. We opened this place to feed people's souls as well as their bodies."

"It is not enough to go to church on Sunday and then live the remainder of the week without God," John said. "The spiritual path of meditation is active twenty-four hours a day. Sri Chinmoy teaches us to keep the mind pure and the heart open to God. He also meditates on us, infusing our bodies with light."

I was a sponge, soaking up this new information: feeding souls; feeling purpose in one's life. It was exactly what I wanted: a cleansing of the impurities in my mind and body, a recovery of who I was before I met Sly—a scrubbing of my soul.

"Where is Sri Chinmoy from?" Carlos asked, his head cocked to the side as he listened intently.

"A small village in India," Mahalakshmi said. "His family studied with Sri Aurobindo, a yoga master and ascetic."

Carlos said he was interested in meeting Sri Chinmoy. *Did I want to meet this guru, too?* The sound of dishes clinking together, and pots banging in the kitchen, hummed around me. In that moment, I wanted nothing more than to experience what these new friends were living. *Could a guru map out my road in life and show me a safe path through the universe?*

We finished the meal with *gulab jamun,* round, doughy balls soaked in sugary syrup. I sat back in my chair, relaxed, content, and filled with thoughts about my next steps, my future. A new possibility was unveiling before me, a communion with my place in the divine plan. The warmth and happiness in the restaurant made me want to stay there. I felt at a turning point in my life.

Carlos and I thanked Mahalakshmi and John. We shook hands and said good-bye to disciples who seemed awed by Carlos, and we bundled into our coats for the walk to the car. John drove us to our hotel in the city, while Mahalakshmi stayed to close the restaurant. Bounding over the parkway, our conversation waned in the late hour. Lights from Manhattan's skyscrapers shimmered across the East River against the gray-black sky. Musty subway odors seeped through John's open window when he paid the toll for the Midtown Tunnel.

He stopped at the curb outside the Fifth Avenue Hotel. Washington Square was two blocks up, the lighted arch glowing over Greenwich Village.

"Thank you, John," I said, climbing out of the backseat.

"You're welcome. Please call me Mahavishnu. Our names have spiritual meanings that Guru gave us. Mine means 'the great Vishnu'—the god who preserves divinity. Mahalakshmi's means 'the great Lakshmi'—the goddess of beauty."

"They're exquisite," I said.

We pulled our suitcases out of the Volvo and waved Mahavishnu back to Queens. A bellman appeared and took our bags inside.

Riding the shaking elevator to the eighth floor, Carlos leaned over and brushed his lips across mine. I tipped the bellman, closed the door, and slid out of my coat. What a magnificent night. My life felt changed—renewed and energized.

New York was wide awake at midnight: horns honking,

traffic lights blinking, strangers scurrying along Fifth Avenue. I sat down at the window and played back the ideas I had been introduced to.

I felt as though fingers, gentle and prodding, had peeled back a dark curtain over my soul and exposed it to the changeless, enduring presence of God.

Carlos set up his cassette player, and Miles's "In a Silent Way" eased into the room.

11

The Pendulum

I fell asleep cradled in Carlos's arms and awoke with his chin resting on my head, my leg across his legs. Bits of last night's conversation floated through my mind. I knew I belonged here on this spiritual adventure with him, seeking something divine through this catalyst of music.

Strips of white paint peeled from the corners of the ceiling above us. The phone rang. I twisted my body toward the nightstand. "Hello?"

"Hi. This is Mahalakshmi. How are you today?"

Her English was so proper. "Fine, thank you."

"I hope I didn't disturb you, but Guru—rather, Sri Chinmoy—has asked me to invite you and Carlos to the United Nations for meditation today at noon. Do you think you can make it?"

I turned to Carlos. He hadn't moved, but was listening to my conversation, one eye open. I was intrigued by the invitation and hoped he was, too. "Can you hold the line, please?"

Burying the phone in the bedcovers, I repeated Sri Chinmoy's request to Carlos.

"Sure," he said. "I'd love to."

"Thanks, Mahalakshmi. We'll be there."

Carlos and I took a taxi across Manhattan. Centuries of living oozed from the buildings, the sidewalks, the people. San Francisco was nascent and tame by comparison. Soot clung to Manhattan's stone facades, poured on by trains, buses, cars, and ships. The boroughs were separated into ethnic groups, yet everyone met as equals on the frenzied battleground of the city.

Dozens of flags representing member countries stood tall along First Avenue in front of the United Nations. The U.N. Chapel was across the street from the stately gray office building on Forty-sixth Street. Mahavishnu and Mahalakshmi stood outside, waving at us from the cab. We followed them into the sanctuary to a row of umber-toned pews that faced a paneled dais in a room the size of a small auditorium. Opulent yet simple, the room was half-filled with forty or more disciples—young men dressed in white, and women in flower-patterned saris—sitting alongside people in suits. Nearly everyone's eyes were closed. Carlos and I sat between Mahavishnu and Mahalakshmi. I straightened my back and closed my eyes, hearing only the faint rustle of clothes against legs as newcomers filed into the pews.

The creak of a door and a low murmur of voices caused me to open my eyes. A round-faced man in a peacock blue flowing garment glided into the room and climbed the stairs to the dais. He was of medium height, his head bald, his hands folded at his chest. He bowed and walked to the podium, gazing intently at his audience, a slight smile on his lips.

At first sight, Sri Chinmoy looked as Mahavishnu and Maha-lakshmi had at the airport: austerely clean, with an otherworldly glow outlining his body. Brown-skinned, like Paramahansa Yogananda in photos I had seen, Sri Chinmoy's nose was sharp and his ears pointy. I turned my gaze within, breathing deeply, trying to expel all images from my mind in order to meditate, but thoughts swept through my head like a ticker tape on Wall Street: Kitsaun's face—*How I wish she were here with me to experience this meditation.* My English professor—*Will I return to school?* A volley of Sly's sneers and mischievous smiles veered through my mind as well. I silently asked God to purify me and forgive my past so that the painful choices I had made would stop haunting me. My chest heaved and fell, my breath calmed, and a feeling of grace brought tears to my eyes. I sat in peace, finally silent inside, yellow-white light beaming in the air whenever I looked up.

When I looked at Sri Chinmoy his body looked frozen. His arms were raised high in the air, his hands pressed together, and his eyes moved up and down rapidly.

What is he doing? I peeked a glance at Mahalakshmi on my right. She was looking at Sri Chinmoy, her mouth in a soft smile. I closed my eyes again, concentrating on my heart gently rising and falling in the center of my body. For thirty minutes, no sound was uttered. I wondered whether Carlos was feeling peaceful or whether thoughts were running through his head. Sri Chinmoy sang one long, nasal "Om" and then bowed. Everyone stood and filed out of the church, disciples with their hands pressed together, bowing as they walked past the guru. I looked at Carlos; we smiled and leaned into each other, not ready to leave.

Mahavishnu asked Carlos and me to meet the guru, walking us to the front of the room. Sri Chinmoy smiled widely and made cooing sounds, his hands hidden in the pockets of the winter coat he had put on. "I'm very happy to meet you," he said, his voice inflected with a slight accent. "Please come to my house for meditation tonight."

He turned and walked through the door, which was held wide by two young men who quickly followed after him. His flowing Indian dress hung shiny and soft under his brown tweed coat. Carlos bowed and touched his hands to his heart.

"Come to our house later and we'll take you to Guru's," Mahavishnu said. "We'll go to the studio after."

Carlos nodded. He grasped my hand, and we stood watching people leave the chapel. I felt stunned, as though knocked down by floodwaters that had washed me clean. An exhilarating freedom was awakened inside me, as though my soul had been asleep until this moment of spiritual illumination, as though meditation on my own was just a hint of what could be experienced. I looked at Carlos—his face was flushed.

"I feel different," he said, looking in my eyes. "I felt something divine in that meditation. Did you?"

"I saw light. For the first time, I felt the bliss we've read about in meditation books."

We walked ten blocks, letting the experience settle in our hearts before deciding where to go. We took a cab back to the Village and ate lunch in a tiny health food store on Eighth Street. A cockroach ran by on the shelf behind the lunch counter as I lifted my avocado sandwich to my lips. "A New York good luck charm," I said, and smiled.

In the late afternoon, we took a taxi to Mahavishnu and Mahalakshmi's house in Queens. They asked if we had trouble saying their names and told us that we could call them the Mahas. Carlos and I looked at each other and laughed. We confessed it was hard to say "Sri Chinmoy." "That's why the disciples call him 'Guru,' " Mahavishnu explained.

"A guru is to be venerated above normal people or spiritual aspirants because he has reached oneness with God," Mahalakshmi said. "When we are invited to his home, like tonight, we are being blessed to feel the transcendent power of God that he receives in meditation." We drove the few blocks to Sri Chinmoy's house. Disciples walked down the street, twilight's shadows dancing on softly billowing Indian saris. *Do they all live in this neighborhood?*

"Is what Sri Chinmoy wears also called a sari?" I asked.

Mahalakshmi opened her car door. "No. The men wear *dhotis* tied around their waists like a sari, and a long shirt that hangs to the thigh, called a *kurta.*"

We climbed the stairs and entered the guru's home. Carlos and I took off our shoes, leaving them beside the Mahas' on the enclosed porch. Each step I took in my stocking feet took me further into this new world. Here we were in the house of a realized spiritual master. Walls were painted high-gloss white. Soft, baby-blue carpeting looked like a waveless ocean. No furniture cluttered the main room that I supposed was once a living room. Only a long, two-foot-tall throne, ornately painted with gold leaf, stood in front of the windows. There, Sri Chinmoy sat cross-legged, wearing an emerald, flowing *dhoti*. The *kurta* hung loosely from his broad shoulders. The only visible parts of his body were his chestnut-hued hands, neck, and very shiny head. Sri Chinmoy's eyes glistened like gold nuggets when he smiled.

"Oh, ho!" he exclaimed as we walked into the room. "You have come." His face gleamed as he narrowed his eyes into meditative slits, watching Carlos and me sit down on the floor beside Mahavishnu and Mahalakshmi. Disciples were lined up in rows facing Sri Chinmoy. I smiled at the woman beside me.

"We are so glad you have come to our humble meditation," the guru spoke softly. "Of course, we are here to meditate on God and bring down the Supreme light from above. Let us go within."

Wafts of incense smoke curled from a table beside the throne. Sri Chinmoy straightened his back and looked up, as though seeing God through the ceiling. He parted his lips, his face molding into a plastic-looking mask. I took deep breaths, swaying in the longing that pulsated from my heart. Thoughts faded, and I was overtaken with the peaceful silence in the room.

Sri Chinmoy chanted "Om" as he had at the U.N. meditation. He looked down at Carlos and me, and then he closed his eyes.

"You are both soulful seekers of the divine Truth. I can feel God's blessings entering into you. Do you have any questions?"

I could not speak. What could I say or ask in front of all these disciples who had been meditating so much longer than I?

Carlos said meekly, "I have followed Jesus and am wondering if meditation with you is okay with him." A few disciples laughed.

Sri Chinmoy said, "This is a very good question. Many of my disciples come from churches and synagogues. We are a path, not a religion. You might think of Jesus as one of God's eyes and me as the other. Through both eyes you can see the Almighty. We are working together to give you the vision of God."

Carlos bowed. I was glad he had asked that question. We had both been raised to believe that Christ is the way to God and heaven.

A girl with waist-length wavy brown hair asked, "How can I make the most progress in the spiritual life?"

Sri Chinmoy closed his eyes. "If you cry only to please God in His own way, if you cry only for your progress, then you are bound to get all the experiences which God has in store for you. Imagine you have a bicycle inside you. When you ride a bicycle, you have to pedal it all the time. You cannot balance motionless at one point. While you are meditating, you have to aspire all the time; otherwise, you will fall. In the spiritual life, movement has to be constant. Either you move forward or you move backward. So, good girl, always pedal forward, always aspire to please God in His own way."

It was as though we were students in Sri Chinmoy's class. In a way, sitting at his feet reminded me of times with Sly. He had created a student-teacher atmosphere, even with candlelight, similar to the candles burning on the table beside Sri Chinmoy. Many nights I had sat at Sly's feet, looking up to him as he talked about his music and danced before his friends as though we were his disciples. I felt cautious at the remembrance. Sly had not been a window to divinity. I hoped it was not possible to get caught in a similar trap with a man who professed to be holy.

I glanced at Carlos, his face shining with light. He caught my stare and smiled. Carlos had a spiritual core like mine, with a hunger to live for God's truth. We would figure this out together.

"Dhruva. You have a question, good boy?" Sri Chinmoy gestured to a man in the row behind us.

"Guru, what is the difference between getting high on drugs and getting high in meditation?" A few snorts of laughter sounded around the room.

"Do not laugh. This is very important," Sri Chinmoy said. "Of course, people may ask how I know the difference since I have not taken drugs. But, I have meditated and have realised the Highest. The use of drugs is not proper. Those who take drugs are damaging their subtle nerves and spiritual faculties. It is the same with drinking and smoking."

I could feel my face flush. He continued. "Those who take drugs get an experience that is unnatural and forced. But when one meditates and enters into the living Consciousness of God, at that time one sees the real Light, knows the real Truth, and feels the real Ecstasy. By taking drugs and using artificial means, people are unconsciously, if not deliberately, negating the real Truth."

I felt like everyone's eyes were on Carlos and me. Sri Chinmoy smiled at Dhruva. "But do not waste your precious time brooding on the kind of life that you lived in the past. I do not ask anybody to repent. It is true that repentance purifies the soul. But at the same time, if you are constantly repenting your past, then you will have no time to aspire and look forward toward the light of the future. All right?"

I needed to hear that it was not necessary to look back. I spent a lot of time examining my past mistakes.

Sri Chinmoy waved his hand and said, "It is late. Go rest." Disciples stood and walked to the front porch. Carlos was surrounded by young men reaching to shake his hand. I looked back at Sri Chinmoy on his throne. He threw a dazzling smile in my direction. I quickly looked down, embarrassed by his attention.

Mahavishnu drove back to their house to drop off Mahalakshmi before he drove us to Manhattan.

"What do you think of our guru?" Mahavishnu asked.

Carlos was quiet for a few seconds. "I think he embodies God's wisdom."

Mahavishnu waited.

"I'm curious about the teachings," I said.

"Do you think you would like to become a disciple?" Mahavishnu asked.

"When Larry Coryell stayed at my house," Carlos offered, "he had that photo of Sri Chinmoy meditating, and it scared me." Carlos shook his head as though trying to get the image out. "Maybe I didn't want light at that time. I've changed, but I don't know if I'm ready to be a disciple, man."

"What does one have to do to be a disciple?" I asked, remembering the words of compassion Sri Chinmoy had spoken that had touched my broken heart.

"Guru says that his meditation path is a boat, and he is the boatman taking us to the Golden Shore," Mahavishnu said. "When he accepts a disciple, he concentrates on the seeker's soul to ask God if the person is meant to follow his path. If the answer is yes, he gives the aspirant's soul an inner meditation. He brings our souls forward and gives us inner instruction. He enters into our consciousnesses and gives us the capacity to receive and manifest God's Light. We consider Guru our spiritual father."

"Does every disciple have to look alike—wearing the saris, the men with white clothes and crew cuts?" I asked.

Mahavishnu chuckled. "It seems a sacrifice to look like a disciple in the beginning. Mahalakshmi and I have been disciples two years. I had long hair, too," he said, glancing at the dark curls hanging down Carlos's back. "But those are only outer suggestions. Wearing white helps us remember to keep our mind pure. The only real rules are that we have to meditate every morning, become vegetarians, and attend meditations at Guru's centers every week. There's a Sri Chinmoy Centre in San Francisco, too."

Neither Carlos nor I said anything. I reflected on all we had seen. Ram Dass's book, *Be Here Now,* gave me the same peaceful feeling, yet I had never heard a philosophy like the one spoken by these people. It was as though life's meaning was touching my heart, sprinkling truth inside my body. And the disciples were beautiful. The women wore no makeup, the men had little hair, yet their skin shone and their eyes were lustrous like pearls. After being in Sri Chinmoy's presence for two meditations, my life seemed changed for eternity.

Mahavishnu pulled up in front of the Fifth Avenue Hotel.

"I'll just run up and get my guitar," Carlos said. We held hands walking into the lobby and took the elevator to our room. Carlos picked up his guitar and kissed me. "I'll be back after we lay down the tracks in the studio."

I closed the door, carefully turning all the dead bolts. Through the window, looking down on the street, I watched them drive off.

Was a meditation teacher what we needed to show us the way on this new road to spiritual truth?

Could a teacher open doors to my soul that were shut tight by my mind? I felt liberated when I sat cross-legged in meditation—at one with a universal God who was beyond religion and boundaries of human thought. Even in this small hotel room, an openness to truth hummed within me.

12

Like a God

$\mathcal{T}$wo days later, Carlos sat on the windowsill beside the radiator. "Mahavishnu asked me about becoming a disciple again when we drove back from the studio." Down the street, sunlight fell on Washington Square, but the twelve-story apartment building across from our hotel blocked its rays from our room. I perched at the end of the bed facing him.

"I'm beginning to feel pressured," he said. "I prayed for a teacher, and I loved the meditation at the United Nations, but I didn't know having a guru would mean I would have to dress differently and have short hair—like a square."

I walked the few steps to the window and touched his soft cheek; my fingers followed the line of his cheekbone. "Maybe you should keep searching. The meditation *was* peaceful, but maybe there's another guru you're meant to follow. Or maybe you don't need a guru at all."

"I just don't want to cut my hair. Because I had tuberculosis in high school, I got deferred from going to Vietnam. I did not believe in being regimented and controlled then, and I do not want to be in a spiritual army now." Carlos's eyes were red with the war he was fighting in his mind and heart.

"Don't rush your answer. Tell Mahavishnu you need more time." I paused and then said, "I didn't know you had TB."

"Yeah. It was awful. No one in my family visited me. I was in San Francisco General Hospital for two months. People were dying in beds all around me. Finally, I had to get out. Ron brought me clothes, and I put them on in the bathroom and walked out. I was afraid I would die if I didn't leave."

How could his family not have visited him? I kneeled on the floor and wrapped my arms around Carlos's waist. His family was so different from mine. They had not been present to his child's heart. I wanted to share the love I had so generously been given as a child; to soothe him with my steadfastness. Carlos's only mainstay in life was his desire to play the guitar. I was beginning to understand why he worked so tenaciously. He was taking care of his life, securing his place on the planet, healing his fractured childhood.

"Mahalakshmi asked me to help in the restaurant while you're in the studio. I didn't know what to say because I don't know how much longer I'll be staying."

"I would love for you to stay until we finish recording."

"I would love to be with you, but what about my college? I can't drop out again."

"Maybe you can work something out with your teachers."

It seemed like months since I had been to San Francisco State. I knew I would have to choose once more. Pursuing a career or pursuing love? Maybe meditation would give me an answer.

"Come on." Carlos beckoned as he stood up. "Let's go down to the record store."

My stride matched Carlos's as he struck out in his snake-skin boots. We linked arms, lovers in Greenwich Village. I leaned into the scent of his leather jacket and Maja soap. Inside the record store, we flipped through dozens of albums, new and used, looking for Coltrane, Miles, Aretha, Billie Holiday—any imports we would not be able to find in San Francisco. Two young men behind the counter stared at Carlos. He did not notice. With albums under his arm, he walked to the register to pay. The one wearing love beads and an earring stuttered, "A-Are you Carlos?"

"Yeah, man," Carlos said, reaching out his hand to the startled fan. I loved that he was always gracious.

"I love your guitar, man," he said, shaking the fingers that strummed the strings.

"Thanks." Carlos pocketed his change, and we walked back to the hotel, a brisk breeze blowing our long hair.

The next morning, Carlos took a cab with me to Parsons Boulevard, a street in Sri Chinmoy's neighborhood where disciples had businesses devoted to spreading the meditation message. In the middle of Long Island's crowded streets—made dark and foreboding by overhead trains, looming brownstones, and dank, acrid subway odors—the white storefronts with smiling disciples gave the impression of openness and safety. We met the Mahas at the Smile of the Beyond, a diner owned by a disciple named Swadhin. Just as Sri Chinmoy had given Maha-vishnu and Mahalakshmi new names with spiritual meanings, we were meeting many disciples with Indian names who lived and worked in Queens. Sri Chinmoy even named the businesses.

Carlos and I sat down on red vinyl stools, Mahavishnu and Mahalakshmi beside us. Swadhin leaned on the counter, his glasses askew. His hair was slicked back like a gang member from *West Side Story*. His face was round, a row of perspiration across his forehead. An apron was tied barber-style around his waist, and he wiped the Formica in little circles with his towel while he talked with his customers. Carlos and I looked over the menu and ordered veggie burgers, while Swadhin joked with Mahavishnu.

"What time do you think you'll be back from recording tonight?" I asked, searching Carlos's eyes. Our hands were clasped between us.

"The engineer's having a hard time getting my sound, so it'll probably be late."

In jest, I poked my lips out as though displeased. I knew Carlos's music came before everything else in his life. After more than three months together, I accepted the line of demarcation between his guitar and me. As much as I wanted to be the great love in Carlos's life, I did not feel competition with his passion for his art. I would never demand he choose between us—not because I knew he would choose his guitar, but because I realized early in life that each person comes to earth with something unique to give to the world. Carlos's gift was his music. Although I was still searching for my purpose, I knew I would never let him come before my destiny when I found it.

Swadhin twirled our plates onto the counter. In front of us, a poster-size photo of Sri Chinmoy—dressed in white, smiling, and holding an open yellow rose—hung suspended by a wire. We faced our images reflected in the eight-foot-wide mirror covering the wall and bowed our heads to bless our food. Books of Sri Chinmoy's teachings were stacked on shelves near the door, price tags on each spine. Disciples sat together in booths, chatting while they ate. They all had such clear eyes and transparent joy.

I cut my veggie burger in half and ate, glancing through the storefront windows onto Parsons Boulevard. A trail of people walking quickly down the hill passed those laboring up the hill.

"Why don't you two stay at our house instead of the hotel?" Mahalakshmi asked. "Carlos can drive to the studio with Mahavishnu."

I looked at Carlos. I still had not decided whether I was staying until the recording would be finished.

Mahavishnu said, "That's a great idea."

Carlos looked down. "We don't want to impose."

"And I have to figure out how long I will be here," I said.

The Mahas spoke at the same time: "We want you to stay!"

Mahalakshmi said, "Think about it and let us know."

I nodded my agreement. "All right," Carlos said. "We'll let you know tomorrow. Thanks." We walked outside and parted with a kiss as Carlos slid into Mahavishnu's Volvo. I stood waving as they drove off to Manhattan. Mahalakshmi and I started up the hill to her little Subaru for the drive to their restaurant, where we had eaten the first night.

"Annam Brahma is more than a restaurant," Mahalakshmi said. "It's a holy abode where we feed customers a higher consciousness along with their vegetarian meals." Sri Chinmoy had named Annam Brahma and the translation from Sanskrit is "Food is God."

My first afternoon helping at the restaurant, Mahalakshmi explained that we had to wash our hands and keep our hair back to meet the health code of New York State. I worked in my jeans and sweater, my hair pulled back into a ponytail. The kitchen had a big commercial six-burner stove and double-door stainless-steel refrigerator. A table with chopping boards was in the center of the room, which was really only big enough for a couple of people to move around in. Along the wall, large canisters with handwritten labels were stacked: lentils, rice, noodles, flour. Bottled spices sat on a stainless-steel ledge above the stove. Mahalakshmi asked me to mix milk, eggs, and sugar for individual custards. As I stirred, I looked out a window onto a dark garbage area and thought how different it was from the beautiful Mill Valley garden outside Carlos's kitchen window.

Though at least five disciples had been working the night Carlos and I first came to Annam Brahma, only Mahalakshmi and I were doing the prep work. She did not carry on casual chatter; she told me about the life of a disciple. "We meditate every morning at six A.M., but you can also start the day by chanting 'Supreme, Supreme' as soon as you open your eyes." She told me that Guru meditated on all his disciples every morning at 2:00 A.M.

I took a taxi back to the hotel around five o'clock. Night closed in on the Manhattan streets, the city crowded with pedestrians and buses, and lights in offices turning on floor by floor. In our room, I ran a hot bath to soak off of my skin the smell of the peanut oil we'd used to fry the Indian flat bread, and thought about the different possibilities for my future. I was twenty-one. Mom said I needed to buckle down and finish my education. Carlos wanted me to travel with him, in his musical realm. I was happy and I was learning, even though it wasn't in a university. What was my place? Was it to gain spiritual knowledge through the meditation practice, or should I return to academia? Both stimulated my heart and mind. Being with Carlos, traveling with him, was the major question. I would assimilate firsthand knowledge of places through walking streets, visiting museums, and meeting local residents—but all on Carlos's timetable, not mine. I lit the candles on our makeshift shrine and sat in the silence, waiting for direction.

When Carlos walked through the door after recording, I said, "I would like to stay in New York with you and work with Mahalakshmi." My heart had chosen spirituality.

"You're sure?" he asked. "You won't regret not finishing your semester?"

"I can start again in January. I'll just end up with a couple of incompletes. I would rather be with you."

"Yes!" Carlos raised his arms above his head and then pulled me into his chest, squeezing me close.

The next day, Carlos and I moved to the Mahas'. They gave us the guest room with twin beds. We slept together in one bed, Carlos's leg swung over my waist, me crushed to his torso. Mahalakshmi knocked gently on our door at 5:30 the following morning. I unpeeled from Carlos's body, my feet hitting the floor before my eyes opened. I stumbled to the shower and stepped into the hot, stinging water, chanting, "Supreme, Supreme" under my breath. It felt strange using "Supreme" instead of "God" or "Jesus," and I saw Sri Chinmoy's brown face instead of a long-haired Jesus of the Bible.

After kissing my sleeping mate good-bye, I drove with Mahalakshmi to the restaurant. She lit candles in the alcove that arched above a very un-human-like photograph of Sri Chinmoy. In black and white, the guru's head was a floating gray shadow with eyes at half-mast in the silver frame. I leaned toward Mahalakshmi and whispered, "It doesn't look anything like Sri Chinmoy." I felt ill at ease before the strange image, which barely looked like a person.

"This photograph was taken by one of his closest disciples many years ago," she said. "Guru was in *samadhi* [supreme enlightenment and oneness with God]. He asks that we meditate on this photo each day to invoke his highest consciousness." I sat silent, letting myself be drawn into the vastness of the consciousness captured by the photograph. After five minutes, Mahalakshmi bowed her head. We stood and walked to the kitchen, ready to work. I slipped a white apron over my head and read the menu with the list of ingredients tacked on the wall. Mahalakshmi pushed the play button on a tape deck above the counter. "This is a tape of Sri Chinmoy singing." A vibrato-inflected tenor voice sang out, "Supreme, Supreme, I bow to thee." In the background I could hear the small Indian organ, called a harmonium. Nasal, tinny, unlike any of the jazz or rock I listened to, or the classical music I had learned as a child, the strange music filled the kitchen.

Mahalakshmi and I chopped broccoli and carrots, soaked beans, sliced cheese, and talked about Sri Chinmoy and the path of bhakti yoga. "Why do the women have to wear saris and the men white?" Mahavishnu had said it was only suggested, but I had not met a New York disciple who did not wear the uniform sari or white pants and shirt.

"In the Eastern tradition, especially yoga," Mahalakshmi said, "purity is the highest goal. To follow God, we must keep our minds on consciousness from above, not on sexual energy, which Sri Chinmoy calls 'the vital.' To follow Guru, we must not be bound by desire or ego, which fashion feeds, but must give up all vanity for faithfulness."

I kept chopping. *Purity is good, but I love clothes. Would I have to give up fashion and style to be pure?* Sri Chinmoy's voice droned scratchily from the cassette. A collage of new questions bombarded my mind: *Even though Sri Chinmoy had said he and Jesus were one, isn't devotion to any person like worshipping an idol? Where is the balance between love of God and human love?* I did not want to transcend my physical desires for Carlos. I daydreamed of being wrapped in his arms at night, snug in his love. I was also happy to feel God's love in meditation. *Could not both exist together?*

I finished dicing the vegetables for the minestrone. "What would you like me to do with these veggies?"

"Sauté them in olive oil in the soup pot for ten minutes."

I had cooked only simple dinners at home, and scrambled eggs and bacon for breakfast. My specialty had been beef stroganoff over noodles. The recipes for Indian cuisine and large quantities of ingredients were a culinary course for me.

The phone rang. I scooped the finely chopped vegetables into a bowl while the oil heated. Mahalakshmi spoke quietly into the phone. "Guru would like to speak to you," she called, holding the receiver out to me.

My heart beat quickly. *Speak to me?* I turned off the burner, wiped my hands on a towel, and pressed the receiver against my ear. "Hello?"

"Hello, good girl." His voice was lilting and jovial. "How do you like working with your new friend?"

"I love it," I answered shyly.

"Please learn our ways from her. She is a very good disciple. You have my infinite blessings, love, and gratitude. Your inner captain is your soul. You will never exploit God's forgiveness sky. All right? Very good. Ommm . . ." Click. The phone buzzed.

That was incredible. Sri Chinmoy had chosen to speak to me. He had said that I could never exploit God's forgiveness. All I wanted was for God to forgive my past. If Sri Chinmoy's meditation could promise me that, then I wanted what he offered. I was desperate for anything that could cleanse me from my past mistakes.

"I think he hung up," I said—more of a question than a statement, as I put the receiver back on the base.

Mahalakshmi smiled sweetly at me and turned back to the stove. I breathed deeply, trying to remember each word he had said and the tone of his voice. I wanted nothing more than to purify myself. Did I want to become a disciple if Carlos did, or would we look for another teacher together? The whole spiritual world was open to us. No matter what path we chose, our lives would never be the same.

"You know," Mahalakshmi spoke over her shoulder, "disciples come from every walk of life. Some were record-company executives, professors, drug dealers, students, and even hobos."

We looked at each other and laughed. Mahalakshmi could not have known about my past, but her statement relieved my anxiety. I was glad I did not have the most wicked or unusual past life compared with those people, who looked like angels to me.

"Guru doesn't allow drugs, alcohol, cigarettes, or swearing," she said. "He wants us to meditate at least a half hour each morning, read his books twenty minutes each day, and meditate for protection before we drive." *That didn't sound too difficult.* "We choose to treat our bodies as temples. Guru's consciousness protects us from darkness if we walk in oneness with him."

Late that night, Carlos and I hid in our little room. "Mahavishnu said Sri Chinmoy told him my soul has asked to be on his path," he whispered. Carlos's breath was warm on my forehead as we lay in the hollow of our twin bed. My lips pressed against his bare chest as I listened to him search his core. "Let's go back to the U.N. Chapel for Sri Chinmoy's noon meditation. This time I'll know if it's God's will for me to join the meditation path—and maybe you will, too."

The path of meditation was being traced on my heart. I had found a new passageway to God very different from my Christian upbringing. My communion with God had begun with prayer, a plea for God's Spirit to enter into my body. Meditation was an extension of that connection, a gathering of inner power with the lightning bolt of heavenly vision. I had not come to New York to find a guru, yet I loved being with Mahalakshmi and learning about the spiritual path.

Wednesday morning, the chapel seemed filled with even more light than the week before. Carlos and I sat near the front of the room, waiting expectantly for a sign from God.

Sri Chinmoy entered in a flaming red *kurta* and *dhoti* that glinted off the walls of the room. Incandescent rays of gold waved behind him as he stepped up to the dais and raised his hands to his forehead. Stillness spread over me. I do not know how long we meditated, but my heart soared to a new height. When thoughts came into my mind, they were about working at Annam Brahma and the idea that maybe one day I could run a divine enterprise. After meditation, everyone filed out. The Mahas told Carlos and me that Sri Chinmoy had asked to speak with us.

We were led to a small room down a hallway. One of Sri Chinmoy's attendants opened the thick wooden door. Inside, Sri Chinmoy sat behind a small table. Two chairs faced him. He motioned for us to sit; then he lifted his face toward the ceiling, his lips parting to reveal a luminous spread of white teeth against his brown skin. "You have both meditated very well today," he murmured. I bowed my head. "It is my joy to tell you that the Supreme has told me you are both meant for my path. Now it is up to you to accept or reject. All my love and bless-ings."

Sri Chinmoy stood and walked past us, laying his hand briefly on my head before reaching the door. His touch left a palm print of heat. I remained bowed until he left the room. When I raised my head, Carlos sat still, his eyes closed. His ponytail hung over his shoulder. After a few moments, he whis-pered, "Now I understand the notes that John Coltrane played when he recorded 'Ascension.' I feel healed from my anger at the breakup of the band. If we join the path, my quest for light will be complete. Do you want to become a disciple with me?"

"I love the meditation and the ideas Sri Chinmoy expresses about truth and light. I feel hope here. If becoming a disciple will give me more of that, I'm ready."

We embraced, sealing our commitment to follow Sri Chinmoy.

The Mahas waited for us in the front of the chapel. Mahavishnu clasped Carlos's hand and put his arm around his shoulders when we told them our decision. "I'm so happy, brother," he said.

Mahalakshmi hugged me. I felt their oneness with us. "Guru said he would like to accept you as disciples at a special meditation," she said. "We'll see you later." They turned from us and disappeared down the street.

Carlos and I walked through Manhattan feeling the intense energy of the city and our decision. Carlos turned and caught my chin with his hand. "Will you go to London with me?" he asked. The band would be leaving in eight days.

"Why?" I asked.

"Because I love being around you and want to share my music and King's Road—even the bad English food—with you." He laughed as though remembering a boiled meal or a fantastic concert played at Great Albert Hall.

I wanted to say yes, but saw my own life shrinking in the mosaic of Carlos's career. Carlos was eagerly inviting me to his fiesta, his life. Mom had always told me I was loyal. *Am I crazy to be loyal in love when I had been so hurt before?* Carlos stared into my eyes as people brushed past us on the sidewalk. I could not resist loving him. "I'd love to go," I said. I knew I made a difference in Carlos's life. He had told me more than once that he adored my soul. Learning from his musical digest of blues, jazz, rock, and Latino rhythms complemented my own gospel and jazz heritage. I only prayed that what Carlos could teach me about love would remain as gratifying as it felt right now. Now I had to work on my bravery to call Mom and Dad to tell them I had decided to put off college once more.

We spent the afternoon in Greenwich Village. Carlos and I walked downstairs to a subterranean salon on Eighth Street. Two hairdressers' eyes opened wide as they recognized the long-haired, mustached man at my side. "May we help you?"

"I need a haircut," Carlos said softly.

"Please sit here," the tall brunette with layered waves said. "An inch?" she asked.

"Um, to here, please." Carlos held his hands beneath his ears, his face blank, his eyes clouded.

"Oh no," she said, clamping her hand over her mouth. "I'm sorry, but are you sure?"

I sat in the swivel chair next to Carlos, observing the scene. "Don't make it any harder for him," I urged.

Carlos gulped. "No, I'm not sure, so you'd better hurry."

Shampoo. Snip, snip, snip. Tears welled in my eyes. The handsome, young rebel man whose free-flying hair had been part of his antiestablishment image sat before me shorn clean. He looked younger, like a high school boy. His skin glowed, and his eyes reflected the pain of the sacrifice he had just made.

Mahavishnu shook Carlos's hand when we returned to their house, congratulating him on his monk-like haircut. Mahalakshmi was at her restaurant, Annam Brahma. Ranjana and Lavanya, the two young women who drove Sri Chinmoy to meetings and were in his inner circle, came to the door with a package for me. Ranjana was about five feet ten inches and angular like a two-by-four, her pale skin lit like a paper lantern. Lavanya was shorter and had a warm smile and soft eyes beneath brown hair held back from her face with a gold barrette. I opened the rose-tinted tissue. Inside were a sari, blouse, and slip. The silky fabric was deep yellow along the bottom, rising to a soft wheat color painted with thin stalks of bamboo. "Thank you," I said, clutching the sari to my heart. "It's beautiful."

"I'm sure Mahalakshmi can help you put it on," Lavanya said. They smiled and walked back down the stairs, turning to wave as they climbed into a blue Rambler, Ranjana behind the wheel.

This entire experience was becoming surrealistic. I felt as though I was in the audience, watching someone else's life be transformed into an astonishing fairy tale.

Mahalakshmi came home and showed me how to wrap the sari. I stepped into the white cotton slip and tied the drawstring around my waist. I put my arms into the short, cotton blouse and snapped it closed. Mahalakshmi walked around me in circles, tucking the slippery yards of fabric into my slip. I felt my past moving farther into the background. Even the few blissful months I had had with Carlos were being transcended by this conversion to discipleship. We were not going to be living only for ourselves: God was now our daily communion, Sri Chinmoy our guide.

With the curling iron, I rolled my shag hairstyle to frame my face and rubbed clear gloss on my lips. Carlos dressed in the white shirt and pants Mahavishnu had brought him from Parsons Boulevard. Standing together in the mirror, we looked like people we did not know. Carlos's short hair gave his eyes room to glow, but he looked so "straight." The sari made me look chubby in the middle—I tried to flatten the bunched material at my stomach. We felt uncomfortable in our new attire, but were determined to conform to this required outer appearance in order to make spiritual progress.

The ceremony was at Sri Chinmoy's house. By the time Carlos and I walked in the front door, I was spinning with nervousness. I felt as though I were flying above the house, watching the whole process from out of my body. Ranjana and Lavanya scooted apart to allow Carlos and me to sit directly in front of Guru. At least twenty disciples were sitting behind us, but I did not focus on them. I kept my head down until Sri Chinmoy sat on his throne; then I lifted my eyes to meditate on him. In my peripheral vision, Carlos shimmered in his white.

"Carlos and Devi," Sri Chinmoy spoke in a soft drone like the harmonium on Mahalakshmi's cassette. "You have now entered the inner world where you have accepted me as your guru. The outer world of turmoil has surrendered to the inner world of delight and peace. Your souls are crying out for the infinite Light from the inner Sun that we all have. I will give you realisation. Your lives are written on my heart. I am at your service forever."

The candlelight pulsed into a wondrous glow, making the room radiantly bright. The night passed as a peace-filled dream—my heart, like a prism, reflecting and receiving the effulgence of God's light. Afterward, the disciples served us plates of curry and rice. We ate very little, we were so excited.

Congratulations followed us out the door when we left Guru's house.

"How do you feel?" I asked Carlos back in our twin bed at the Mahas'.

"I hear new notes to play, new songs. You?"

"I'm thrilled thinking about what is ahead. I feel clean and pure."

Before Carlos and I left Queens to fly to Europe, Sri Chinmoy called us to his house for a private meditation. His eyes rolled heavenward as he entered into a trance on his throne. "You have been initiated into a new life, a blessingful, prayerful life, dear ones." As he spoke, his eyes fluttered. "I am your spiritual parent. I offer you my highest love and gratitude for the service you will offer the Supreme through me. Hmmm."

We bowed, and I felt an intense love. It was unlike human love. It was almost fragrant, as though petals of a most delicate ginger flower were floating above us. Sri Chinmoy's eyes were closed, and we took that as our cue to leave his home and go out into the world.

13

London

November 1972

✳

$\mathcal{T}$he night Carlos and Mahavishnu completed their musical collaboration, they danced into the house like fireworks from heaven. One of Sri Chinmoy's books had a poem, "Love, Devotion and Surrender," that Carlos felt represented his spiritual journey, and he chose the title for the album.

The next morning Carlos and I rose early to finish packing for our flight to London. I tidied our little guest room, stripped the sheets, folded blankets, and left a note leaning against Sri Chinmoy's photograph thanking Mahalakshmi for her hospitality. Hugging the Mahas good-bye, I had to fight not to cry. So much had happened in the month we had known them. I was sad to part with our new friends.

We flew into Heathrow International Airport. I thought of the time I had come to London with Sly. The memory of snorting cocaine in the bathroom of the Bally shoe store on King's Road seemed like another life. I chanted "Supreme, Supreme" to push the image out of my mind. Carlos, by my side in his white disciple clothes, myself in a sari beneath my long woolen coat—we were definitely not the same people we had been the year before.

We walked to the bus that would carry the band to our hotel. Barry Imhoff, the tour manager, was the first face whose mouth dropped open when he saw Carlos's hair. Michael Shrieve said, "What happened, man?"

"Remember John McLaughlin's guru? We joined his path."

Michael rubbed his chin. "Whoa. That's drastic."

Carlos and I slid into a row near the back of the bus. "We have to try to stay awake all day to get our bodies on this time," he said, hugging me. I listened, smiling in sleepy agreement as we leaned back against the soft, high-backed seats. All I wanted to do was rest my head on his shoulder and take a nap.

At the hotel, we opened our suitcases and set up our shrine. We centered Sri Chinmoy's and Christ's photos on the coffee table, placing a brass incense holder to the left and a votive candle in front of our two spiritual guides. Carlos, intent on staying up, rushed to change into jeans, then spirited us off to Kensington Market in a roomy, box-like black taxi with a horn that sounded like a circus clown's. There were many Indians living in London, so I did not look out of place in my sari. We stepped into a boot maker's shop in a marketplace. Smells of leather and polishes hung thickly in the room. Carlos shook hands with the craftsman. "How've you been, man?"

The shopkeeper smiled, pumping Carlos's hand. "We're doing all right, my friend. Thanks for coming back."

Carlos strolled down a row of the high-heeled cowboy boots he loved to wear. He chose three pairs—a creamy light brown, a bright red with white stitching, and a dark green. After paying for his treasures, we strolled through the other market stalls. Carlos paused near a curtained entryway. "I've been to the psychic here," he said. "She predicted our band was going to break up."

"You're kidding!" I had never been to a psychic. I did not think they were legitimate. "When was this?" I asked.

"The last time our band was in London. I knew things were falling apart, so I asked her what she saw in my future. It really scared me when she told me, but when I went back to the hotel, I knew in my heart that if the band broke up, it would be the best thing for all of us."

I did not know whether I would ever believe a psychic, but here was proof that at least one prediction came true.

We stopped in a diner, both of us craving fish and chips but settling for grilled cheese sandwiches and French fries, to abide by the vegetarian diet of disciples. We were becoming delirious with fatigue and laughed at our increasing clumsiness as we tried to stay awake. Back at the hotel, we crawled into bed, passing into a dreamless state, our bodies on New York time.

I awoke while it was still dark, washed my face, brushed my teeth, and began stretching. I reached my arms toward the ceiling, bent over and touched my toes, and then pushed my right leg straight out along the floor behind me, following with my left. Lowering my torso down to the floor, I lifted my head and neck while lying on my stomach. I had learned this asana, "Salutation to the Sun," at the yoga studio in San Francisco. As I flowed into the movements, I awakened fully to my inner connection with the unknown. An orb of peace radiated in my chest, and I relaxed into the awareness that God's radiant spirit cared for me and held my energy in the universe. As long as I had faith in the infinite Presence, I would be fine.

Slowly, I stood and again stretched my arms above my head.

I felt Carlos's eyes. He called me into his arms. *I could do this every morning,* I thought. *Easily.*

"Good morning," Carlos said, wrapping his legs around me as I slid under the covers. He kissed my face and pressed his body into mine. His touch connected my dreams to the reality of his love, like a long, narrow river flowing between us.

"I was dreaming of angels," he said. "Do you believe in angels?"

His hands were soft, pressing against my back. Even the calluses on the tips of his fingers where he memorized notes on the guitar strings were smooth.

"I don't see them as cupids or women in white gossamer robes who fly," I said. "I see them as spirits that hover around our lives to protect and guide us. What do you think?"

Carlos rested his head on mine. "I see angels as God's divine messengers, as warriors who speak to us to help us gain knowledge."

We lay together talking about reincarnation and the fear of dying, which Carlos did not have. I told him how, while growing up, I had learned to pray without ceasing, no matter where I was.

Our beliefs and openness to spirituality united us in a way that I had never been close with anyone before. I felt deeply in love after having thought I could never love again, because I was

speaking, living, and acting from what I believed to be true—
that I was more than my body or even my mind, and my purpose was to discover and expand this reality. I believed it
synchronous that Carlos and I had met, and I wondered if it was
part of God's plan.

Carlos had a press conference and band rehearsal in the afternoon. After he showered, he pulled out his notepad and pen
and began writing a music set. He hunched over, concentrating
on choosing the sequence of songs they would perform in concert. "Every note, its time of manifestation in the show, is
important," he said. I sat beside him, reading, looking up occasionally to see the crease between his brows, the twitch of his
mustache.

Carlos stood up. "I'm going downstairs to do some interviews. You want to go? I will leave for rehearsal from there." He
ripped off the sheets of paper that held his notes, put them in
his bag, and walked to the closet for his jacket.

"Sure."

The band members gathered in the hotel ballroom behind
a skirted table. Men and women from various newspapers and
magazines sat with tablets, cameras with gigantic flashbulbs,
and tape recorders waiting for the first words. Michael Shrieve
was soft-spoken, his eyes holding wisdom and kindness. The
bassist, a tall, lanky, Afro-topped man named Doug Rauch,
seemed distant and mentally removed from the press conference, pulling his hair while looking up at the ceiling. Armando
Peraza, the conga player Carlos revered so much, slapped Carlos on the back and talked in his ear. Carlos told me how Armando had carried his conga across fields in his native Cuba,

fighting off ruffians who tried to steal his drum on his way to gigs. When he first came to America, he played with Mongo Santamaria and George Shearing. Armando knew my dad's music. "You're Saunders King's daughter? Wow, man. I've been listening to him for years," he said. His dark brown face broke into a smile, and he rubbed his forehead with his thick, callused hands.

Mingo Lewis also played congas. He had got his gig with Santana when Michael Carabello protested the changes Carlos was making in the band and did not fly to New York for the Madison Square Garden show. Carlos had asked whether there was anyone in the audience who played congas, and Mingo jumped onstage. Chepitó, the timbales player, was the only band member I tried to avoid at all costs. Diminutive in stature, with long, curly hair styled like a woman's, he had said crude remarks to women, which I'd overheard after one of the Winterland shows. He looked over at me at the time, as though hoping I would react, but I looked away, embarrassed and furious. I had told Carlos what he'd said. "He had an aneurysm in his brain a couple of years ago and has not been right since," Carlos said. "He's an exceptional musician, but a difficult person." I considered that an understatement.

Tom Coster—the keyboardist Carlos and I heard playing with Gabor Szabo at the El Matador Club when we had first begun dating—was from the old school of jazz. He improvised beautifully and could read charts like no one else in the band. Tom told corny jokes that made me laugh. Richard Kermode also played keyboard. He had been in Malo, Carlos's brother Jorge's band. Together, the band was a rhythmic brotherhood whose personalities and differences merged into one musical force onstage.

I sat in the back of the room watching the press conference and the attention placed on Carlos, his music, and the band. Most questions were directed to Carlos, and when he spoke, the journalists were quiet. He answered questions about his short hair with an explanation of his spiritual quest. The press did not linger on the subject, wanting to know about the music, the songs. Carlos was comfortable in the attention and adulation. *Could Carlos love me, one person, when he is adored by thousands? Should I allow myself to care so deeply for him, when there is a great chance I could be hurt?* I sighed. My soul seemed to whisper: *Live true to love. Give Carlos the sacred that flows through you. He will reward you with the sacred in him.*

His soft, luscious voice came from the microphone. I measured the width of his shoulders, the profile of his face, the directness with which he looked into one's eyes before answering a question, and I longed for our love to survive.

Carlos left for rehearsal. I asked the concierge for a map of the city so I could walk from our corner of Hyde Park to Harrods department store. London was cold and gray, with a chip of winter in the air. Store windows were festooned with Christmas trees and lights. Harrods was a glittering, warm madhouse of people, clothing, housewares, and food. I sent Mom and Dad a foil-wrapped Christmas pudding, even though I was unsure what it was. I caught a taxi to Buckingham Palace and watched the guards march from their stands to the closed arches of the monarchy's castle. In a fancy tea shop where I barely understood the inflections of the waitress's English, I drank a pot of

Darjeeling tea and ate a buttery scone, which took away the early evening cold.

On the afternoon of the concert at Wembley Pool Arena, the band bus rolled and dipped through London streets, tumbling past cathedrals and walled gardens with topiary bushes and park benches. Most of the band, including Carlos, were withdrawn, quiet. Only Chepitó threw out jokes like rapid-fire sticks on drum skins as we drove into the backstage parking area. Pulling up alongside the two semitrucks that transported the band's tons of musical instruments and sound equipment, we disembarked in a line, heading for the heavily guarded stage door entrance.

Fans were lined up behind the metal barricade, screaming, "Carlos, can you autograph this?" "Michael, we love you!" "Carlos, can we get your picture?" "Chepitó, Chepitó!"

Chepitó danced over to the fans, his fluffy black hair blowing as he stepped daintily in his black high-heeled boots, sweet-talking two young girls who giggled at his attention. The rest of the musicians waved briefly, following the manager inside to the hospitality suite.

Carlos left the group and walked to his tuning room. The other musicians hung their wardrobes and snacked on fruit and cookies from a heavily laden buffet table. Armando wrapped each of his fingers with half-inch strips of white tape. The skins of the congas tore through his calluses if he did not protect his thick, powerful hands.

I found a soft chair, plopped down, and opened my novel. Heads popped in and out of the dressing room as technicians did their jobs. Loud bantering ensued between Killer Kahn, the production manager, and the local crew as they hurried to bring in extra lights. Chepitó's high-pitched laugh floated down the hall. I could hear the shuffle of feet moving upstairs in the arena as the audience took their seats.

Twenty minutes before eight, I walked to Carlos's tuning room. His technician was leaving with a guitar in each hand to place in stands on the stage.

"Make sure you watch my signals tonight, man," Carlos said, leaning over to light two candles. "I don't want to have to look for you if the monitors aren't working right." He blew out the match as sharply as he ended his sentence and sat down on the floor, crossing his legs. A picture of Jesus was perched on an amplifier next to a photo of Sri Chinmoy. I sat on a white metal road case and meditated with him for five minutes. When he rose, he gave me a quick kiss, opened the door, and swiftly headed straight down the hallway for the stage. I followed behind, waiting for Killer to tell me where I could sit.

The band ascended the stairs, spotlights lifted, and a roar erupted from the crowd. Killer led me to a road case on the side of the stage beside the sound engineer who mixed the stage monitors. The first note was the echoing ring of a brass gong. A spotlight swung on Carlos, and the audience leaped to its feet. No one introduced the band. Carlos offered no words of welcome. A musical train of notes, rhythms, and percussive blasts railed, rallied, swooped, and gained momentum. A swirling aura of light-filled music blew through every pore of my skin.

I concentrated on each musician for a few moments, my eyes moving in a circle, looking at the different grimaces and faces each one made. I was mesmerized by the talent with which each musician picked notes, like fruit hanging ripe from sun-blessed trees, juices dripping in their hands. I was in a trance. Chepitó threw his timbales' sticks out into the audience, the spell broken as I turned to watch fans fly into a frenzy in the section of seating where the sticks landed.

Carlos was a speechless conductor: He tiptoed across the stage, dark eyes flashing as he connected with each musician, willing them to play their hardest, their best. Standing directly in front of Armando, he stomped his heel, biting hard on his lower lip, snapping his head on the beat. When he was pleased with the rhythms Armando played, a wide smile sprang onto his face. He strode to the keyboards, bending and swaying, pushing Tom to dig deeper into his solo.

At concert's end, when the final chord was held, Michael pounded the drums and cymbals in a fury. The audience was on its feet, screaming. I stood on the side, impressed with the musicality of the set, the creative realm that had carried me along for two hours. It was like a play—the notes telling a story with the rise of suspense in the fast songs relieved by ballads like "Samba Pa Ti."

After three encores, Carlos walked into my arms. His T-shirt, drenched with the remaining essence of his performance, soaked me as he held me close.

"It was a great show," I whispered into his moist ear. Carlos's body was steaming.

"Thank you. We tried our best. The band played better than at Winterland! I was so high from the music, I didn't know where I was."

We walked to the hospitality suite. Carlos was almost air-borne. Guests of the band filled the backstage area, their bodies packed together tightly. Laughter looped through the room. The musicians, high with the show's energy, hugged friends and high-fived the promoter and representatives from the record company. The euphoria of the concert heated the backstage like a fireball. Carlos grabbed two bottles of mineral water and led me to the tuning room.

The review in the British press said, "The gods descended from Mount Olympus," praising Santana's musicality and power, and confirming that Carlos had chosen the best musicians and songs to complement his new direction. In the next week, I flew with the band to Germany, Sweden, and Switzerland. Carlos's life was dedicated to making each performance better than the last, and we listened to Miles Davis, Herbie Hancock, and Wayne Shorter—jazz artists I knew about and loved, too. Carlos said, "These are the geniuses of American music, the masters." He knew the name of every song on every album, every musi-cian who played on each track. Carlos and I meditated early every morning before exploring Europe's walking streets, mu-seums, and brasseries, returning to the hotel in the afternoons when shops closed and people went home to rest. I had never visited cathedrals so magnificent, with intricate stained-glass windows that told spiritual stories, nor had I seen such delicately carved stone statues of the Virgin Mary. Each historic landmark made an impressive imprint on my memory because of my ex-hilaration of seeing it on Carlos's arm. We were like walking fire-works, attentive and scintillating at every moment.

When we arrived in Berlin, the sky blended into sodden gray buildings. The hotel was square, sparsely furnished, and felt as cold inside as outside. Carlos left for the show, and I took a taxi to the Berlin Wall. The photographs in the fortress-like museum chilled me—the construction of the wall dividing East and West. Tanks lined the Friedrichstrasse as I walked a few blocks, past guards patrolling with long rifles slung over their shoulders. The darker the afternoon became, the more sorrowful I felt, as though the horrors of World War II idled as ghosts in the German streets.

After the show on our last night together in Montreux, Claude Nobs the promoter had a dinner for the band. His chalet in the Alps was hung with colored lights, and Carlos and I danced in a romantic spell while he ignited cherries flambé.

Carlos and I parted at the airport so I could return to New York to keep my promise to Guru to help Mahalakshmi. The band was traveling on to Holland and France. Tears pooled in my eyes as Carlos and I hugged. I had not been away from him since we met five months before in July, and it would be almost two weeks until we would see each other again.

I slept fitfully in the window seat, my head covered with the airline's small, scratchy blanket. In my hand was a wet, shredded Kleenex that I dabbed in the corners of my eyes. I was miserably lovesick.

Mahalakshmi met me at the gate, her cheeks red from the windy December afternoon. She drove while telling me the latest news about Sri Chinmoy, and she asked whether I felt up to going to the evening's meditation.

"Sure, I just need a shower to wash off the hours of travel." I moved my suitcase back into the guest room, feeling as though I were lacking a part of myself without Carlos. We drove up the parkway to Norwalk, the night chill seeping through the car windows. Houses nestled in clumps of trees, amber lights softly glowed, and I thought longingly of having a home like one of these, warm and welcoming.

The Connecticut Meditation Centre had been in existence nine years. The house was a lovely saltbox, painted Wedgwood blue, with lantern porch lights and cars filling the gravel drive. Other disciples arrived, and we walked together in silence: a brood of pilgrims traveling together to meet our earthly deity. Stones crunched under my feet as we neared the rambling, two-story country house. Across the large front porch were about fifty pairs of shoes—all different sizes; some old, some new. Coats and parkas were lying across a window seat.

I followed Mahalakshmi into the meditation room and sat down cross-legged behind her, looking over her head at the photos of Sri Chinmoy that hung on the walls.

Closing my eyes, I inhaled through my nose, pulled my shoulders back, straightened my spine, and then exhaled deeply through my mouth. I imagined my breath passing in and out of my chest, slowly. Calm feelings enveloped me; my heartbeat became faint, muted. My sadness about leaving Carlos began to dissipate. In and out, my chest heaved and collapsed in a slow, steady rhythm.

A thought that Carlos could be here sitting next to me, sharing our spirituality, came to my mind. But the reality was, he was a musician. He would always travel. It had made me unbearably sad to leave him in Europe, but I was not one to remain sentimental or become immobilized by pain. Was not this transcendence of the temporal the reason I was looking for life's meaning? Of course I was sad, but I had to find peace within myself—whether Carlos and I were together or apart. Mystics claim that the presence of God's Spirit makes one strong and that meditation is the way to know peace and God's omnipotent power. Church had taught me that God would answer my prayers. I would never need to depend on someone or something outside of me: Life's happiness lay within my own soul. I had felt extreme contentment before. Even as a child, when my friend Karmen and I walked to her church, Saint Emydius, and she slipped the lace covering onto her head before we entered the pew, I felt the Presence. I knew in my heart that God was everywhere.

In the distance I heard the muffled rustle of fabric and the soft hum of Sri Chinmoy's voice. My eyes sprang open. Disciples rose to their feet, bowing as he walked in, shiny red satin *dhoti* hanging below his heavy brown overcoat. His face beamed. He moved his head from side to side as he walked down the aisle, looking at us. He reached his chair, pausing to smile resplendently before sitting down. His small feet crossed at the ankles; he sat back, lamplight shining on his bald brown head.

We meditated in silence, my neck barely able to hold my head up as I wove in and out of contemplation and dream. My life was a flight between oceans and mountains, past and present; every person sitting around me was a new friend; and I accepted it all, drifting further and further away from my calamitous past.

14

Given a Chance

*M*ahalakshmi took me on a tour of Parsons Boulevard, to Guru Stationery, where I bought letter paper with Sri Chinmoy's aphorisms printed on each page. A tall man named Ashrita introduced himself to me and said, in an amazingly loud voice, "Gosh, Debbie, it's so good you came back to be around Guru. You'll make so much spiritual progress here." His clear, white skin framed flashing dark eyes. When we left the store, Mahalakshmi told me that Ashrita was Guru's messenger. If someone needed to reach Sri Chinmoy, they called the stationery store and Ashrita gave Guru the message. Only a handful of disciples could telephone Sri Chinmoy directly: Ranjana, Lavanya, Ashrita, Savyasachi, and Dulal, the leader of the New York Centre. The remaining 890 disciples, like me, had to send communiqués through these five.

The New York skies wore a heavy winter cloak. I wrapped my woolen scarf tighter around my neck as we traversed the Queens neighborhood. Back at the Mahas', I read Carlos's itinerary, reminiscing about our days together in London and the night in Montreux when we danced in candlelight at the promoter's mountain chalet.

Mahalakshmi and I worked side by side at Annam Brahma. I chopped vegetables, cooked rice, and blended sauces. She showed me how to slice eggplant, salt it, and then lay it on paper towels to draw out the bitterness before breading and frying it for eggplant parmigiana. She coached me in disciple etiquette while we worked. "We do not ever point our feet toward Guru. It's disrespectful. We do not touch him, either."

"Why?" I asked. I had never known a person I could not touch. There were many unusual customs on this meditation path.

"Guru is a vessel of divinity. He brings down infinite grace and compassion from God. Because he meditates on such a high plane of consciousness, he is hypersensitive—and just as he receives energy from the Supreme, he also receives our impurities. If we touch him, all that we are thinking and feeling enters into him because he is our spiritual father. So, we try not to saturate him with our human frailties. Ramakrishna, the great Indian avatar, died of cancer that came to him through his disciples' impurities."

These concepts and beliefs were all new and, although they were foreign in origin, I accepted them, excited to be learning the customs of another culture.

Working at Annam Brahma, the hours passed quickly. We put in almost ten hours a day at the restaurant. I made and drank a sweet *lhassi* every day, perfecting the mix of yogurt, rose water, and honey. Sri Chinmoy said that disciples would have boundless energy by living pure lives devoted to God. I felt energetic, but collapsed into bed each night after work. When we went to meditation, I felt sleepy; but as I breathed in—focusing on Sri Chinmoy's face—the light I received raised my spirits and gave me strength. Sometimes disciples nodded forward in a swooping motion as they fell fast asleep during meditation. It was hard not to laugh as they straightened themselves and tried to look alert, as though nothing had happened.

Disciples were the only friends Mahalakshmi had. She mentioned that her mother lived in the English countryside, but said she did not visit often. I began to see that the meditation path was a separate world, a protected environment that was self-sustaining and so full that it precluded time to socialize outside the center. I did not even consider that being separate from my family would ever be required of me. We were closer than ever. Maybe Kitsaun would come to meditation with me.

On my last morning in New York, Sri Chinmoy called me to his house for a private meditation. A wind of fury sped through the streets, blowing the last leaves of fall into the gutters. Again I was sad to be parting from Sri Chinmoy and the disciples who had mentored me, but I was joyous to be returning to San Francisco, where Carlos would arrive only a few hours after me.

"Please," Sri Chinmoy said, "sit down."

I sat on the carpet facing him. He wore luminous peach satin. "You will go back with all my blessings, good girl. Carlos will bring the impurities of the world, and you will give him my blessingful light and love. Now, let us meditate."

I concentrated on Sri Chinmoy's eyes. The room began to

spin. My body felt weightless as I floated in the rays of Guru's meditative trance. When he bowed, I bowed and raised myself from the floor. My vision was blurred with tears that had risen from some inner emotion over which I had no control.

I hugged Mahalakshmi outside JFK airport. "Thanks for everything—working at Annam Brahma and letting me stay with you." I grabbed my suitcase from the car and ran into the terminal, waving as the automatic door closed behind me.

The plane landed in San Francisco, and I pulled my sky-blue fleece coat over my sari. Carlos had bought the coat for me at Mary Quant in London, and I loved it. My hair was curled around my face, and I wore no trace of makeup. I claimed my suitcase and walked to the international terminal to wait for Carlos's plane. I had not been alone much in Queens and savored having time to myself, even if it was at the airport.

I stood outside the metal doors to customs, my palms clammy. After two weeks apart, I wondered if our fledgling romance might have lost some of its fire. Even the transcendent hours of meditation could not take away the fluttering nervousness I felt. I first spotted Barry, the road manager; then, above the slow-moving line of travelers, I saw Carlos's head, his pale lemony skin, shorn curls, and off-white suit. I froze, waiting for recognition that he was as excited to see me as I was to see him. I hated my insecurity, but felt dwarfed by the love Carlos received from thousands of fans each night. Carlos smiled and waved, holding my gaze with his dark eyes. I surged forward through the crowd and dove inside his warm arms, which transported me to the comfort of his manhood and the memory of his arms and legs entwined with mine. In the crush of bodies, he held me, his soft lips parting to receive mine.

"You taste so good. I've wanted to hold you in my arms since the day you left," he whispered. "Just feeling you gives me strength."

People pushed past us, shoving us closer together. Blood rushed through my body, pounding in my pulses. "I've missed you so much," I whispered.

Kitsaun met us outside. She looked radiant, taller. I noticed her staring at my sari with the intensity of a seagull diving for a fish. She would expect a full explanation of the past month's activities. I embraced her, holding on for a long time, and lingered in the sisterhood that I had missed. She drove us across the Golden Gate Bridge, past Tam Junction and around familiar roads, asking me about Europe and wanting to hear about the meditation path. "What does the guru do?" she asked.

"He meditates in front of us, teaching with his consciousness as well as by answering questions about the spiritual life," I said. "His followers work in businesses they own so they can keep their minds on meditation and purity."

"Sounds interesting," she said. "But I don't see why you have to dress like you're in India. Why the sari?" She turned onto the Mill Valley Road, where Carlos's mountain chalet sat at the end.

Carlos said, "It's all about identification with the divine, taking us away from the ways of the ego and desire."

Kitsaun wasn't convinced about the direction of our lives, but she seemed open. She drove back to the city, leaving Carlos and me alone: one continuous, complete heart.

15

Purity of Heart

December 1972

✳

$\mathcal{I}$ had traveled nearly twenty thousand miles across America, the Atlantic Ocean, and Europe—and no place was as beautiful to me as the San Francisco Bay area. The redwoods, firs, and pines standing still on Mount Tamalpais as though waiting for rainfall to reawaken them; the creek spinning through Old Mill Park, smoothing stones and pebbles; neoclassic sandstone buildings on Market Street that were rebuilt after the 1906 earthquake—all welcomed me back to the splendor of our home. When we first ventured to meditation in San Francisco, the Farallon Islands floated out on the ocean in the last sunlight of the day. We drove across the Golden Gate Bridge, sailboats breezing through the swirling waters between steel pillars that plunged hundreds of feet below. Christmas lights flickered on in the Embarcadero office buildings. Carlos turned the black Volvo hatchback onto Park Presidio, and we headed to Noe Valley.

Meditations were held in a Victorian house on Sanchez, a street so steep that cars parked sideways so their brakes would not slip and cause them to careen down the hill. Sevika and Saumitra, the Centre's leaders, seemed younger than twenty-one. Like other disciples, they were innocent and unguarded, friendly and open. Sevika wore her long brown hair pulled back into the popular disciple ponytail. Her narrow, long nose and thin lips gave her face a gaunt look, but her body was strong and well built. She wore her sari a little shorter than the ankle-length style of the New York girls. Saumitra's above-the-ears haircut accented his bushy eyebrows and penetrating eyes. They lived in the Centre, a simple, unpretentious house.

The dining room served as the meditation space, with a large, ornately framed transcendental photo of Sri Chinmoy on a table, votive candles sending up shimmering white light. Carlos and I sat down cross-legged with five disciples who were already in the room. After fifteen minutes of silence, Sevika stood and read from one of Sri Chinmoy's books: "Pray with fear: God sheds bitter tears; pray with love: God smiles with the beauty of the Golden Dawn; pray with all you have: God wings toward you to grasp you. Pray with all that you are: God becomes your liberation." She bowed to Guru's picture and sat down again, facing the shrine.

The words flowed with my slow breathing, and my heart communed with my inner source. When meditation ended, I felt refreshed and inspired—at one with God.

Sevika caught up with Carlos and me in the hallway as we were walking to retrieve our shoes and jackets. "Would you like to stay and eat with us?" Her face held an eagerness that was almost pleading.

I looked at Carlos. "Thanks," he said quietly, "but we have reservations at a restaurant."

Sevika's shoulders sagged, but she smiled and said, "I'll call you tomorrow, Debbie. Maybe we can work on a project together next week."

"Sure, that would be great." I put on my coat. Carlos opened the door.

Saumitra called out, "Good night, brother. Good night, sister!"

I smiled.

"What?" Carlos asked.

"They're so sweet."

"It's almost unreal," Carlos agreed.

"That's what the New York disciples were like: always smiling, bouncing with energy and joy."

Carlos put his arm around me. "That's how I feel around Mahavishnu. I don't need food or sleep. Just meditation and my guitar."

We drove to La Traviata on Mission Street. Zef, the owner, hugged us as we entered, and seated us in a corner booth. Sonorous opera music filled the restaurant. Scents of fresh-baked bread, tomatoes, and crushed garlic seemed to emanate from Zef's apron and clothing.

By the time we drove back to Marin, Panoramic Highway was enveloped in fog. Our headlights reflected soft light back to us from the clouds clawing along the street. The tower house was warm, protected from the wind by the hillside across the road. We lit candles and talked until the whisper of our bodies became more important, calling us into a spinning circle of lovemaking. Carlos's hands were like silk along my body, and for long moments we watched each other, caught in the pleasure of longing. I loved the sounds of tree branches brushing the side of the house when I was in Carlos's arms.

Most nights I stayed in Mill Valley, and I went home to Mom and Dad's when I needed different clothes. My parents were accepting of my living arrangement—either they genuinely loved Carlos, or perhaps they remembered the trials of their early years together and had compassion for me. Sometimes I spent a night or two in my old bedroom. Kitsaun was living at home again, and we went to movies and talked late into the night. She met Carlos and me at Shandygaff, and we told her about the Centre; she promised to visit a meditation soon.

Carlos stayed up until 2:00 A.M. every night, practicing his guitar downstairs in his studio, and he rehearsed Monday through Friday in the city with the band. I wrote poetry, shopped for groceries, or met Sevika at the Centre to help transcribe cassette tapes of Sri Chinmoy's lectures. New York disciples wrote us group letters that held new language and ideas. Disciples called Guru their "father" and God "the Supreme." Their letters persuaded us to deepen our connection with Sri Chinmoy. The head of the New York Centre, Dulal, wrote that we should "live it, practice it, breathe it, eat it, touch it and become intoxicated with the Supreme's nectar." The disciples shared a fervent enthusiasm to spur one another to be more and more absorbed in spirituality. I ingested this information and coerced my mind to accept what disciples called Transcendental Reality—the truth of higher consciousness: It was a study of Hinduism, like a college course, about India's culture and cosmic theology. Part of my mind readily accepted the new ideas and spiritual concepts. Yet deep within, the teachings of my childhood that Jesus Christ was the way to God was an impediment to this new theology. Martin Luther King, Jr., had accepted the teaching of nonviolence from Mahatma Gandhi. Other Indian values of truth, such as nonpossession, physical labor, fearlessness, celibacy unless one was married, and equal respect for all religions were ideals that I wanted to incorporate into my daily life. Although some of the beliefs were similar to Christian thought, I had never studied them with a contemplative spirit, and I felt that I was expanding my soul.

Being in a relationship with Carlos was like standing beside a radiant, iridescent peacock with its tail feathers fully fanned out in a blue-green rainbow. Everywhere we went, people wanted to shake his hand, praise him. Women actually asked to kiss him right in front of me. My heart felt trampled in the outpouring of devotion to him. On the one hand I accepted the culture of devotion accompanying Carlos's fame. On the other, I couldn't conceive of being so fanatical about another human being and I often told people, when they oohed and aahed over my good fortune to be with him, that "each person has a gift to offer the world," and I was sure they were special, too.

But, clouds blew in through the window of my insecurity and disrupted my peaceful meditative world when I answered the telephone and someone was breathing and then hung up. My intuition told me it was a woman calling to speak with Carlos, but that she was afraid to ask for him when she heard my voice. I wondered if it was his former girlfriend, Linda, and worried he was not over her, and when it happened more than once, fretted there were others, and allowed the voiceless phone calls to poison my joy. I rationalized that if Carlos was seeing other women, it should not concern me. We were not married, but we were together so much, I did not believe he had time for another relationship. Carlos and I had a closeness that assured me we would be together for a while, and I purchased flower bulbs to plant in his garden, as though I would be there in spring to see tulips and daffodils push up along the walkway outside the kitchen window.

Sevika called me every day. She planned ways for the San Francisco Centre to make money to buy books and tapes from the New York Centre, and she wanted to sell clothes at the Alameda Flea Market. I had so much I was not wearing from my old life. I took Sly's goat coat, my tight, eight-button sailor jeans, and the purple taffeta hot-pants suit I had not worn since L.A. to sell at the flea market. Carlos reluctantly gave some snakeskin boots and black leather pants.

Sevika put Sri Chinmoy's picture on the table with the items for sale. Saris were enough of an attention-getter, but the transcendental meditation photo really raised eyebrows. An older couple walked by us, looking at the photo, and then stared and shook their heads—and the man mumbled, "Damn gurus come to America, brainwash our kids, steal our money."

I was mortified. I felt the same despair from the man's negative comments that I had felt growing up with people staring at my father's coal skin next to my mother's white. Their eyes had held scorn, even hatred, as they openly stared at us walking by. We never said anything, just stared back, holding our ground, keeping our heads high.

With Sevika, I could swallow my discomfort because it did not hurt like racism. And I felt it was my duty to help her. I was the only other woman in the Centre. I also had fun learning more about Guru from her perspective, which was much holier and funnier than Mahalakshmi's. Sevika acted as though Guru were present at every moment. His invisible spirit-consciousness was like a ghost constantly at her side. Being with Sevika was like being in New York. Before she drove, she prayed aloud for Guru to protect her. Yet she had a boisterous sense of humor and told jokes nonstop. She worked tirelessly on project after project, including sewing a bright gold satin *kurta* and *dhoti* for Sri Chinmoy that required tedious hand stitching. Her eyes often were red-rimmed from working until the wee hours of the morning. What drove her was divine love. When she spoke Guru's name, she swooned with devotion.

Carlos took me to his parents' home in late December. He had bought them a duplex in Noe Valley near Twenty-fourth Street. Mrs. Santana hugged me and spoke to me in Spanish. She and Carlos had the same butterscotch skin; Mr. Santana was brown like me. His mother's hair was straight and thick, a golden color. She was tall, with a wide girth and imposing strength. Her voice was musical and kind. Carlos had to interpret their words, as my high school Spanish was not good enough to understand what they were saying. The house was immaculate, and we sat at their dining room table eating a delicious meal of *chile rellenos* and refried beans that Mrs. Santana had cooked. Mr. Santana held Carlos's hand in his own, gently squeezing it as he spoke softly to him. He wore a black suit, the jacket cropped short, with polished silver buttons looped with chains across his white shirt. He was going to play violin at La Cantina with his mariachi band. Mrs. Santana fluttered from the kitchen to the dining table, trying to include me in her fluent Spanish conversation.

When we left, Carlos said, "I think that went all right."

"What do you mean?"

"I have not been close to my mom since I left home. She and I fought a lot."

"About what?"

"Mom wanted us to live according to her rigid sense of right and wrong. I was a hippie, and we couldn't talk about anything, so I moved out, roaming San Francisco with my friends and playing my guitar to make money. We played at weddings and at the YMCA in the Mission. I stayed at Gregg Rolie's and Michael Shrieve's houses a lot."

Carlos and I told each other stories about our families and began to understand that although we had been raised worlds apart—his father old-country macho, and his mother traditional stay-at-home; my father a social rebel, and my mother an independent woman who worked outside our home—what we had in common was a desire to be kind and to trust in love. He accepted me wholeheartedly like a limb of his body and called me *muñeca*—"doll" in Spanish. I called him "sweetheart." Carlos was a name that belonged to the world, and I wanted the part of him that wrapped spiritual love around me—soft, tender, generous, and mine alone.

We flew to New York to attend Sri Chinmoy's New Year Meditation and rented a car to drive to Manhattan, rushing so we would not be late. A gust of Manhattan's cold brittle wind pushed me up the stone steps of Hunter College Auditorium. The double doors opened to a marble foyer, where a poster of Sri Chinmoy hung, his face an expression of meditative bliss.

NEW YEAR MEDITATION WITH SRI CHINMOY,
SELF-REALISED MASTER
HUNTER COLLEGE AUDITORIUM,
DECEMBER 31, 1972, 7:30 P.M.
MAHAVISHNU JOHN MCLAUGHLIN
WILL PERFORM ON GUITAR

The words were framed in hand-drawn gardenias. I was surprised to see Mahavishnu's name like an advertisement. It seemed artless and begging, as if Sri Chinmoy needed a famous person to sell his spirituality, incongruous to what I believed God could do without human assistance. People stood outside the doors to the auditorium. One of Sri Chinmoy's male attendants opened a side door for Carlos and me. Disciples bustled through the large theater: Two men carried a wooden platform onto the center of the light-flooded stage, bending deeply as they set it down. A woman followed, her sari dancing around her. She laid a thick square of foam on the wooden seat and draped gold brocade over it, smoothing the fabric with her hands. The plain wood was transformed into a throne, accented by flowerpots of poinsettias and chrysanthemums along the front of the stage.

Mahalakshmi waved from down front and walked quickly to us. "I'm so glad you could come. Guru wants you to sit with the New York Centre. We're in the middle first three rows."

She led us to our seats. No New York disciples were talking. They sat straight-backed with their eyes closed, absorbed in their own consciousnesses, finding an inner silence in the midst of the preparations. I wanted to sit by Mahalakshmi and catch up on disciple news, but the focus of the devotees was the night's meditation. Carlos and I sat down. Mahavishnu slid into the seat next to Carlos and embraced him in a bear hug. "I'm playing acoustic tonight. Want to join me? We can do 'Naima' or 'A Love Supreme.' "

Carlos looked surprised. "I don't have my guitar," he whispered.

Mahavishnu smiled. "I brought an extra Martin."

Although Carlos loved spontaneous jam sessions, he usually played his own instrument.

Carlos looked down at his hands for a few moments. The stage lights cast an adobe glow over his skin; he looked so mestizo against the white shirt he wore. A long line creased his cheek, like a dimple pulled sideways. His lips pursed together as he thought.

Carlos raised his head, eyes twinkling. "Okay, man."

Mahavishnu motioned for Carlos to follow him. Carlos left his coat on the seat next to mine and walked up the stairs onto the stage, disappearing behind thick velvet curtains. Doors at the rear of the auditorium opened, and seekers filed into rows behind the disciples.

Lavanya and Ranjana descended the stage stairs. Light glinted off their saris—Ranjana's threaded with gold, and Lavanya's embroidered with tiny round mirrors. They were dressed as though going to a ball. Their lives were a puzzle to me: Although they were together much of the time, I never saw them talk to each other or display outer signs of closeness or even friendliness. They carried themselves with an air of knowing, but their faces—often without emotion—were aloof like wax figurines. They sat in the first row directly in front of the throne. Sri Chinmoy emerged from the side, walking stiffly, as though already deep in trance. His brown head topped a flowing white *kurta* and *dhoti;* his hands were clasped loosely in front of his body. He sat down on the edge of the throne, his feet in sheer, white striped socks.

"Om," he chanted forcefully, the word resonating until the sound melted into absolute silence. "Om," he chanted again. An aura of white light radiated around Sri Chinmoy's face, his neck extended like a heron ready to fly and his eyelids half-mast in dreamlike whiteness. On Guru's shoulders rested blossoms of white and red carnations woven into a thick necklace hanging to his stomach. He sat back on his throne, the garland around his neck rising and falling with each breath.

Mahavishnu walked onto the stage. Fans began whistling and clapping.

"Whoo! All right!"

Applause crescendoed around the auditorium. Carlos walked out in his bare feet, carrying a guitar by the neck with both hands. His head was bowed. A hum of voices said, "It's Carlos. That's Carlos Santana." Louder cat calls, whistles, and clapping.

Mahavishnu and Carlos sat down on the stage floor behind a six-inch-high microphone on a stand. They tuned their strings to each other. The auditorium grew silent. Their four hands moved

My mother, Jo Frances, age twenty, Chicago, Illinois, 1945. When I was
growing up, Mom, an outspoken Irish-American woman, worked full-
time in an era when it was acceptable, if not expected, that women stay at
home with their children.

A promotional shot of my father, Saunders King, in the 1940s. Dad embodied all of the melodies that were important to me: power, Blackness, loving everyone no matter what his or her station in life, and upholding truth.

From left: my mother Jo Frances, my grandmother Virgie Willis, and Aunt Nita in San Clemente, California, 1946.

The Saunders King Quintet at the Backstage Club in San Francisco, circa 1940. From left: Joe Holder, bass; Eddie Taylor, tenor sax; Saunders King, guitar; Bernard Peters, drums; Eddie Walker, trumpet.

Here He Is!!!
The King of the Blues
SAUNDERS KING
and
ALADDIN
got HIM!

First Release ...... Week

"ST. JAMES INFIRMAR'
and "LITTLE GIR
ALADDIN NO. 30

Order From Your D

For That Magic Touch

Newspaper ads
promoting my father's
performances.

Dad sang and played
guitar with his band, the
Saunders King Orchestra,
and often sat in with
Billie Holiday, Charlie
Parker, and T-Bone
Walker. One of Dad's
most famous songs,
"SK Blues," was written
before I was born.

OPENING TONIGHT

NEW YORK Comes to SAN FRANCISCO

Café SOCIETY Style ENTERTAINMENT

BILLIE HOLLIDAY

ESQUIRE MAGAZINE'S
AWARD WINNING
BLUES SINGER

ROSE
(CHI-CHI)
MURPHY
Direct From
GEORGE WHITE'S
SCANDALS

SIRKI de
VYSENOF
PAUL DRAPER'S
Only Rival
Whole Production
Direction of
SIRKI de VYSENOF

Dance To The
RED HOT RHYTHMS OF
SAUNDERS KING
Decca Recording Orchestra

Club SAVOY
ARRELL at POWELL··Phone EX. 2626

Delicious
6 COURSE DINNERS
FIRST SHOW
7:30 P.M.

I am one year old in this picture with my mother, 1952.

From left: my sister, Kitsaun, age four; my mother; and me at age two, Berkeley, California, 1953.

Kitsaun at age nine and me at age seven with our German shepherd Ki in front of our home in San Francisco, California, 1958.

My second-grade class photo. I am third from the right, top row, 1958.

Cheerleading for Lowell High School, San Francisco, 1968.

Washington Square Park, New York City, in 1969, during a visit with my sister and our friend David. I would be attending college that fall and was excited about my coming independence.

From left: Kitsaun, Grandmother Sarah King, and me in 1970. I learned about the peace of God during the two weeks spent with my grandmother each summer.

My family in 1970: Jo Frances, Saunders, Kitsaun, and me.

Carlos and me shortly after becoming disciples of Sri Chinmoy. Greenwich Village, New York City, 1972.

My parents in the 1970s. I came from a strong home with parents who talked to my sister and me and gave us spiritual values on which to build our lives.

José and Josefina Santana (Carlos's parents) on the occasion of their fiftieth wedding anniversary, 1990.

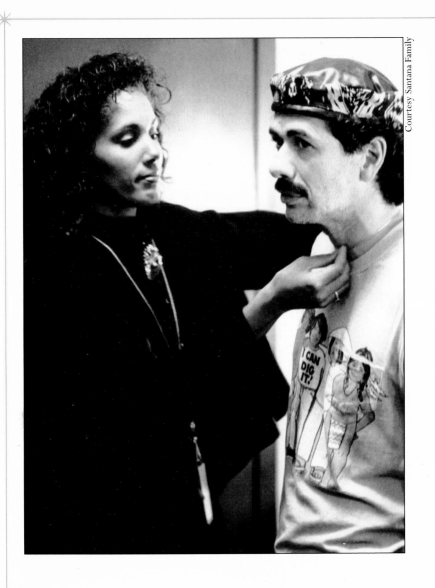

Carlos and me backstage at the Blues for Salvador benefit concert for the NEST (New El Salvador Today) Foundation. Oakland, California, 1988.

Our children, from left: Stella, age five; Salvador, age seven; and Angelica Faith, three months, in Hawaii, 1990.

In 1996 I attended a week long writing workshop with my friend Lynn DiGiovine at Mabel Dodge Luhan House, a historic artist colony in Taos, New Mexico. Writing grounded me in the direction I wanted to travel and made me feel whole.

Carlos and me at the World Shoe Association Show in Las Vegas, 2003. Carlos Santana Footwear is a licensing division of our River of Colors lifestyle brand.

Kitsaun and me before the California Music Awards, March 29, 2001.

Our family, San Rafael, California, 2003. Clockwise from top: Salvador, Stella, Angelica, Carlos, and me.

Carlos and me, San Rafael, California, 2003. Thirty-one years. We now understand that to love deeply, one must live without judgment and with compassion.

ever so slightly as the melody of John Coltrane's "Naima" whispered across their guitar strings. Sri Chinmoy sat up tall, his eyes fluttering as the two guitarists bent over their fingers, absorbed in the music. Carlos's soft legato chords were a perfect foil to Mahavishnu's rapid arpeggio runs. Trading solos, their tonal qualities blended as one voice.

Sri Chinmoy maintained his meditative tranquility. The final chord was followed by cheering, as though we were at a concert rather than a meditation. Sri Chinmoy bowed toward Mahavishnu and Carlos, a smile beaming from his face. The guitarists walked off the stage. After many shouts of "Encore! Encore!" did not bring the men back, I heard the rustle of some people leaving.

The New York girls went onto the stage to sing. I would have died if I'd had to follow Carlos and Mahavishnu, even though many of their fans had left, but the women closed their eyes and folded their hands; Bengali words tumbled from their lips as the remaining nondisciples squirmed in their seats.

The meditation ended, and Sri Chinmoy left the stage. Carlos walked toward me, fans surrounding him, trying to shake his hand. When he reached me, I thought, *He's glowing.*

"You're glowing," he said, looking in my eyes.

"So are you." I laughed.

Savyasachi came up behind Carlos. "Guru would like to see you both in the back room." He led us down a hallway behind the stage to a door cracked and yellowed with age. The air held the scent of fresh gardenias. Carlos and I waited while Savyasachi slipped inside the room. I shifted my heavy wool coat from arm to arm. Carlos leaned back against the wall, his eyes closed. The door opened, sending light cascading into the hall. "Guru can see you now," Savyasachi said.

Sri Chinmoy sat in an orange-cushioned recliner, his Buddha-like smile gently beckoning us. Carlos knelt at his feet, his eyes looking down at the floor. I knelt next to him.

"Dear ones, I am so happy you came to this special meditation." Sri Chinmoy's voice creaked like a door, its hinges needing oil. "While I was meditating, your souls approached me, asking for a blessing. When you were playing your guitar, dear Carlos, the Supreme told me your spiritual name. This name I will give you in the next few months. When you receive this name, a new, fruitful consciousness will dawn in you. Your soul flew to me also, Devi." I smiled at the way he pronounced my name with a *v* instead of a *b*. In Hindi, *Devi* means "goddess." I hoped that *Devi* would become my spiritual name.

"The Supreme gave me your spiritual name also. Together, the two of you will run like deer to the golden shore. You have pleased God with your purity, your aspiration. In August we will have a special gathering at my home for you to receive your soul names."

Carlos and I bowed, feeling that we were making progress in our spiritual lives. Each Indian name embodied the divine qualities of the disciple's soul. We stood up, gathered our coats, and backed out of the room. The next day we left for San Francisco.

Carlos continued rehearsing every day with the band. They were scheduled to begin their tour in San Diego on January 30, my birthday. His suitcases were laid out on the bedroom floor. He folded T-shirts, jeans, and a snakeskin jacket into neat piles and laid cowboy boots on their sides. Carlos made copies of albums he wanted to listen to on the road and lined one whole side of his suitcase with cassettes. We went to his management office in San Francisco to meet with Barry Imhoff, the tour manager, who worked under Bill Graham. Bill owned the Fillmore West in San Francisco and the Fillmore East in New York City, world-renowned concert venues, and ran his concert-promotion and band-management company across the street from Fillmore West on Geary Boulevard. Carlos held my hand, and we walked by the thin-faced lobby receptionist into the main room. Heads turned to watch us. I continued to be stunned when people paid such attention to Carlos and, in turn, to me. When the band was onstage, I understood who Carlos was in the musical world—his gift of melody and time, his fame. But alone, he was my sweet friend and lover, not a famous celebrity.

Music streamed from radios and cassette players in different corners of the office—mixing drums, screaming guitars, and bass. Every inch of every wall was covered: photos and posters of the Rolling Stones hung alongside Led Zeppelin; Peter Frampton; Bob Dylan; Crosby, Stills, Nash, & Young; James Brown; Joan Baez. A huge photo of Santana onstage at Woodstock with Bill playing cowbell in the wings was suspended outside Bill's office door. Dried flowers were strung over windows. A framed wheel of tickets was displayed, one from every venue in each city played on the Who's tour—a Plexiglas window box with photos of Pete Townshend and the band in performance. The office was a rock-and-roll museum. I sat on a leather couch outside Bill's office, waiting for Carlos while he met with Barry and Bill, and I made small talk with Bill's personal secretary. My eyes took in a lectern outside Bill's door; it had a microphone perched in the center and lights strung in an arc over the top. I asked her what it was.

"His soapbox. If Bill wants to make an announcement or yell at someone, he turns on the mike and the lights and we all hear his message—loud and clear."

I had not forgotten Bill's voice yelling at me across the Winterland lobby, and I hoped Carlos would come out before Bill felt a need to get on his soapbox today.

As I watched Carlos prepare to leave on tour, the blues descended on me. I listened to Miles play "Concerto de Aranjuez" and felt miserable. I had grown addicted to Carlos's arms around me, his lips on my neck, his soft voice in my ear. Our last night together, I followed him downstairs to the studio, a large square room void of natural light, its walls lined with mocha-stained cork panels to absorb sound. A jumble of conga drums, bongos, B-3 organ, guitars, tambourines, maracas, and trap drums filled the space. An end table held a pile of music magazines. Tops of amplifiers were crowded with samba whistles and ceramic angels, candles, and incense holders. Carlos sat on a small stool, fingering notes on his guitar while listening to Wes Montgomery.

I sat down across from him. He looked up, smiled, and blew me a kiss. I leaned against the six-foot-tall, carved-wooden mermaid that stood in the center of his music room, feeling her smoothly chiseled hardness along my back. I was jealous of her when Carlos first brought me to Mill Valley: She was powerful, physically perfect, her bell-shaped breasts pro-

truding so sensuously, like fine instruments to play. She towered over me—she was a goddess he could have anytime he
wanted, like real women I could not measure up to with my
skinny legs and small breasts. But I was not jealous now. He was
leaving her, too, for the road. I felt a bond with the nymph,
who, like me, was abandoned for Carlos's insatiable true love:
music.

Clouds hung over the bay billowy and dark the day I drove
Carlos to the airport for the flight to San Diego. "I'm not leaving you," he said as we stood in the breeze outside. "You are in
my heart. Wherever I go, you go with me."

I tried to smile, but tears fell just the same. I pushed my
body close to his, wrapping my arms around him so I could
squeeze myself inside of him. We walked to the gate, and the
band boarded. Loneliness was sitting in the pit of my stomach.
I drove back, crying, to the Mill Valley house. The little black
Volvo was my consolation. I could drive Carlos's car, inhale his
peppermint tea scent, and feel as though I were inside of him.
The house, so cozy when the two of us were together, felt isolated in the dark night. I got into bed, curled my knees to my
chest, and picked up my book, trying to ignore the sounds of
raccoon feet on the deck.

Kitsaun finally came to a meditation with me. Sevika and
Saumitra could not believe how alike we looked and acted. Kitsaun was a smidgen taller than me, her face angular like
Mom's—the same high cheekbones—my face rounder—like a
chipmunk, I always said—like Dad's. Twenty-two months
older, she was my guide as well as the tester of waters I would
be wading through after her. We had always shared friends, read

the same books, and, when younger, taken the bus together to civil rights rallies. We were different, too. Kitsaun had worn a 'fro that rivaled Kathleen Cleaver's, and I'd worn a long scarf flattening my hair. Kitsaun's eye for assessing a situation was clear—like an eagle's. She stuck with projects, whether sewing my orchestra outfit in junior high, finishing a term paper, or telling the raw truth. I was a hummingbird who flitted from interest to interest. People thought she was hard because she was fiercely vocal about her beliefs. I knew she was compassionate and hurt easily. I appeared soft and gentle because I smiled when speaking and served compliantly. But inside, I was strong—a composite of Mom's color-blind passion and Dad's staunch wariness. Kitsaun and I wore an invisible link of sisterhood that allowed us to forgive each other when we made mistakes. Mom had repeated throughout our lives, "Don't let anyone or anything come between you and your sister."

After the meditation, Kitsaun turned to me as we walked to our cars. "The disciples are so homogeneous. And why do you have to wear saris?"

"Sri Chinmoy says they help our purity."

Kitsaun gave me a sideways cut of her eyes and pulled her lower eyelid down with her index finger, which meant in our silent sister-speak, "Get real." But she had felt something, too, and said, "I like the quiet. Maybe I'll come back."

I used all my wiles to convince her that meditation with Guru was the answer to our inner search and that we could continue to work for civil rights by creating peace within. There were few experiences we had not shared, and I did not want to be on the spiritual path without her. I was working to absolve myself from my past sins. Although we did not talk about her time with Jake, or the drugs, I knew she could stand to do the same.

Sevika said that Kitsaun could send a photograph of her face to Sri Chinmoy with a letter asking to become a disciple. "Many seekers can't see Sri Chinmoy in person before they become disciples, so he meditates on their soul through their eyes in the photograph. His heart knows immediately if someone is meant for his meditation path."

Kitsaun mailed a letter telling a little about her life with the photo. A few days later, she called me. "I'm accepted," she said, sounding pleased. Sevika had called Kitsaun to say that Sri Chinmoy had meditated on the essence of her soul and she was now a member of the San Francisco Centre. She was on the path with me!

16

Surrender

$\mathcal{T}$he theme of our discipleship became "surrender." As I worked next to Sevika, the term came up daily: Surrender all that you are, all that you think, all that you envision for yourself—to the will of the guru. Every time a message came from Sri Chinmoy, it seemed there was something we had to relinquish. Carlos had touched on this when he named his recording with Mahavishnu "Love, Devotion and Surrender," but neither of us had foreseen how intrinsic this would be to the meditation path.

Sri Chinmoy asked disciples to do things the Supreme told him in meditation. Carlos and I had been together seven months when Sri Chinmoy invited us to New York and asked to speak privately with Carlos. Ranjana greeted us at Guru's front door and sent Carlos upstairs to talk with Guru. I followed her into the kitchen, where she was making a curried potato and pea dish for Guru and asked me to help.

I washed my hands and started pushing the stainless-steel peeler across russet potatoes while Ranjana clicked on a tape recording of Guru singing in Bengali. Her chestnut brown hair was pulled into a ponytail high on her head. Her eggshell-thin skin was powdery pale with the flush of winter-red cheeks. My heart was racing, wondering what Guru was talking to Carlos about.

My head was bent over a handful of peas when I heard Carlos's soft voice calling me. I looked up and he motioned for me to follow him. I washed my hands and walked with him into the meditation room. Guru was sitting comfortably on his throne, leaning to the side on his elbow.

"So, good girl, Carlos and I have had a heart-to-heart talk. He will tell you all about it. Now let's meditate."

I sat next to Carlos watching Sri Chinmoy's face. The room disappeared in a wash of golden light. I folded my hands in front of my chest, showing my devotion to the light that was coming into my soul. When Sri Chinmoy bowed, Carlos and I bowed, gathered our shoes and coats, and walked outside. I turned to Carlos. "What kind of heart-to-heart talk?" I asked anxiously.

We descended the stairs to the sidewalk and turned left, heading back to the Mahas'. Carlos took my hand, but walked in silence. At the corner, he pulled me to him. "He asked me if I loved you."

"What?" I couldn't believe they had been talking about us! I felt embarrassed. "What did you say?"

Carlos looked into my eyes. "I told him I love you with all my heart."

Why did Sri Chinmoy want to know if Carlos loved me? "Then what did he say?" The pitch of my voice was getting higher in my ears.

"He asked me what's keeping us from getting married."

"Married?" My heart was pounding. I was deeply in love with Carlos, but marriage had not entered my mind. I was only twenty-two; Carlos twenty-five. My freewheeling, no-bra-wearing spirit of the 1960s did not need the institution of marriage to define my relationship with Carlos.

"Yes, married." Carlos's penetrating eyes searched my face. He held my soul in his gaze.

"What else did he say?" I asked, resisting the urge to pace.

"He said that you are the one who can help me make the fastest spiritual progress."

"Do you want to marry me for me, or because Guru said you should?" I asked him, now staring into his honey-colored eyes, a flash of anger rising.

"I love you, Deborah. I want to marry you because I want to be with you always." We started walking. "What about you?" He pulled my hand, forcing me to turn and face him. "Do you want to marry me for me, or because Guru thinks we'll make fast spiritual progress together?"

I looked into his amber-hued mestizo face, his chiseled cheekbones, his fragile smile, trying to see the truth. "I would like to marry you because you have a heart of gold and I love you." My arms reached out around his winter coat, wondering if he knew how afraid I was. I had been crushed by Sly. My heart was like a car that had been in a very bad accident. Carlos's loving had repaired it, made it look almost new, but inside I was still shaken and dented.

His arms circled my back, rubbing up and down, igniting a flow of energy. I buried my face in his chest, and then we kissed beneath the bare limbs of the sycamore tree.

We surrendered to the meditation teacher; but, unconventional to the core, we did not want a traditional ceremony, bridesmaids and groomsmen, a reception in an elegant hotel, or fancy invitations. We asked my uncle U.S. to marry us. When he asked "Where?" I asked him if we could come to his house. He said he and Aunt Bitsy would be thrilled to have us married in their home in Oakland. Uncle U.S. was Dad's older brother, and the only one who had followed their parents into the ministry. Not quite as tall as Dad, who elegantly stretched to five feet eleven inches, Uncle U.S. was a joyous man with a round belly, whose glasses sat low on his nose, giving him a professorial air.

We would have to fit the ceremony in between tours, so I coordinated Carlos's schedule with Uncle U.S.'s. First we needed a marriage license, which I had no idea how to obtain. I called the Marin County Hall of Justice to find out how to get married, and then Mom to ask if we could come over. Sitting in their living room, Carlos asked Dad, "I'd like to have your daughter's hand in marriage."

I squirmed in my chair across the room, watching Dad's reaction.

He didn't flinch or answer quickly, but beside me, I saw Mom's face light up with a big smile. Dad sat up straighter, then cleared his throat. "If Deborah is sure this is what she wants, you have my permission."

I was mortified at the old-fashioned ritual I was taking part in, but glad it was over. Later that evening, Mom, Dad, and I went out to dinner together. "You know, Carlos is from a different culture than you are, Dobs."

"You mean because his family's from Mexico?" I asked.

"Yes. Their ways are different," Dad said.

"Carlos has been here twelve or thirteen years. I think he's pretty American now."

Dad did not respond, and Mom told me much later that she had wanted to kick him under the table and scream, "Whoopee!" She was happy I was going to settle down and she would not have to worry about me as she had when I was living in Los Angeles and called her with the "horror stories" of my life with Sly. She was thanking God.

Uncle U.S. reserved April 20 at his house. I invited Aunt Daisy, and Aunt Bitsy would be there, of course. Carlos said he would tell his parents.

The day of our ceremony, I awakened feeling nervous. The sky was the hue of lapis, with no fog drifting past our mountain road into Mill Valley.

Carlos pulled on the slacks to his white suit. His face was half-shaved; he grunted trying to put on his tie. My sari kept sliding out of my full-length slip. I yanked the five yards of fabric off, letting it billow to the floor, tied my slip string tighter around my waist, and started over.

"We have to be there in forty-five minutes," Carlos called out to me tersely.

"I'm almost ready. They can't start without us, you know!"

I knew how to get to Uncle U.S.'s house as well as I knew how to get to my parents' home. But, as Carlos exited the 580 freeway onto MacArthur Boulevard, I told him to turn left rather than right—and we headed for Berkeley instead of Oakland. "Make a U-turn," I screamed, rather indelicately.

"Oh God," Carlos groaned. "I hope I don't get a ticket!" He swung the car around, heading back toward Uncle U.S.'s house.

"Turn left here," I guided him onto Dover Street. "There's the house, the dark brown one."

Carlos parked, leaving both hands on the steering wheel, and put his head down. His back began to quiver. A laugh squirted out of his mouth. I joined in. "This is nerve-racking," I said, laughing. We looked at each other, tension melting.

A twinkle bounced from Carlos's eyes into my heart, and the muscles in my shoulders relaxed.

"I love you," I said, with a yearning to feel his soul always one with mine.

"I love you, too." Carlos's tie hung loose. He had never worn one before. "You ready?"

I nodded yes. "Who's bringing your parents?" I asked, opening the car door and gathering my sari in my hand.

"I didn't invite them," Carlos said. He bent over, locking the car while I stood on the sidewalk, my mouth open in shock.

"But, you said you would call them," I said.

"My mother and I weren't on speaking terms for years—remember, Deb? When I took you over to meet her at Christmas, everything went well, but I didn't want her to come in now and try to control me. She would have wanted a big wedding in a Catholic church."

Carlos put his arm around my shoulders and guided me off the Oakland sidewalk into the street. I swallowed hard and cleared my throat. I didn't know what to say. It was too late to invite them now, and I remembered Dad's caution about marrying into a different culture. Would Carlos's parents accept our marriage when they were not even invited to the ceremony? It felt strange to leave them out, but there was no point in my worrying now.

The front door of my uncle and aunt's house opened wide. Kitsaun stood there, hands on her hips, looking like Mom. "What's taken you two so long? Chickening out?"

We laughed, climbed the stairs, and hugged her as we walked inside the living room with its flowered couch and cushioned side chairs. Mom and Dad walked over to meet us, Dad firmly shaking Carlos's hand. Mom's eyes shone like the brass buttons on the navy blue suit she wore. Dad's soft face was scented with the splash of his lemony aftershave. They both looked beautiful. Mom patted Carlos's arm while she held my hand. I introduced Carlos to Uncle U.S. and Aunt Bitsy, who greeted us with a hug into her full bosom as we explained that Carlos's parents were not coming.

The noonday sun streamed into the living room. We made small talk, and Dad helped Carlos knot his tie. Uncle U.S. stood. "I'll get my robes on," he said, walking into his small study between the living room and their bedroom. When he came out, looking official in the loose-fitting, pleated black gown, we all stood.

"Who will be the witnesses?" Uncle U.S. asked. Aunt Bitsy and Dad nodded their heads yes.

Carlos took my hand. Kitsaun stood behind me with Mom. Dad stood behind Carlos. I felt loved and protected, although my stomach nervously twitched. Uncle U.S.'s preacher's voice began, "Dearly beloved . . ."

I entered a dream state. "I will," I answered when asked whether I would take Carlos to be my lawfully wedded husband, but the rest of the ceremony—as Uncle U.S. read from the leather-bound book open in his hands—was a blur.

"You may now kiss the bride." Carlos was wearing his platform boots from London. I had taken my shoes off when I came in the front door, so he was much taller than usual. Our kiss was soft and sweet.

Hands clapped around us. Dad hugged me. "May you always be happy, Dobs." Mom hugged Carlos, and Kitsaun wiped big tears from her cheeks, smiling at the same time. Uncle U.S. filled out the marriage certificate: "I hereby certify that on the 20th day of April, 1973, at Oakland, in the county of Alameda, state of California, under authority of a license issued by the County Clerk of Marin County, I, the undersigned, as a minister, joined in marriage, Carlos Santana and Deborah Sara King. . . ."

The "reception" was given by Aunt Daisy, in her two-bedroom apartment on Stannage Street in Albany. While we had been saying our vows, she was home, cooking Louisiana-style gumbo. Carlos and I drove to her place, following my parents and Kitsaun. I was giddy that we had accomplished the task of getting married a month after being given the command from Guru. I had no idea that marriage would be any different from living together, and was embarking on our new journey with an open mind.

Daisy had cooked for our family every weekend since my childhood. Her home was always fun—fresh baked pies sitting on her counter, bowls of peppermints on the coffee table, fried chicken popping and crackling on her stove. She batted her eyelashes with a coy charm that kept us laughing as she told us stories about her young years in Hollywood: rubbing elbows with Lena Horne; being romantically pursued by Louis Armstrong. "I'm so happy you all came. Carlos, you know I was in the movies—you're not the only star in this family." She winked at him, snapped her fingers, and shook her hips.

The final course was homemade sweet potato pie in a buttery crust. After Carlos finished, he stood up. "Thank you all for a wonderful wedding day. I'm late for band rehearsal, so I'd better go." He planted a kiss on my lips.

Mom's and Daisy's mouths opened in surprise. I smiled. "Kitsaun, can you give me a ride home?" I knew he had rehearsal. We had struggled to fit the wedding in between his commitments. Carlos walked from Mom to Dad to Daisy, hugging each one.

Moments after he left, he returned through the screen door. "Dad," Carlos called to his new father-in-law, "I locked my keys in the car. Can you help me get in?" We all laughed wildly.

Monday, Carlos called his mother to tell her we were married. When he hung up the phone, he said, "She's speechless. I think she's in shock."

We took our mothers, Kitsaun, and Carlos's sister Laura to New York the next week for a wedding celebration with Sri Chinmoy and the disciples. The trip raised a slew of questions when they saw the adulation the disciples gave Sri Chinmoy, and the community of seekers so impressed with a human leader.

When we returned, Mom and Dad asked to talk with me about Sri Chinmoy. Dad sat in his easy chair in the living room. Mom sat on the couch, looking out toward the Bay Bridge. "What does this guru teach?" Dad asked.

"He teaches meditation and the path of love and devotion to God," I said.

"What's wrong with the church's teachings? You've studied the Bible all your life. Why can't you meditate on the Word?" Mom's lips were tight. "God is no more in Sri Chinmoy than He is in you or me."

"There's nothing wrong with church, Mom. But people only go there on Sundays. Sri Chinmoy has us meditate every day, and he meditates on us, helping our souls make spiritual progress." I was repeating what Saumitra had told me. "It's like the yoga class we took together at Walt Baptiste's studio on Clement Street, Mom. Quiet and soothing."

"Yes, I meditated with the guru when I was with you in New York. Those disciples looked at him as though he were God, bowing to him and looking spacey. But when we were at yoga, we weren't asked to join the group and wear saris."

I wish I had been able to recognize the truth in Mom's words then. But at the time, the inner journey of meditation was replacing the ritual of church I had grown up with. It was a new lens through which I was viewing the sacred, and I did not comprehend that I was focusing too much on the man rather than on the message. "That's true, Mom. But Sri Chinmoy instructs us in how to find God inside ourselves, not only in heaven."

Dad clicked his teeth with his tongue. "God is everywhere, but you have to watch the messenger," he said. "Not everyone who meditates is from God." Dad was visibly unhappy with Kitsaun and me following a guru's teachings. Rather than try to please him and Mom by denying my belief in meditation, I felt upset that they were challenging us.

"And gurus from India are just a fad," Mom said. "It seems like everyone has a guru nowadays—that doesn't mean they're real."

I had to bite my tongue. I felt peace in the meditations and was clinging to testimonies of disciples whose lives had improved from following Sri Chinmoy; and I was inspired because the path was a contrast to the life I had been leading. No one has an exclusive ownership of Truth, and I knew even then that it was my faith in God that provided my soul with guidance and light.

Dad said, "Be careful, Dobs."

"We will," I answered. "Don't worry."

Mom and Dad did not look pleased. Even though we were adults, that did not stop them from checking on us. I didn't mind. They had always been invested in whatever Kitsaun and I did: They went to football games when I was cheerleader, choir concerts when Kitsaun and I sang, and they had come to L.A. when I was with Sly. Always looking in and watching out for us. Our family was close, and Mom and Dad did not need permission to care about our business. We shared experiences and conversations at dinner and in front of the TV. Dad had even asked his friends to follow Kitsaun and me around the city when we were teenagers.

Mom and Dad did not elaborate about their struggles or exalt the bravery their interracial union had taken. They had shown by example that we could be whatever we wanted, and let us know the world could be hostile to us because of our brown skin. They would always stand by us.

"Don't forget who you are," Dad said, "and where you came from."

Mom took a deep breath and crossed her arms over her chest. "You kids have common sense. Just think for yourselves."

Sri Chinmoy's next message from the Supreme was for Carlos and me to open a vegetarian restaurant in San Francisco. "This will be our premier divine enterprise for the West Coast," he told us.

We did not hesitate to say yes. I loved the work I had done at Annam Brahma, and this would be an opportunity for me to create something meaningful in my own life. Carlos offered ten thousand dollars to begin the business, and I drove around the city searching for an empty building for the restaurant, settling on a storefront at the corner of Church and Market Streets.

Carlos composed new music and recorded *Borboletta*. Then he packed his suitcases for the road. Part of me wanted to leave with Carlos, to sit beside him on the airplane, disembark in Tokyo, and travel with the band for the six-week leg of the tour. In the same moment, adrenaline pumped like sugar through my body as I wrote lists of supplies we would need to set up the restaurant. I did not know whether I could successfully live split in two—wanting to be in San Francisco and on the road, wanting to work on the divine enterprise and also watch Carlos perform on the other side of the world, wanting to live my life away from him, or live his with him. I plodded on, riding my roller coaster, hanging on to the crash bar, knowing how lucky I was to be torn in two by love and opportunity.

I partnered with Carlos's accountants to sign the rental lease and buy insurance; I ordered building permits; and Saumitra helped me find an architect and construction crew. Kitsaun gave notice at Frank's clothing company and came on board full-time. For two months, Saumitra and the architect were busy adapting the building to serve our needs while I created a menu and Kitsaun wrote lists of items we would need for preparation of the vegetarian entrées, soups, salads, and sandwiches we had selected for the menu.

Checkbook in hand, Kitsaun and I stood in Dvorson's restaurant supply store between rows of eight-foot-high metal shelves filled with gigantic stainless-steel whisks, serving spoons, casserole pans large enough to bathe a toddler in, gallon blenders, industrial-size coffee urns, and soup pots up to our knees. Sunlight gleamed on the sides of the pots, flashing silver before us. The restaurant was becoming visible. I savored the excitement and thrill.

"We'll need good knives that we can sharpen ourselves," Kitsaun said, lifting up a twelve-inch-long Hinckel. "And we'll need small spatulas for spreading mayonnaise on bread for sandwiches, as well as one of these Hobart food cutters to chop vegetables." She checked off items on her list, her face serious, her angular cheekbones set high in her sandalwood skin.

I picked up a plate, edges scalloped with a delicate pale green design. "This place setting will look nice with pale yellow walls, don't you think?"

Kitsaun peered closely. "It's difficult to tell. Let's ask if we can take a sample with us to compare with the paint."

I nodded. Kitsaun's business mind and organizational skills

were essential to putting the structure of the restaurant to-gether. She had helped me decide to have the restaurant de-signed cafeteria-style so that we could operate with the small staff of disciples, as there were only five in the Centre who could work in the divine enterprise.

Her artistic mind and impeccable eye for detail supported me as the business moved swiftly forward and I managed con-struction, people, and a budget.

We climbed into Kitsaun's clunky old BMW, the backseat and trunk holding our cache, and drove to Mom and Dad's on Harold Street. As we opened the garage door and carried soup pots, foot-long cooking spoons, and the sample plate into the hallway outside her bedroom, we saw Dad watching us from the living room window, hands on his hips, whistling "When Your Lover Has Gone."

Mom came home from work just as we finished. "Hi, girls. What do you have there?" She was breathing heavily after her long walk up the hill from the streetcar stop on Ocean Avenue. Her thin face was flushed red. Brunette hair fell softly over her brow. She pulled off her tan jacket and sat on Kitsaun's chair, next to the pile of recipe and management books.

"Hi, Mom," I said, holding a bundle of white aprons in my arms. "We're starting to buy equipment for the restaurant."

She looked around. "Everything is so big!" Mom was a Depression-era minimalist. She had miniature handwriting, wore her clothes until they were almost threadbare, and liked small sizes of almost everything. She smiled wanly and walked upstairs. We could hear Dad's voice booming through the floor, "What are they doing?"

We couldn't hear Mom's reply, but we fell onto Kitsaun's bed—laughing at how ridiculous we must have looked to Dad, lugging huge pots and pans, whisks, and plastic tubs into Kitsaun's bedroom, our saris flapping behind us.

From an 1,800-square-foot, empty storefront, we built a cafeteria-style restaurant that Sri Chinmoy named Dipti Nivas—"the Abode of Light." Perhaps more than anything else I had done since leaving L.A., the birth of our restaurant became the manifestation of who I was as a spiritual person and strong woman. I wrote an employee manual and job descriptions, determined shift times, and trained the workers based on the mission statement I wrote: "to serve humanity by offering pure, fresh food prepared in a peaceful and loving environment."

Carlos continued touring and recording, and the restaurant became my "child." Sevika was our bread baker and turned out loaves of light, whole-wheat ecstasy taken from a recipe in *The Tassajara Cookbook,* from a famed Zen monastery down the California coast. We opened in September 1973 and had fifty customers our first day. I had never stood on my feet eleven hours straight before, and could barely keep my eyes open on the drive home to Mill Valley. Every morning we would be back early—washing vegetables, cooking marinara sauce for spinach lasagna, and cutting up fruit for the fruit salad with honey-and-yogurt dressing. Rushes of customers came at lunchtime and from five until seven in the evenings. In between, people trickled in, giving us time to prepare for the following day and review what had not worked. We had a few failures of the recipes I chose: Carrot soup did not survive the first cauldron. And once, I made spanakopita, a Greek spinach dish with intricate layers of flaky dough, spending more than an hour with the process of chopping, mixing, and drizzling butter over the masterpiece; but during the final layering, I was called away and forgot to add the spinach that was draining in the colander by the sink. That casserole was a disaster.

1974

Within a few months, Dipti Nivas became well known in the Bay Area. A reputation for delicious casseroles and low prices brought customers from Sonoma, Oakland, San Jose, Berkeley, and Marin. They joined the local "regulars"—the name we endearingly called those who ate lunch and dinner with us many times a week. R. B. Read, columnist for the *San Francisco Examiner,* wrote that our restaurant was "a vegetarian delight," with meals of "truly gourmet quality." Kitsaun and I jumped into each other's arms, overjoyed that our hard work had been publicly recognized and our restaurant praised.

We hired more employees and became noticeably more efficient. Hundreds of diners ate at Dipti Nivas each day. I was able to work one shift rather than all day and night. My schedule began at 2:30 in the afternoon and ended at closing. When I arrived at the restaurant, I meditated; then I layered a tossed green salad over brown rice and smothered it in blue cheese dressing; I ate at our desk in the cramped office, or at a table in the low-seating area if we were not busy. The staff was never allowed to eat in the kitchen. I was a stickler for cleanliness and posted a sign on the wall: DO NOT TOUCH FACE OR HAIR WITHOUT WASHING HANDS AFTERWARDS.

During my shift I worked as cashier: I would ring up sales,

oversee the flow of food from kitchen to counter, and make sure the shakes, sandwiches, casseroles, or sundaes were placed on customers' trays before they left the cash register to sit down. Because we were cafeteria-style, we did not take reservations. Sometimes strangers sat together, happy to get a table at all when we were busy.

My spirit was buoyed by the hum of voices and the laughter that chimed through the dining room. *I'm twenty-three years old and these people are enjoying the menu I created.* I could not believe I was managing a restaurant loved by the people of San Francisco, a grand city with many award-winning gourmet restaurants. Regulars told us that one of the reasons they kept coming back was that they felt energized and full of light eating our fresh food. I swam in God's mercy, feeling that my time apart from Carlos was being rewarded.

Kitsaun managed the early-morning chores and often finally left at six or seven at night, after the dinner rush. If someone called in sick, she would work two full shifts. She thrived in the exhausting labor and, like me, was consumed with Dipti Nivas. When the doors were locked at ten at night, I emptied the sandwich bar—wrapping cheese, bread, and tofu salad, and saving sliced tomatoes for fresh marinara sauce we would simmer the next day. The busboys washed the last dishes, pots, and pans; then they swept and mopped the whole restaurant and turned off the dining room lights before taking the streetcar home. Every day they washed hundreds of plates, cups, bowls, and saucers without complaint, their faces red and rippled with perspiration. They scrubbed stainless-steel casserole pans lined with cheese and sauce baked to a hard crust, while suds sloshed on their white uniforms. All that we did was for Guru.

The restaurant work purified my heart, and the simple act of serving our customers balanced the life I had as Carlos's wife. Mom and Dad had raised Kitsaun and me to understand that fame was inconsequential to one's character. Mom was never in awe of musicians Dad knew, and Kitsaun and I had grown up hearing famous names without any reaction or fawning from any of our relatives. Sevika told me she had overheard a young woman in line at Dipti Nivas say, "If I were Carlos Santana's wife, I wouldn't work here." But I remembered L.A.— and I knew I would rather be at the restaurant than anywhere else.

My goal was to be a light to the world. The more work I did and the more projects I took on, the more motivated I became. I yearned for people around me to know God.

17

Let Go

$\mathscr{C}$arlos wrote to me from Hong Kong, "Here I am, two o'clock in the morning, all wet. We just had a water fight and it seems like everybody in the hotel was involved. Of course, I started it (this time), but everything is all right now. The security guard came over and we all cooled it." It was a three-page letter about sold-out shows, how similar Hong Kong was to New York, and that a typhoon was coming. In the middle of the news, he wrote, "I love you with all that I am. Please don't feel lonely, for I am always with you in everything you do and say. You are my first and only love, for you are my physical aspiration for the Supreme.

"How are my children, the cats, and how are the cars running?" he concluded.

From the beginning of our marriage, I was Carlos's link to home, to family, and to spiritual growth. And he was my link to thinking more freely and to embracing a life with open boundaries. Like an immense John Coltrane saxophone solo, Carlos taught me to not think about the constructs put on me by society. His upbringing did not teach him to fear some One in Heaven, the way mine had; and he was not impressed with authority. My years as a Girl Scout—earning badges by collecting old newspapers to take to the dump, visiting the elderly, and singing simple songs about friendship—had trained me in good works. Carlos offered me independence.

I flew to Brazil to meet the band and to spend a week on the road, enjoying the stadium concerts and hearing how their music had changed since I'd last heard them perform. The Rio de Janeiro show was in a soccer stadium. I sat to the side of Carlos's equipment, out of the audience's sight, watching his lanky body skate across the stage, his guitar plugged into a Boogie amp: the umbilical cord to his sound. He cajoled his guitar to speak the melodic language of his muse. Fans danced sensuously across the field. As Carlos strummed the first, slow, tremulous notes of "Samba Pa Ti," the crowd gasped, and then a wind of ecstatic screams reached the stage. Fans struck matches and lighters, holding the flames high above their heads, flickers of light appearing one by one, ignited milliseconds apart like fireflies across the sky. From the field to the top of the bleachers, people swayed in unison, their faces glistening with emotion. Every note Carlos played resonated from a familiar place inside me. Dad's guitar playing held the lineage of Charlie Christian, T Bone Walker, B. B. King. They lived through Carlos's hands, too. How Dad wrote a song, fingered the frets, how he played the world through his Gibson, had foreshadowed Carlos's music in my life and carried the stories of jazz and blues innovators whose music had lived through times of great suffering.

The audience went wild, begging for more after the concert ended. But after three encores, Carlos refused to return to the stage. He was dissatisfied with his equipment and how he had sounded through the stage monitors. Even though the crew tried to convince him the speakers in the arena had sounded magnificently clear, Carlos could not be consoled. It was the first time I heard him yell at his roadies and not go back onstage when the crowd was still screaming for more.

The promoter took the band to a dinner club that had tables on an outside terrace beneath palm trees. Platters of seafood, vegetables, and rice were placed in front of us. Carlos pulled me onto the dance floor when the house musicians played a slow song. I shivered from the flame of his body close to mine, and we floated cloud-like, sounds of the concert still echoing in my ears. My heart caught in my throat singing out my love for Carlos, although only I could hear. I felt Carlos's anger leave, and the heat of his body engulfed me. Santana's manager, Barry Imhoff, snapped his camera—the flash lighting in my eyelids as I rested my head on Carlos's shoulder.

In our room, we sipped champagne, the last drink of alcohol I had as a disciple, and Carlos folded hotel stationery into airplanes, flying the white birds from our balcony to the beach.

Every nuance of Carlos's life endeared him to me. He knelt to speak with children playing in alleyways, pouring coins into their hands. In our room, we listened to Weather Report, sharing the magnificence of Jaco, Wayne Shorter, and Joe Zawinul's solos. I learned when to fade into the background and observe Carlos's life, when to participate. On hotel beds, we discovered where one of us began and the other ended.

We meditated each morning in soft candlelight. I concentrated on the rise and fall of my breath. Sometimes I heard no sound. Other times, the flush of a toilet in another hotel room, or the bell of the elevator stopping on our floor, caught my attention. When the distractions lodged in my mind, I prayed as I had as a child, "The Lord is my shepherd . . ."

Phone calls back to Kitsaun at Dipti Nivas assured me that she was handling the restaurant just fine. After seven days of travel—hearing hundreds of horns honking in the metropolis of Buenos Aires, and seeing the red clay of Brasília and its angular, modern buildings—I flew home to San Francisco, eager to return to the restaurant and our customers. On the road, I had been treated like a queen, staying in beautiful hotels with soft feather beds, ordering room service that arrived on silver trays with roses in crystal vases. But, as much as I loved the road and being with Carlos, it was his journey, his work, and I was an extra appendage. At Dipti Nivas, I cooked curries, chopped vegetables, and rang up customers at the cash register, caught in the activity that fueled my creativity. It was hard work—and I loved it.

In December, I met Carlos in Osaka, Japan. I felt as though I had been transported underneath America, to the other side of the world. We rode the Bullet Train from Osaka to Tokyo, traveling 340 miles in three hours. One cantaloupe cost twenty dollars, and a glass of orange juice in the hotel restaurant was six dollars. Japanese women dressed in high-fashion European couture as well as in traditional Japanese kimonos. We visited Buddhist shrines and Shinto temples, and I read about Amaterasu-O-Mikami, the Sun Goddess, a chief deity of the Shinto faith. Other than the Indian goddess Kali, she was one of the only female gods I knew about. We saw thousands of golden Buddhas lining temple walls, and we were taken to Kamakura, where the famous Daibutsu Buddha stood more than forty feet high.

I had not realized how much traveling I would need to do to be with Carlos. I loved airplane flights, seeing countrysides from trains, and trying to guess what a hotel would look like before I arrived. Bill Graham often traveled with the band, and over time I began to know him. We made plans after concerts to meet in the hotel lobby the next morning to run together. Bill had a powerful, strong presence, and his body moving next to mine gave me adrenaline to pump my arms harder and push my legs farther. We talked as we huffed and strode through Vienna, Geneva, and Munich, places he had known as a child, and I got to know Bill through the stories he told of not even remembering his parents—he was two days old when his father died, and nine when his mother sent him to France for school. When Hitler's regime began persecuting and murdering Jews, Bill and his schoolmates were put on buses and sent away with almost nothing to eat but oranges. He exchanged the innocence of childhood for toughness and survival walking from Lyon to Marseilles, on a train to Spain and Portugal and on a ship to Casablanca, without parents and with the sound of torpedoes sizzling in the sky. As we ran, I thought about the trauma and humiliation Bill had endured that had produced the stony exterior and fighting spirit that had bullied me and others. Two of his sisters survived Auschwitz, and Bill was sent to a Hebrew shelter in New York, where he waited nine weeks for someone to pick him out for adoption. Compassion, love, and respect were what I grew to feel for Bill after our runs. We interacted in business as I assumed more responsibility for Carlos's schedule and finances, and I saw with new eyes the fearless warrior Bill had learned to be as a child.

In the summer of 1974, Guru held a special ceremony in his backyard to give Carlos and me our spiritual names. Every August devotees from around the world stayed in the Queens neighborhood to celebrate Sri Chinmoy's birthday, and to attend meditations. Carlos could be in Queens only five days between his Philadelphia and Saratoga Springs shows, so he met me there. We sat among a small group of devotees as butterflies lit on the maple leaves above our heads and a warm breeze filtered through my sari. Sri Chinmoy proclaimed that Carlos was to be called Devadip, meaning "Lamp of God," "Eye of God," and "Light of God." I was given the spiritual name Urmila, meaning "the Light of the Supreme." The bestowal of names signified that we had made spiritual progress. Carlos returned to his tour, telling his road manager and band members to call him by his new name. The press was puzzled but followed Carlos's request. Mom and Dad were less than enthusiastic to hear Kitsaun call me Urmila, and they continued to address me as Deborah, the name they had given me to honor a woman of great strength and intelligence in the Bible.

Carlos and I had always wanted a family, but were told that Sri Chinmoy's philosophy was that children were a hindrance to the meditative life. We asked Sri Chinmoy when it would be time for us to start a family, and Guru told us, "Wait. Wait." Dipti Nivas kept me busy to exhaustion, and Carlos's schedule of touring and recording kept us apart. Abruptly, Mahalakshmi and Mahavishnu left the meditation path, which jolted Carlos and me. Sri Chinmoy said they would fall in spiritual consciousness without him, and we debated if this could be possible. I continued to manage Dipti Nivas and attend meditations as if nothing were different. Then, early in 1976, I became pregnant. I don't know if my diaphragm failed, or if I subconsciously wanted a child so badly, I'd forgotten to use it. Through the disciple phone chain, I sent a message to Sri Chinmoy, asking him to call. I hoped he would offer us his blessing. But, in his grainy voice, he told me, "Do not worry, dear one. The soul has not yet entered your body. You can have an abortion." This sounded authentic to what an illumined master would know, but I was flooded with disappointment and sorrow. My desire to fulfill my own needs was not enough to refuse to follow his direction, and I trusted Sri Chinmoy could see planes of consciousness I could not. Now, my immaturity seems appalling, but at the time, I completely believed Sri Chinmoy was an avatar, a holy man, someone whose grasp of divinity was higher than mine. I did not consult Carlos, because my allegiance was to God and I had heard directly from God's messenger. I scheduled the abortion for a time when Carlos would be in Los Angeles, recording. He never saw my tears or noticed my emotional numbness. Carrying the secret of my act, I clung more to Sri Chinmoy's edicts and followed his way to God by denying my own inner voice. The mourning period was exactly one year until I could sit before my shrine and my first thought was not how sad I felt. It is interesting to me now that Guru never considered the aliveness of a woman's psyche that is connected with such intimate decisions. He never asked how I was doing with the choice I had made.

Carlos and I were on different time zones in our own house: I awakened at 5:00 A.M. to meditate, run, and go to work. He still stayed up until 2:00 A.M. practicing his guitar, and he rose long after I left the house. Music was his life; meditation and service, mine. It was a recipe for separation in even the closest of marriages, but with rock-and-roll as a backdrop luring Carlos away from home on a regular basis, even our devotion to God could not protect us from life's temptations. Sri Chinmoy's goal of keeping disciples busy so that the world would not draw us away from spirituality only served to separate Carlos and me more. He began going to clubs when he was home, and I was too tired to go out with him. What he really wanted was to escape the same rigid box he had left his parents' home to be free of, and he was sick of obeying Sri Chinmoy's orders. I was stuck in the cycle of obedience, and wholeheartedly subscribed to the disciple life. Carlos could not talk me out of it. If I had known it was disconnecting us, I might have been able to pull back and examine where I was; but I did not comprehend Carlos's need, nor see how I was justifying and blindly accepting Sri Chinmoy's demands.

This continued until one Friday night in early summer of 1978, when our schedules coalesced and we went to a small club in Burlingame to hear a local band. On the drive over, I talked about how Kitsaun and I were planning a remodel of Dipti Nivas. Carlos talked about his upcoming tour. We parked on Hillside Drive and walked inside the club. Heads turned and voices whispered as we came through the doors. "Carlos is here." "Santana's here."

We were led to a table in the front, but Carlos asked to sit farther back. I took off my coat and ordered sparkling mineral water, aware of eyes on us. After the band's set, a young woman with dark curls around her face walked up to our table. "I want you to have this," she said, pushing a gold bracelet into my hands. The angle of her face and her smile were directed at Carlos, and my stomach flip-flopped at the husky intonation of her voice.

I opened my mouth to say thank you, but Carlos stood up and ushered her away, his hand on her elbow. He bent over, talking to her in a way that suggested he knew her well. She looked vaguely familiar. Then I remembered—she was a Bay Area musician, and I had seen her before.

My heart sped, and my insides felt as though they were catapulting across the room. The stage spun before me. I recognized in one horrible moment that Carlos was having an affair. When he turned to walk back to our table, I stood up and put my coat on. I had to get outside. Carlos followed me through the smoke-filled room. I burst through the doors, as though the fresh air could save me from what I had discovered. This man whom I adored, who had vowed that spirituality was the highest value in his life, who meditated each morning, who married me in my uncle's home—had chosen to break our covenant.

Carlos opened my car door. I fell into the car as though I were drunk. Rage, sorrow, and a broken heart made me dizzy. I did not look at his face when he got behind the wheel. He put the key in the ignition, but did not turn the car on.

"Do you want a divorce?" I asked.

"What!" Carlos screamed. "What are you talking about?"

"It's obvious that you and that woman have something going on. I've been through this before. I'm not going to live with you while you carry on with other women. We're married. That means something to me."

"This was nothing," he said in a choked whisper. "I love you."

"Love is one thing. Fidelity is another," I said, sounding like a schoolteacher instead of the brokenhearted lover. *Why can't I cry?* My mouth was dry. My eyes were dry. I was stunned, reduced to giving a nagging lecture. "Let's just go home," I said. "I need to pack."

The hour drive from Burlingame to Mill Valley was excruciating. Road sign after road sign announced that my world was splitting apart. Like a train charging through my mind, the woman's face chased me. I had left the bracelet on the table. *What was that supposed to have been? A gift for the wife from the girlfriend?* All the pain of previous years raged through my body. What I had learned from Sly's twisted world was that it mattered to me if he slept with other women. Maybe it was my parents' long marriage and their image of togetherness—the bond they had forged fighting racism to seal their love—that made me want a pure intimacy with Carlos. Maybe it was my idealism that two people could love each other only, even in the hedonistic world we lived in. Trust and loyalty were essential to me in any relationship, friendship or marriage. I felt shattered knowing I had shared my body and soul with a man who had been making love to someone else. What had been a triangle with

God at the top and Carlos and me sharing the foundation was now a series of disconnected lines. I stared out into the night, piecing together the past months. I had been caught up in planning the remodel of Dipti Nivas, in running, in learning Guru's songs, and in teaching meditation. *When Carlos had gone out to clubs, he must have been meeting her.*

We drove in silence until we reached the gravel drive to our house. Carlos spoke: "I'm sorry. I don't want you to go."

I jumped out of the car, slammed the door, and ran to the house. The key would not turn in the lock. When it did, I turned off the burglar alarm, marched up the hall stairs, and dragged my suitcase from the attic.

Carlos was standing in the living room, his head hanging on his chest. "Where are you going?"

"I don't know, but I'll leave in the morning. It's too late now. I'm just going to pack."

I walked to our bedroom. Over the window hung a quilted banner I had bought at a country fair. Appliquéd letters spelled out: IF YOU LOVE SOMETHING VERY MUCH, LET IT GO. IF IT COMES BACK, IT'S YOURS TO KEEP. My eyes spilled over with the waters of heartbreak. I opened drawers and filled my suitcase with saris, slips, underwear, running clothes, and toiletries. On the top, I placed Guru's picture and some of his books. I would have to move in with Kitsaun. I had a room there where I occasionally spent the night when Carlos was on the road. I could not believe this was happening. *Should I ask Carlos if he is sleeping with her? He didn't deny it when I told him that's what I thought. Why couldn't he have denied it?*

From the studio beneath our bedroom floor, I could hear

the beautiful notes Carlos's fingers were playing on his guitar. They pierced my heart; tears dropping like a storm on everything I packed. I sat on the floor, looking at Guru's picture—asking, pleading with God for help. The music stopped downstairs, and Carlos soon stood over me. "Please don't go. I promise I won't see her again. I love you."

"I love you, too. But if you loved me, you wouldn't have done this. I can't live like this. It's too painful. It's everything I went through with Sly."

"I'm not Sly," Carlos said firmly.

I wanted to scream, "Bullshit!" but my years of meditation would not let the words leave my lips. I looked up at the ceiling we had painted when we first began living together. "I don't know who you are right now." I walked into the bathroom and locked the door, turning on the shower and letting it run for five minutes before I took off my clothes and stepped in. I did not move as the water sluiced over me. Too much was churning inside for me to move on the outside. My thoughts went over the past few weeks—every day, every detail—as I looked for something I must have done, some lack I had, to have made Carlos share the most intimate part of himself with someone else. I had left Sly knowing I had not been enough. He'd needed many women, different women—certainly not me, not my upbringing, not my love of purity. He had been a pimp before Sly and the Family Stone, for God's sake! But with Carlos, I'd thought I had found a soul mate, an eternal lover. *What a fool.*

I had seen Carlos's eyes when women flirted with him from the audience and backstage after shows: a glint of passion; a thrill of the chase. It was so obvious they wanted to be with him. His melodies were an aphrodisiac, and he held his guitar as though it were a woman, caressing the neck, bending his knees into each note. Silent promises emanated from the stage—of sensuality, of tenderness—enough to weaken any woman's legs with desire. I towel-dried my limp body in the bathroom, dressed, and slowly opened the door to our bedroom. Carlos was not there. I could hear him playing his guitar downstairs.

I slept fully dressed on top of the bed, waiting for morning. When I woke up as the orange glow of sunlight spread through the gray mist outside, Carlos was asleep next to me, under the covers. My wedding ring felt as though it weighed twenty pounds. I sat up, looking at Guru's photo. *I've got to call New York. Guru will tell me what I should do.*

I walked to the sliding-glass door, opened it quietly, stepped onto the wooden deck, and pulled my wedding band off my finger. I tossed it over the railing, watching the gold spin into the redwood grove below. I picked up my suitcase, tiptoed out of 88 Marin View Avenue, and drove my Audi across the Golden Gate Bridge, wiping away an ocean of tears.

18

Marathon

Sri Chinmoy and the disciples rallied around my broken heart, and I moved in with Kitsaun, searching for my deepest self within the breach of my marriage. Kitsaun had moved to a house in our old neighborhood in San Francisco, close to the places I had grown up and felt secure in. Saumitra and Sevika helped me paint and decorate a downstairs bedroom that became my new home. Carlos accepted my departure—he continued touring and living his music, which really was his sacred passion. I decided to train for the New York City Marathon; quite a few disciples were planning to run the 26.2-mile race. Running in Golden Gate Park—past the polo fields to the Great Highway, around the windmill standing stately and immobile—brought me deeper into myself. *Runner's World* magazine provided a training schedule of long runs and short runs that built up to a seventeen-mile distance a few weeks before the race. I ran hard and long and began to sift through who I was—with and without Carlos—to separate love from life, realizing I had used spirituality and meditation to try to protect myself from getting hurt. When I ran, my life ran alongside me. I saw how the choices we make can hurt others and how careful I had always been to consider others' feelings. But no one is immune from the human struggle of making choices for oneself that injure others; and although Carlos's choices had crushed me mightily, I perceived glimpses of my heart's transcendence and joy.

In my morning meditations I became stronger by accepting being alone, although I was gravely disappointed that human love was not forever. My work at Dipti Nivas was a wonderful healing balm; and if I lapsed into a self-pity party, wanting to collapse into tears, the customers always said something that drew me out and demanded I serve the ideal I had created.

The outcome of my separation from Carlos was that, after two months on my own, I enjoyed tremendous relief in not having to worry about whether he was being faithful to me, whether we were communicating well, or even how I looked. All of the constraints I had assumed as the wife of a rock star were sheared from my life while I hung out with myself on the hills of San Francisco—where I had first learned to think and live as an individual. There was a moment of revelation that ruffled through me like a great wind, and I knew I would be a magnificent person with or without Carlos.

But it was not as freeing for Carlos, and after three months apart, he returned from Europe and asked to see me. I was nervous that I was not ready to hear what he had to say, but I stood in a belief in my feminine power, holding on to the strong, spiritual bond I had created with myself. He walked to me as I stood in Dipti Nivas, and slid his knit cap from his head. His scalp was bare. "I shaved my head to conquer my pride and my desires," he said. "I want to be with you."

His smooth-shaven head frightened me. He looked a bit like Mr. Spock. I wanted to deny I was moved by his gesture. I wanted to say that it was too late to win me back—but the grandness of his act gripped my heart, and I couldn't speak. "I have so many feelings, so many fears," I told him. "I know I love you, but now that you say you are ready to turn from your impurity, I don't know if I can change my life from what it has become."

"What do you mean?" Carlos's eyes reddened.

"I've been living without the pain of worrying whether you love me. I've been free from striving to be enough to keep you."

"You have always been more than enough. I love you. I was running from the Centre, not you."

I was torn into fragments of love for myself and love for Carlos; afraid to believe him, yet understanding the seriousness of his shaved head.

Carlos opened his arms—and the memory of our love bent me. I walked into his embrace, the bareness of his scalp lying against my temple, and I released the safe, closed person I had become. Sri Chinmoy called on the phone, having been alerted by the disciples that Carlos was back, and encouraged me to return to my husband.

I felt as though I were in a dream when we drove home to Mill Valley listening to Wes Montgomery and John Coltrane ballads on our way up the mountain. Obedient to Guru, but not really sure on my own, I had returned to the mountain chalet where Carlos and I had first fallen in love. The cats mewed when I came into the house, and I bent to stroke their smooth, silky fur, biding my time to face Carlos and talk more. It was thrilling, but frightening, too.

Carlos said, "I'll be upstairs in the meditation room." Thankful for time alone to adjust, I opened my toiletry bag and placed my creams and toothbrush on the counter. The towels beneath the sink smelled damp and musty from sitting unused for three months. I showered and climbed the outside stairs to the meditation room in the tower. The fresh mountain air soaked into my body. I had not missed Mill Valley when I stayed at Kitsaun's, but now that I was back, the view of the redwoods and bay reminded me of happy times. I turned the doorknob of the meditation room. Books and candles were just as I had left them three months earlier. I sat next to Carlos on a pillow before the altar, closed my eyes, and felt a brush of heaven's peace inside me. The next morning, we drove to Stinson Beach and ate breakfast in a ramshackle café, then sat on the sand and watched the choppy sea become a waveless line at the horizon. I felt awkward, as though on a first date with someone I did not know. Carlos's soft words prodded me to be his friend again, and he picked up my hand every few minutes, kissing my palm. "I have something for you," he said.

"What?"

Carlos put his hand in his pocket and slowly drew it out. When he opened his fingers, my gold wedding band sat in his palm.

I was completely surprised and overtaken with emotion that he had my ring. "How did you find it?"

"Jorge did. He searched the forest for me." Carlos slid the band on my finger. I stared at it, shocked that Carlos's brother would humble himself to comb through the pine needles in the backyard for my wedding ring.

"I can't believe he found it. I threw it into a tangle of ferns and redwood trunks." It felt heavy, like this reunion of husband and wife. But I wore it with the hope that our marriage would survive.

On the winding ascent back to our home, I massaged the back of Carlos's neck, like I always had when he drove and I was beside him. He pressed his cheek to my hand. I wanted our marriage to survive. I still loved Carlos madly and believed in the idea of us working together to bring God's message of light and truth to the world. My entire existence prayed I could forgive him for not being faithful to me and that I could regain trust and openness with him. Each day I awakened amazed that I was back in Mill Valley and I moved cautiously with my heart. Maintaining my training schedule for the New York City Marathon allowed me autonomy and solitude to heal my wounds.

I flew to New York for the 26.2-mile footrace. Seventy-five of us were running from different Centres. Sundari from San Francisco had trained with me. Guru held a special meditation for us the evening before the marathon. We filled the pews of the Bayside Church, Guru on his throne above us. After meditating, he said, "You are all divine runners. You will be carried to the finish line by my transcendental consciousness. Now go. Get a good night's sleep." His smile spread across his face, candlelight twinkling on his white teeth.

At 6:00 A.M. we drove in vans and cars to the starting line at the Verrazano-Narrows Bridge. A mammoth fear that I would not finish quaked inside me. The 26.2 miles loomed ahead like 100 as I thought of my hours of training. In the chilly October morning I stood with hundreds of runners at the four-hour sign, wearing trash bags that we would toss on the side of the road when we were warmed up. We hopped from foot to foot, adrenaline pumping and teeth chattering, waiting the ten minutes it took just to cross the starting line after the gun was fired.

New Yorkers lined the streets, yelling encouragement. I ripped off my garbage bag at three miles. At mile fifteen, on the incline to the Queensboro Bridge, my legs became heavy. My prayer was to finish, no matter what. Volunteers handed out orange wedges and small paper cups of water and electrolyte-charged juice. Cups crunched under my feet as I ran past water stations. A disciple I began with moved ahead of me. Runners walked along the perimeter; some limped. Perspiration coated my chest and back. I kept my eyes frozen on a runner a quarter mile ahead of me, watching his back as though attached to him by a lifeline. My feet pounded through the neighborhood of Hasidic Jews—where men with ringlets poking out from felt fedoras stood with their families on door stoops. Voices called out, "Go on, sister!" as I strode through Harlem. At mile twenty-two, I walked for a couple of minutes; but when my calves began to tighten, I started shuffling along again. I was in a battle between my mind and body. My body wanted to sit along the curb and watch the other runners go by. My mind was determined to reach the finish line. Kitsaun's words about my training miles being deposited into a bank that

I was now drawing from kept rolling through my mind. My right foot felt wet.

In Central Park, hundreds stood cheering below the gigantic digital clock that ticked at the finish. The last quarter mile, my feet barely lifted above the asphalt. Someone threw water on another runner, and it splashed onto me. I tasted salt dripping from my upper lip. When I passed through the final chute, the clock said four hours, eleven minutes, and three seconds. Guru stood to the side, taking movies. I waved and smiled—jubilant! My time was more than two hours after the winner, but I did not care. I had finished!

"Keep walking," yelled a volunteer on the other side of the finish line. "Don't stop or your muscles will cramp up!"

I staggered across the field where thousands of runners were standing, chugging beers, or splayed across the grass. I headed toward Tavern on the Green, where disciples had been told to meet. Seeing the sky-blue flag with Guru's photo silkscreened across it, I walked dizzily toward it. Sundari was lying on a table, her legs being massaged by Nandita; Sundari had finished five minutes before me; Gayatri, my friend from the Connecticut Centre, ran up and gave me a hug. I began shaking with exhaustion and emotion. I had done it. No matter what else came in my life, knowing I had run 26.2 miles would sustain me.

I bent over to untie my shoelaces, and stars spun in front of me. I flopped down on the ground and carefully took off my shoes. Blood covered my right sock. I peeled it off. My toenail was black and blue; blood oozed out from under the nail. Gayatri brought me water and a sweatshirt.

Tears rolled down my cheeks. While Carlos and I had been separated, running was my solace, the cornerstone of my survival. I could not believe I had completed what I'd set out to do—three months of lonely determination washed down my face. I was surprised by my courage, and fulfilled that I had accomplished a rigorous goal. No matter what happened with Carlos, I knew I would survive. I smiled and smiled all the way back to Queens.

The next night, I walked from the plane, the muscles in my legs and groin burning like wood in a fire. I looked through the waiting crowd for Carlos in his knit cap. Short, tall, women, men, children jumping up and down—but no Carlos. My eyes darted nervously; my heart sank. Then, from behind a pillar, arms waving a bouquet of yellow roses caught my eye. Carlos's mustached smile spread across his face. I hobbled to him.

"You did it!" he said, pushing the flowers into my hands as he embraced me, the petals crushing between us. "I knew you would finish!"

Warm and welcoming, Carlos's arms were around me again. I smiled, lost in the euphoria of my marathon victory and reuniting with Carlos.

While my marriage was mending, Sri Chinmoy's demands on my time increased. "Give more meditation classes to bring more disciples, Urmila. Run more marathons. Come to New York to be in my divine presence," he told me. I felt as though I would break apart from the pressure, and I began to disconnect inwardly from Sri Chinmoy's control. There was a gaping hole between what his books taught about enlightenment and the psychological and physical requirements of energy, money, loyalty, and selfless allegiance. Carlos watched me, afraid to pull me away, but waiting for a splinter in my devotion. My head ached each day, and I admitted to myself that I was allowing Sri Chinmoy to keep me in bondage of mind and spirit. As disciples, we had no freedom to follow the God of our own hearts. Carlos's fame was used like fly paper to catch new devotees, and though we had once believed the Centre was a refuge from an iniquitous world, we now saw it was a closed, isolated cult filling us with fear of the world we were meant to be a part of. No spiritual teacher could save us; we had to strike a balance between the materialism of the world and the spirit of our souls. Sri Chinmoy was asking us to hide behind him in saris and white clothes, but he was also asking us to deny thinking for ourselves so that we would do whatever he said.

19

Trust Life

1981

✳

$\mathcal{I}$ went with Carlos on the band's summer tour of Japan, and made a visit to the Zojo-ji Temple in Tokyo. On an earlier trip to Japan, I had walked to this holy place and felt peace and tranquillity rising from the silence of the Buddhist meditation. The main hall stands behind the Sanmon Gate, the oldest wooden structure in Tokyo. Worshippers in quilted jackets and cotton kimonos threw coins into a grate, clapped twice, and bowed before entering the shrine. Japanese wooden clogs worn by monks lined the stone entrance. I walked across small pebbles to the side of the temple and began to climb up the hill.

Hundreds of small stone statues dotted the hillside, and each one had a red cloth hood. I breathed in aromatic aloe wood incense and opened my heart to the spirits. Wooden tablets, pushed into the ground, waved light pink and turquoise prayer flags, and some of the statues were draped in baby slippers or knit caps. Folded paper birds blew in the wind beside them. My body trembled in this memorial garden for dead children and aborted babies.

I climbed higher, trying not to stumble into the storm of emotions clamoring in my body, and I sat on a bench overlooking the main temple. A man and a woman held hands and stood motionless by a statue. I opened my mouth—silent cries lifting onto the wind as I allowed the pain of my abortions to pour from my eyes and mouth.

Many of the wooden stakes had names written on them. In Japan, it is not a crime to choose to not have a baby. You can name the child; make a shrine to the soul; and ask God to recycle it to another family in another woman's warm womb. I believed this had been done for me and all women who choose to abort or lose babies without understanding why. Certainly, the Creator of life holds each seed in the eternity of a loving hand.

When I returned to our hotel room, Carlos caressed my face and kissed me softly on the lips. "You look like you climbed to the stars."

"I need to tell you something serious," I said, folding my arms across my chest. This was harder than I had imagined. "Before we separated, I was pregnant."

"What?" Carlos sat up and grabbed my shoulders. His brows forged together. His mouth opened wide. "What do you mean? What happened?"

Carlos looked so surprised, that my head felt like it would explode in desperation and fear. "Guru said that I should have an abortion. The baby's soul wasn't in my body yet. He said a baby would distract us from our spiritual lives." Grief still lingered in my heart.

"Why didn't you tell me?" Carlos slumped down onto the couch, his face contorted in sadness.

"I didn't know what Guru would want us to do. He'd told us to wait to have a family. I was afraid you might want to leave the Centre and have the baby even if Guru told us not to. But I was hoping he would give us his blessings. And I thought he knew everything then. I believed he would tell me the right thing to do. My mind was blinded by my foolish devotion."

Carlos's dark eyes winced as he reached his arms out to hold me. We rocked from side to side, each lost in our own thoughts. "It's going to be all right," Carlos crooned. "We'll try again to have a baby." He paused. "You still can, can't you? They didn't hurt you, did they?"

"No."

Carlos lifted my chin, forcing my eyes to look into his. "I want to have babies with you, but it *is* your body and your decision, as much as it hurts me." He pulled me into his chest, his broad hand pressing against my back, rubbing up and down my spine. His body was rigid, not soft against mine. "I still don't understand why Guru says you can't have a family and be spiritual."

I lay in his arms, thinking of the garden I had just walked in. "When I stood alone in the cemetery, I was not afraid," I said. "I knew with certainty that a loving spirit was with me. Sri Chinmoy says that having a family will lessen our dedication to the spiritual life. I think he fears that having children will expose us to a higher love. He forced us to remain obedient to him by making us fear that we cannot be spiritual without him, telling us that it is our efforts to live a perfect life, doing only what he sanctions, that will allow us to be one with the infinite Spirit of creation. But as the breeze blew by me on that hill, I knew that his philosophy is merely one view of God. My goal is to trust God's eternal connection with our spirits so that I can step out on the edge of a thousand-foot-high cliff and know that God has miracles beyond what I can see. Even if we stumble into the abyss, God will be there. My faith is in the daily rising of my soul's sun."

Carlos nodded and whispered in my ear, "We are one with God and each other. No matter what happens, we are one. I love you."

I wrapped my arms around his back and closed my eyes, feeling his body breathing in rhythm with mine. "I sat at the temple with the souls of my babies. I'm at peace with leaving the Centre and going on with our lives. Everything exists within us. Our teacher, God, our love, our healing." Carlos squeezed me into his body, swaying back and forth, like a strong covering for our journey.

Sri Chinmoy exploded when he received our message that we were leaving the Centre. It reminded me of the fury of Mount Saint Helens, which had erupted a few months earlier in Washington State. A whole portion of rock face fell, creating landslides and a total ash-out for twenty miles. Sixty people died. Sri Chinmoy called us in Mill Valley, his voice dripping with pain and disappointment. "You have twenty-four hours to change your minds or the door will be closed forever." I did not answer, but set the receiver on its cradle while taking in his words. Before, if Guru had said the door to his spiritual path would be closed, terror would have flamed through my body. Now I felt calm. We had seen other people leave, like our friends Mahavishnu and Mahalakshmi, and we knew it would not be easy. Yet it was piercing to hear him say the same words to us that I had heard him say to others. Sri Chinmoy's philosophy was that anyone who left his Centre could only fall to the depths of darkness. We sent a message to him that our minds were made up. Disciples called us day and night, putting pressure on us to stay. Although it became emotionally trying, the most difficult shift was to accept that Sri Chinmoy was not the illumined spiritual teacher that his disciples proclaimed. Carlos and I had outgrown his make-believe realm and had unbraided our mental dependency on him as our link to God. We sought the God-ness that existed inside us. The knowledge that God could not be contained in one man was so liberating, I felt as though light were dancing in my body: My mind could hardly hold the possibilities before me. No more "Yes, Guru"; "Whatever you say, Guru." No more bowing to a frail form of divinity. I could rekindle the friendships I had abandoned in my busy life as a devotee. How I would live and whom I would believe were entirely in my control.

Kitsaun was very upset and cried when we told her of our decision to leave, because we had not shared our thoughts with her before we decided to go. But she had always maintained an independent spirit, and soon she parted ways with Sri Chinmoy also. It was even sadder for her to watch us sell Dipti Nivas, but we'd tried to give it to Sri Chinmoy as a San Francisco enterprise and he had refused to accept it.

The restaurant had been one of the best experiences of my life. I had learned patience by managing people who had different levels of skill and commitment; I had grasped the systems of purchases and orders; I had grown to understand my own determined desire for perfection. We put the restaurant on the market, and it sold quickly. I went to Europe with the band, purchasing new clothes in Cannes that cut close to my body and allowed the sun to warm my skin. I didn't miss wearing saris—they had been an oppressive covering of my individuality and style, besides a physical barrier to moving freely through life.

During sound check in Fréjus, France, I sat on a sloping hill above the ancient Roman-built amphitheater, peace rippling through my soul. On the gentle breeze, I heard the women in my family together with the mothers of the universe singing through my spirit. It was as though they were unwrapping patriarchal dominance from my life, like binding from my feet, and releasing a tourniquet of cloth that had crushed my toes under the soles of my feet, pinching and suffocating growth that was imperative to my movement and power.

Carlos held my hand close to his chest, squeezing and kissing my fingers, so happy that I was his partner and friend rather than Guru's tireless devotee. We were two new people, born out of the dedication to attain higher consciousness through our nine years of meditation. I wrapped my arm around his waist and stayed close to his side to feel who he was. I worked to forgive my own naiveté and remembered there had also been some favorable outcomes from being cloistered in Sri Chinmoy's organization: My body was purified by consuming no alcohol, drugs, or meat. I was physically fit through running. In addition, when obstacles had arisen, I overcame them by deep inner reflection and reliance on my inner stillness. Learning can come from good and bad experiences—it is a matter of how we process and contextualize the information. Carlos and I had pursued light and truth. The path was flawed, but the essence of God's love in our lives was perfect.

For the year it took me to become pregnant, Carlos told the band members, "We're working on making a baby," and he doted on me as never before. His hair curled on the nape of his neck, growing long again. When I became pregnant, he took me to Hot N Hunky in the Castro to eat hamburgers and drink thick vanilla milkshakes. After nine years as a vegetarian, I enjoyed the sizzling meat and grease.

We felt deep gratitude and hope in starting our family, after ten years of being together. To say I felt no regret over my abortions would be a lie. But it spurred me to continue examining what I believed and how my view of truth was rooted in our patriarchal, Christian society. Now that Carlos and I were fulfilling the opportunity to give life, we meditated to welcome the little one into our family.

Without the restaurant, I was restless and looking for meaningful work. For a few months I volunteered at a preschool in the Western Addition and read stories to children because I wanted to offer something to their lives.

Carlos and I also spent time at meetings with Bill Graham and Ray, the tour manager, exploring options for Carlos's career. He was always brimming with creative ideas—people with whom he wanted to play, countries where he wanted to perform that had been off limits for rock music, such as China and Russia. Carlos treasured the original Santana Band's trip to Ghana with Ike and Tina Turner, Wilson Pickett, and the Voices of East Harlem. He still told the story of the tribes that met them at the airport, drumming and dancing; the voodoo doctor who put a curse on one of the musicians; and the musical symbiosis when his guitar danced in rhythm with each pair of dark eyes.

At Winterland Productions, Bill's merchandise company, we met with artists who designed T-shirts, and we were led to a poorly lit room in the basement where the Santana Fan Club's business was handled. Five women stood over a long table, stuffing envelopes and packaging T-shirts, and one woman sat at a battered desk with papers piled high in front of her. She showed me a binder with names and addresses that had been cut from envelopes and pasted onto paper. "This is a list of the fans who write."

I looked through the book, noticing duplicate entries and no sense of order. *There must be a better way to keep a record of our fans.* "What do you send to the fans?" I asked.

"We mail them an order form for T-shirts."

"Do you send photos?"

"Yes," she said, "if they ask for one."

I handed her back the binder. "Thanks."

It seemed an inefficient system. I had been to many of the places Santana had toured, and I felt personally connected to the fans. I had watched their faces light up with the opening chords of "Welcome," and had seen people leap in the air when Carlos hit a note on his guitar, his eyes squeezed shut, his mouth open in an inaudible scream. I had witnessed faces wet with tears during "Europa," and had watched women rip off their blouses and wave them over their heads when the recognizable chords of "Oye Como Va" rolled from the stage. The fans deserved a heartfelt response when they wrote to us, certainly a more personal touch than they were receiving. With time on my hands and a baby in my belly, I decided to take over the fan club. I bought a computer to set up a proper database and asked the manager to have the binder sent to me. With Mom's help, I entered each name, organized by city, state, and country. It took us weeks to type in every one. When we finished, we had three thousand fans registered in the database. Kitsaun volunteered to help, and with her background in merchandising and eye for color and design, we created the first newsletter. She also picked up the mail from the post office box so we could keep the mailing list current. We personally answered any letter by someone who was sick or in need. Within a few months, Kitsaun came to work at the Santana office and did all of the fan club business.

It was rewarding to read fans' letters; sometimes Kitsaun cried at the soulful comments they wrote about the experiences they had at shows. I clipped foreign stamps from envelopes and mounted them in a scrapbook. From just the first year, the postage represented fifty-one countries where people had been touched by Santana's music.

My body was changing inside and out. Having always been skinny, I watched with curiosity as padding grew on my hips and stomach and I expanded to make a home for the baby. I reconnected with my parents on a different level, asking questions about family history and genealogy: Dad's Louisiana

Creole heritage, and Mom's Irish-English roots. Carlos and I talked about our pasts and our future, debated names for the baby, and played Miles's "Concerto de Aranjuez" to educate the baby's musical cells as they developed.

Four months pregnant, I spent New Year's Eve of 1983 with Carlos, meditating in front of a fire, a picture of Jesus leaning on the mantel. The sky was filled with pinpoints of stars floating in navy vellum. I read from Paramahansa Yogananda: "Learn to discriminate in the new year. Examine every impulse that comes, to see if it is the right thing for you to act on. And when your reason tells you to do a certain thing, let neither the fates nor the gods stand in your way." I carried this message with me, folded in my purse, and referred to it when I needed to know I could count on my own mind and heart to chart my course.

My stomach grew larger, and the baby kicked in rhythm, which made me suspect a musician was dwelling there. I shopped for tiny outfits, crib sheets, and baby towels soft as velvet. Carlos and I attended Lamaze classes so I could deliver naturally. When my labor started, I recalled each footstep in the New York City Marathon and kept telling myself that if I could run 26.2 miles, I could certainly get through childbirth. Carlos was a nervous wreck, and his pacing drove me crazy. My labor was long, and I sent him home on an imaginary errand so I could relax and concentrate on my breathing. He returned minutes before Salvador was born, a precious colicky wonder, and we thanked Spirit for the miracle of his life.

I worked to adjust my life from runner, former restaurant manager, and fan club administrator to full-time mom; and I assembled my schedule around Salvador's gurgles and smiles.

Many days I struggled to adapt to the little person in my care. I would call Mom to ask how often to bathe Salvador, when he could eat solid food, and "Can I bring him over so I can go for a long run?" Mom and Dad were ecstatic to have a grandchild. I never could figure out why he slept all night at their house and then awakened at eight in the morning—when he would wake up two or three times during the night at home.

When he was seven weeks old, Salvador went on the road with us to Tokyo, Japan, looking like a miniature sumo wrestler wearing his baseball cap and a kimono. In August we went to New York City for the Jones Beach Show, and Salvador visited museums and shops on Madison Avenue with me, charming everyone he met.

In the elevator at the Parker Meridien Hotel in Manhattan, a man said to me, *Estás cuidando el niño?*

"No," I replied. *"Es mí niño."*

My face heated up, and I was mad as hell that he had asked whether I was taking care of Salvador, as though the child could not be mine because our skin colors were different. I fought to accept the man's innocence. Because of Salvador's pale skin— like Mom's and Carlos's—the man did not know Salvador was my child. His eyes were blue, his fat little arms and toes not even brown in the creases. I instantly understood what my mom must have felt when she'd carried brown baby girls in her arms and people had asked whether she was taking care of them, or worse, had scorned her for marrying a black man. I felt strange realizing that I was repeating the life my mother had lived more than thirty years before. Times had changed—inter-racial marriage was no longer illegal in sixteen states, as it had been in Mom and Dad's time—but people still could not see beyond color. Living with racism was painful, and struck a tender nerve in my core. Carlos and I had not experienced what Mom and Dad had as a couple, but with Salvador I saw a challenging road ahead.

Carlos also assessed his life in context of being a son and a father. He told me that when he was a boy he used to sit outside his Tijuana home, turning the wheel of a bicycle, hitting a stick against the spokes, hoping the spinning rhythm would drown the sadness he felt when his father walked from the house with his violin in hand to play mariachi music in distant towns.

Their family moved to the United States and lived in a small apartment in the Mission District of San Francisco. Carlos chased his own guitar aspirations, listening to blues players on records at his friends' houses when he cut school at Mission High. He wanted to play like B. B., T Bone, and Albert King.

"My dad told me to do anything but be a musician. I couldn't believe he would tell me that after he had spent his whole life playing music. In Mexico, I had worked so hard to learn the guitar and worked strip clubs in Tijuana to buy my first guitar. I was so mad at him that I became more determined to play my music," Carlos said.

"Why did your dad say that? Didn't he want you to follow in his footsteps?"

"Mom was working in a Laundromat, and Dad was playing in Mexican restaurants that didn't pay much, in the Mission. He was frustrated and afraid I would have the same hard life. But when he said it, I didn't understand—I just thought he was trying to stop me from reaching the most important goal of my life. One afternoon when I worked at Tick Tock's, the Grateful Dead pulled up in a limo and I told myself then that if they could make it, so could I. It was music or die."

In December we traveled to Cihuatlan, México, with my mom and dad, Carlos's parents, and Salvador. At the Manzanillo airport, Carlos's maternal aunts, *Tías* Sylvie and Gollita, and *Tío* Cesar, together with many friends and relatives, waited for us. They were dancing with the thrill of having their sister Josefina and all of us in their land. We were taken by Volkswagen bus to Las Hadas, the resort where we stayed, nestled in front of mountains with a sparkling oceanfront beach and luscious magenta bougainvillea trailing along the white buildings. When we visited the *tías'* house, Salvador was the star—his feet never touched the ground. Gollita ran about the house waiting on us hand and foot as she chattered Spanish adorations at her grand-nephew.

The town was a shocking contrast to the hotel. When cars sped through the dirt streets, dust flew everywhere. Mrs. Santana had sent money to her sisters, so their house had two indoor bathrooms, nice furniture, and a washing machine. Sylvie told us another woman in town had a washing machine she had won in a contest, and how happy it made her because she had twenty-two children.

Dad and Carlos played tennis at the hotel and let me in for one Australian set, where we played two on a side, rotating around the court. I loved being on the side playing singles against the two powerhouse men, and I slid back and forth on the red clay to keep up with their forehand smashes and backhand cross-court slices. Afterward, we dined beside the pool under amber lights, Salvador asleep in my arms.

Carlos and his Dad wanted to travel to Autlán, the town where Carlos and most of his siblings had been born. A friend took us in a truck while Salvador stayed with Mom and Dad at Las Hadas. Mrs. Santana was content to stay and talk nonstop with her sisters about her children and what had changed in Cihuatlan.

We drove through land lush with fruit-laden banana, coconut, and papaya trees. The road snaked through farmlands and valleys with thousands of palm trees as far as I could see—a breathtaking, tropical paradise. The sun baked us, and a thin film of perspiration lay like dew on my skin. Fields of sugarcane and corn drifted in and out of view. I asked what the yellow-breasted birds were swooping through the sky. "Garrionsillos," Mr. Santana said.

Small, open-air casitas were situated on each farm, and speckled black chickens pecked the dusty road for morsels of food. I marveled at the beauty and simplicity of this life, where families could live richly off the land. Yet the poverty was so great that many houses were without roofs—brick casas left half finished, with pieces of plastic sheeting or tin covering their tops. Horses stood saddled up and tied to fence posts, and men's faces were weathered and hardened with weary expressions. Outside, in the dirt, toddlers played, watched by older children. I thought how easy my life was, how hard it must be to work this glorious land as a campesino. In fields of lavender flowers, Brahma bulls' muscles twitched to shake off flies; and farmers wearing yellow and white peasant shirts walked behind horses tilling the soft earth.

We passed El Tigre, and wound downhill into a desert of cactus, tall as trees, to Autlán. We parked and extracted our cramped bodies from the cab of the truck, walking to the *zócalo* in the center of town. Carlos had not been there since he'd left at the age of ten. "I can't believe how small it is," he said. "It seemed like a big city when we lived here. It was all I knew."

We walked to the church where Carlos had been an altar boy. He kneeled before the Virgen at the door and touched his dad's shoulder, a poignant, bittersweet moment: Good memories and bad from his childhood and times of strife between his parents that haunted him; but to be home again was exorcising a giant shadow that he had spent years running away from.

We passed a restaurant, and men ran out to us. "Don José!" they exclaimed, and clapped Mr. Santana on the back, yelling across the street to their friends. Laughter. Then faces turned to Carlos, and they spilled out sentences in Spanish, pointing to Mr. Santana.

"Dad's like the mayor of Autlán," Carlos said, smiling. "He's more famous here than I am."

It was dark when we climbed into the truck to drive back to Salvador. I could not wait to get my arms around that chunky boy. I had learned about myself on this trip to Carlos's birthplace: how privileged my childhood seemed compared with Carlos's humble beginnings, and how I do not need material wealth to be happy. I saw how much we have that we do not need, and I wanted to remember Mexico to avoid being swayed by the competitive nature of American life.

Could I be happy on one of these farms in Mexico? I didn't think so. But I could keep my life real in homage to the weathered farmers and shoeless children I had seen and knew Carlos had once been.

20

Daughters

1985

✳

𝒮alvador was the sweetest child, whose language was drumming on bongos in the living room, on pots and pans in the kitchen, or on his high chair during meals. He pointed and sighed when he wanted something, sometimes speaking in indistinguishable words. The summer he was eleven months old, we met the band on tour in Europe with Bob Dylan, traveling to Nice, France, with Carlos's sister Irma, and to Italy and then Spain. The day of the show at the Palaeur in Rome, we boarded the tour bus, Salvador on his knees in the seat next to me, breathing on the window while he watched a waiter at the outdoor café. Carlos sat behind me deep in conversation with keyboardist Chester Thompson. He was telling CT how he had pushed past Dylan's security to ask Bob to jam with Santana—proud that he had received a yes. My stomach turned over, and a thin string of bile rose in my esophagus. I closed my eyes and swallowed. *I must be pregnant.* I waited to tell Carlos until we checked into the Palace Hotel in Madrid. Sunlight streamed through the pale yellow Tiffany stained-glass dome in the gorgeous lobby. We collected our room key and settled in our room. Salvador was napping, and I sat Carlos down. "I'm pretty sure I'm pregnant," I said. "I felt queasy yesterday."

"This will be Stella," he said excitedly. He had chosen that name for our first child, but Salvador had come instead of a girl. Salvador took his first steps in Madrid, teetering from Carlos's outstretched arms to mine, delighted with his freedom, giggling until he drooled.

That night, Carlos read in our room, Salvador asleep in a crib next to him. Irma and I talked in her room, our conversation turning to her childhood in Mexico. "I loved to sing," Irma said. "I was in a band before Carlos, you know."

"You're kidding! I didn't know that, Irma." I knew her as a mother of two sons who were in their early teens.

"Yes. My father encouraged me. I sang songs from the Everly Brothers and Sam Cooke. Mom didn't want me to sing. She didn't have time for things like that. She was so busy keeping us kids in line. She and I fought like crazy."

"All kids fight with their parents," I said.

"Mom was angry because Dad was gone all the time. And we had no money. Carlos and I are strong-willed like her, and we didn't know when to back down so that we wouldn't get in trouble."

Mrs. Santana was always sweet when I was around. She fed us gigantic *chile rellenos* with refried beans and corn tortillas, and *horchata* with ice, and she seemed to love having children and grandchildren around. Whenever she and I were alone, she told me stories of Mr. Santana's infidelities while wringing her hands. She talked fast, and my limited Spanish vocabulary did not allow me to comprehend the whole story. I knew enough of the language to understand that she had been mortified and hurt by his affairs, and at the same time she was proud of her fortitude and love in remaining with José Santana almost fifty years.

I lay in bed thinking about what Irma had said. Mrs. Santana's strength and ability to care for her family—even when her husband led a separate life—had formed a tenuous emotional history for her children. I had learned to approach Carlos genteelly when I was worried or wanted to discuss something bothering me in our marriage: He had quite a temper and had been known to throw a guitar during rehearsal if things were not going right. In talking with me, he often became agitated or worried when forced to listen to viewpoints different from his own. I was like him and Irma—not one who believed in backing down if it meant compromising my truth. I saw now that Carlos probably had never learned to exchange ideas or discuss differing viewpoints in his family. It was the antithesis of the household I grew up in, where we could talk about any subject and debate our ideas with Mom and Dad. They always had the final say, but they listened to our youthful—and many times wild—opinions. We were punished by being grounded when we were teenagers, but were never made to feel shame for our mistakes. Hearing about Carlos's childhood didn't make me relate his father's life with how Carlos would be as a father. He thought Salvador was the most precious gift and I took Salvador on the road to enable the two to be together, since Carlos toured about five months out of the year.

Stella arrived two weeks after her due date, on Epiphany. Nine pounds and four ounces, with black hair curled atop her head, her skin was the color of tea with milk in it. Stella brought a new dimension to my life. I reflected on how I could raise a strong daughter, how to protect her yet nurture her independence and set her free in the world. She developed tremendous spunk and drama, with a bit of Aunt Daisy's movie star qualities. By three years old, she twirled through the house in her ballet leotard and tutu and did not mind putting her hand on her hip to tell us what to do. By the time she was four, I was telling her that her Academy Award was in the mail, even though she had no idea what that was. Her vocabulary was clear, and her voice loud. Kitsaun had taught Salvador and Stella the joy of running through the house and screaming with joy, when they were very young. While Salvador lived in a dreamy musical world, mesmerized by dust particles flying in the air—examining the explosion of matter with light—Stella conducted the sequence of their play with bossy determination. They rode their tricycles through mud and chased lizards from warm rocks into the field of poppies beside the house. Words and giggles jumped from their little mouths as they fit pieces into their wooden puzzles, played with plastic cars on the family-room table, and drew with fat crayons. Delight sprung from every step they took, Salvador enthusiastically gathering copper-colored rocks from the garden, Stella singing about the Berenstain Bears. Their innocence was a rippling rainbow through our house.

Salvador and Carlos played drums together to the music of Third World and Olatunji, the rhythms beating through the floor. With both children in the bedroom right next to us, we were outgrowing our mountain-tower house, our tiny kitchen, and the lawn outside the living room; and we worried about the cars rushing by on Panoramic Highway, so close to our little ones. We moved to a larger home in 1987, and although it was wonderful to spread out and have a yard in which the kids could run a full circle around the house, the space—twice the size of the Mill Valley house—was a yawning cavern for a while.

I returned to college—initially at a junior college to study creative writing and Spanish, and then at a local university, Dominican. I took classes in ethics, world religions, and women and literature, and my soul thirsted for more. The lessons I had learned in life came from books as well as from having created Dipti Nivas, working with the band, and raising a family. In Experience, Learning, and Identity—a course for twenty-eight adult students who, like me, had returned to college to complete a bachelor's degree—we examined the ways we had learned during the years we were in the workplace rather than in school, as well as how we had integrated the voices that had taught us, including our own. We accepted that one form of education is doing the practical and receiving knowledge from life experience. My study in the world religions class confirmed that spirituality continued to be my core, and my explorations expanded to Native American ideals as well as the feminine aspect of God. My awareness of the larger Self, the oneness of all sentient beings, alongside the reading I did in Huston Smith's book *The World's Religions,* made me more conscious of how religious doctrines guide and motivate people's lives. I developed the desire to live less selfishly and with more compassion for all. I became friends with my classmates and saw how many of the women struggled, like me, for time to grow outside of family.

The band was going to Moscow to play in a concert Bill Graham had organized for the end of the American-Soviet Peace Walk. I had never been away from my babies more than two nights at a time, but this was a once-in-a-lifetime experience. Even though I would be gone six nights, I made plans to meet Carlos and the band in Washington, D.C. Salvador and Stella stayed home with my mother-in-law and Carlos's sister Laura. All I knew of Russia was from high school history books and American media that had taught Communism as a repressive economic and political system denying wealth and freedom to the Russian people.

Two hundred Americans and two hundred Soviets were walking from Leningrad to Moscow for peace and to bring global awareness to the threat of war and to bring people together to end an unwanted nuclear arms race. Santana would perform a free concert in Moscow's Izmajlovo Stadium on July 4 with the Doobie Brothers, James Taylor, Bonnie Raitt, and Russian bands.

On the Aeroflot flight, Bill's staff handed out a brief history of Russia—with excerpts from essays about the culture, quotes from a glasnost-inspired Gorbachev, and a page of scheduled press conference and show times. I hoped to learn firsthand about Russian people, the effects of Communism on their lives, and the daily atmosphere of a city of nine million people. I knew being there would give me a sense of life different than from reading about it in books. Tiles in a hallway, the smell of crushed flowers in a meadow, the dark purple hue of figs in a marketplace, the texture of toilet paper—simple, everyday oc-currences would cast impressions of life on another continent.

Approaching Moscow airspace, we flew over green coun-tryside. Small towns were nestled near tall factory smokestacks and twisting rivers, acres of bushy firs and tall beech trees, and smooth lakes with a few boats sailing on the waters. We landed and were greeted by a disheveled and exhausted-looking Bill Graham, who had been in Moscow ten days. Killer told us that the staging and roofing had been trucked in from Budapest, some of the sound equipment from London, a portion of the lights from Sweden, and the stage technicians from Hungary—along with three refrigerator truckloads of food to feed every-one. The logistics had been a nightmare, but the type of challenge Bill loved.

Santana was driven to Solnechny Hotel, a dingy, hostel-type, low-rise outside Moscow. We passed three nuclear reac-tors puffing toxic waste into the atmosphere and entered through electric gates rising out of unkempt grass. The most magical two hours of my trip occurred when Bill sent a bus at midnight to take us to Red Square. The navy sky was broken by a row of thin clouds that opened to a single star. We drove along quiet streets, voices floating through the bus, and I read street names such as Lenin Prospect, imagining the lives of women in this country. A large brick monument said, THE SOVIET UNION IS THE MAKER OF PEACE. Was this government propaganda, or what they truly believed?

Bright red star lights came into view at the top of Red Square. We climbed out of the bus and walked through the cob-blestone plaza in silence. Soldiers stood guard at stone ramps leading to the seven towers surrounding the Kremlin, and the onion-shaped domes glimmered with gold flecks against the black sky. I had seen them so many times in photographs—I could not believe I was standing in their presence. Bonnie sang softly, her voice heavy and clear in the night, as though she were in a choir of hovering blues singers. I watched her face, an aura of confidence shining from her freckled skin, walking with the rhythm of an African tribal chief.

We passed the Lenin Library, Moscow University, and the Bolshoi Theatre on our way back to the hotel. In our room, Carlos and I tiredly climbed into two twin beds that were covered in white linen with red woolen blankets and crisp white sheets. I sank into a soothing sleep.

We awoke to early sunlight casting lace flower patterns across our beds. In the private breakfast room we ate bread and eggs from plates on a buffet and climbed onto the bus for the drive to the city for the press conference. In the light of day, Moscow was weathered and covered in dirt. Each building was lined with cracks, and staircases leaned to their sides. Buses spewed oil-black fumes. Women bent at the waist sweeping the ground with straw brooms. I wanted to jump off the bus and wander down alleys and up stairways to stumble into people who would either show me kindness or avoid my foreign skin—but I didn't feel confident wandering the city without a translator.

At the Soviet Peace Committee Offices on Peace Avenue, four rows of media people worked in the hot room, perspiration dripping from their brows. Bill thanked the committee for making the concert possible and explained that 25,000 free tickets had been distributed to people in offices and factories, as well as to students. The musicians answered questions from reporters who became antagonistic after a while, accusing the Americans of not understanding Russia's political struggles and the Soviet government of giving tickets only to approved citizens.

I met the peace walkers after the press conference. Mildred Walter came from Denver, Little Dove from Seattle, Judy and Shirley from the East Coast. They told of the warm welcomes they had received walking through Russian villages as they had hugged babushkas (grandmothers) widowed since World War II, learned numerous Russian words, and in one month created new lives of understanding. They invited me to go with them to meet Lily Golden, an African-Soviet woman who had lived in Russia since her childhood. I had only the address—Moscow 103473, Seleznevskaya 34-1-25—and Carlos questioned my going alone. I kissed him good-bye and called for a taxi. I was more excited about this event than I was about the concert: To hear stories from a Black Russian woman and see firsthand how she lived, how she perceived her life, was just the experience I had hoped for. The taxi dropped me off in a neighborhood of Baroque buildings with wrought-iron balconies, curved windows, and enormous entrance doors. Ms. Golden, standing in her doorway to greet us, was quite tall—perhaps five feet ten inches—stately, and elegant, with naturally soft, brown hair in African curls. We entered her flat and sat in her book-filled living room. In a deep voice with a lovely accent and words, she told of her father, Oliver Jerome Golden, who was sought out by the Russian cotton industry and asked to bring a group of experts to Russia to improve farming techniques. In Tuskegee,

Alabama, he had been hated and chased, his heart weakened by running from mobs of racist whites. In 1931 he had gone to Russia and taught cotton farming; eventually he had moved his family to the country. Lily had fond memories of growing up in Russia, where she was the darling of her school. She excelled in playing the piano and was a tennis champion. She had married an African man she'd met at university. A respected author, Lily wrote *Africans in Russia,* a chronicle of her life experience, and translated Angela Davis's works into Russian. She served us tea and fruit, and we asked questions for two hours. I was satisfied with stories of her brilliant life, rich in global ideas and culture. My new friends stood in the street with me until a taxi arrived to carry me back to the hotel. The roads were almost empty, and I savored my Moscow adventure in a cab with a driver who spoke no English and me no Russian.

We arrived at sound check on July 4, entering the familiar world of concerts. Izmajlovo Stadium was a football field surrounded by a track. The bleachers had MIRA (the Russian word for "peace") spelled out in orange sheeting, and the backstage area was filled with the buzz of activity that precedes every concert. Carlos nearly ran to his guitar, so happy to be performing in Russia.

Army vehicles drove into the stadium and lined up behind the stage. I counted thirty-nine trucks as soldiers jumped out and ran to the front of the stage, to the bleachers, and around the perimeter of the stadium. The walkers gathered at the gates of the arena as though they had just arrived from Leningrad, and Bill signaled for the release of two hundred doves that soared into the sky above us. Bonnie, James, the Doobie Brothers, and Santana Band members walked onto the stage carrying dozens of red and pink carnations and roses in their arms. Standing shoulder to shoulder, we heard the leader of the Soviet Peace Committee implore each of us to carry the message of peace to our cities and homes. In the audience, people clapped and raised their hands, gesturing the peace sign. James Taylor came on with his mellow sounds, and a Russian rock band, Autograf, performed after Bonnie Raitt. Santana finished the show, flashing musical rhythms of the world. At the finale, more than one hundred walkers, friends, and music lovers danced with the audience. Bill spun on the stage with his arms around a voluptuous folk dancer and stayed through the encore, a medley of "In the Midnight Hour," "Johnny B Goode," and "Give Peace a Chance."

By the time we left the dressing rooms, the stadium floor was cleared except for twenty sweepers moving rubbish fiercely across to the track. It seemed like magic that thousands had stood as one and now were all gone. A smoky orange moon hung in a circle of clouds. We loaded onto the buses, the musicians riding their after-show high, trying to come down by talking. Lights in Moscow shone like Fourth of July sparklers, and dark trees swayed in the breeze.

In our bungalow, Carlos and I packed for our 5:30 A.M. wake-up. I wrote in my journal about the stark, simple ways of this foreign culture and what I had learned about peace during my six-day sojourn. War's destruction is a possibility foremost in the minds of the Soviets, and as a result, the country has an active movement for peace. I realized that each day I take for granted the joy of living with birds that fly in a clear sky, without nuclear reactors in my backyard or memories of the slow whistle and explosion of bombs in my town. I read a letter printed in a book by the Soviet Peace Fund:

> I am in the eighth grade. My family gathered medicinal herbs all summer long and we have decided to donate some of the money we raised to the Peace Fund. None of us wants war. My grandfather died in Leningrad during the blockade; and my father lost his right arm in the war. Even now we are reminded of the war. We want to live in peace; not to go to war against anyone. My poetry may not be very clever, but here are my thoughts and wishes:
>
>> Those who now threaten war,
>> Have not seen war.
>> They want to wipe both you and me
>> From the face of the Earth.
>> We were not born to see that once more
>> There should be explosions, death;
>> Let us preserve peace throughout the world,
>> The People of the Earth!
>
> *N. Ivanova*

After our travel to the Soviet Union, the length of a day and the darkness of night caused me to assess if I was living consciously. Was I appreciating the opportunities in my life? The precious existence of my own family—tender and young, healthy and blessed—brought prayers of gratitude to my lips.

Feeling the clasp of Salvador's hand or hearing Stella's gleeful giggle made me catch my breath. Faces of strangers on city streets, lonely and hungry, clutched my heart. Tenderness for all people was born from my realization that we are all one. I did not understand how people could hate others merely because they lived in a different country, and I believed governments committed a travesty by making enemies of whole populations who had never met as individuals, never had an opportunity to connect. On any level, we can address the division and separation of nations, if only by illumining ourselves. The circumstances I sought to change were symptoms of my soul's longing to find peace and be safe and whole in the world. To this end, I invited friends—Holly, Lynn, Liz, Stefani, Chris, Ayn, and Hilly—to meet once a month to explore our global divinity through meditation, art, cultural exchange, and talking. Each one of us came from a different religious background, and we shared personal traditions when we met. Stefani set out pillows and we drummed; Holly gave us watercolor pens and assigned us to draw a prayer wheel for our lives; Chris gave us guidance to write a letter expressing regrets, grief, and love, ending with imagined forgiveness from the person we held in our minds. Every meeting became a healing, an expansion of our hearts and spirits.

My soul is a world soul. Would I have been different had I not been born biracial and multiethnic? The blend of my lineage certainly afforded me opportunities that a person of one heritage does not have—openness to more than one country and history, relatives with different life experiences who shared similar chromosomes, and attended separate churches, one whose congregation shouts "Hallelujah" by the prompting of the Holy Spirit, and another whose congregation prays silently and whispers "Amen." It is much more than DNA that allows one to embrace difference; it is an alignment with the universe of consciousness and a desire to accept all human beings as smaller images of an omniscient Divine Presence (anthropomorphic God). To identify with the outer characteristics of humans as who they are is too limited for me, yet every day I am aware that my skin is brown. It is indeed a paradox to have this awareness, yet seek to transcend the borders of outer identification.

1989

Four months pregnant with our third child, I went with the children, Mom, Dad, and Kitsaun to Italy and England, where the band was touring. We taxied to Regents Park at the London Zoo, which had a two-year-old gorilla born the same day as Stella. Salvador slinked along next to his favorites, the wolves. In Rome, the children swam in the Cavalieri Hilton pool. We traveled by train from Modena to Florence, where we saw the magnificent Duomo. We toured the Accademia (the Academy Gallery) and, staring up at Michelangelo's anatomically perfect marble statue *David,* Salvador stood with hands clasped behind his back and mouth wide open. We shuffled through the museum with hundreds of others, sharing European history and soaking up art and culture. I will always remember that trip because it was the last time we traveled as a complete, physically healthy family.

One Sunday morning in November, Mom called our house. "Something is wrong with your dad's arm. He says it's tingling."

"Did you call the doctor?"

"I called Kit. She said to call 911."

My heart was fluttering, and I cradled my large stomach in my left arm. "Call 911, Mom. I'll be right over." We lived only ten minutes from Mom and Dad. I went upstairs and told Carlos.

"I'll go. You stay here with the kids," he said.

I was so nervous that I thought I would deliver right then. In October, the Loma Prieta earthquake had rocked through San Francisco Bay, shaking our house and most of Northern California. I had been sure at that time that I would have the baby in the devastating excitement. But *something wrong with Dad?*—I sat down and prayed, waiting for Carlos to call me.

When the phone rang, I jumped. On the other end of the line, Carlos said, "The paramedics are here. They're giving Dad oxygen and taking him to the hospital. Don't worry, I'm going with Mom."

I called our sitter to come stay with the children, and drove to Marin General Hospital. Dad's mud-colored right hand lay limp on the sheet alongside his body, covered by a thin hospital blanket. The knuckle of the index finger lay swollen, making his hand seem five times larger than his wrist. It looked twisted, gnarled, and unusable there on the bed. His eyes were closed.

"He's had a stroke," Mom said, her eyes cloudy. Dad looked up at me and smiled weakly. His eyes darted from the doctors to us. For the first time in my life, Dad looked confused. I leaned my head close to his square face and kissed his charcoal skin. The words that passed through his pink lips were unintelligible, and my throat closed up.

I looked up as Kitsaun came through the door, her face bunched into a worried cry. She wiped her eyes. "The nurses keep saying they can't believe Dad's eighty."

His skin was smooth, and his eyes so bright. "He thought Roosevelt was president when the paramedics asked him," Mom said.

She stood unfaltering through the first few days of Dad's medical tests and physical therapy, but when Dad was moved into a nursing home to regain his strength and mental capacity, her heart began to break. Mom had always been able to look at the positive side of situations and pray her way through every dilemma. She dug into her inner resolve and declared that Dad was going to be fine and that she could take care of him until he would be his old self.

A month later, on a sunny afternoon, our second daughter was born. We named her Angelica Faith, her middle name chosen for the quality I cherished most in the world and what I believed she would stand for: faith in God, the good of humankind, faith in herself.

After one night, she and I came home from the hospital because the showers were not hot enough and I wanted to be with my family. A wise soul looked out at us from Angelica's brown eyes. She brought joy and peace and lifted us above the worry about Dad. As I took care of three children, I also looked in on Mom and Dad, trying to be a bridge to the care Dad needed with physical therapy and outpatient services, now that he was back home. We treasured our history more than ever, since we had almost lost our fortress. I asked Dad about his early years playing music in San Francisco at the Savoy and the Blackhawk. Mom reminded him he had been rejected by the armed services in World War II because his answers to the questions about war had been contrary to that of a model American citizen's. Dad's face broke into a mischievous smile. "I picked up my shoes and was glad to go," he said in a halting voice. For a black man who was persecuted in daily American life, it must have been ludicrous to be asked to kill for a country that did not treat him as a citizen.

The bleeding in Dad's brain from the stroke had erased some of his memories. The stroke made his right foot drag, and he often tripped because his brain could not signal him to raise his toes just an eighth of an inch higher. But it had not taken his charm or clever wit away.

I have a photograph of Dad holding Angelica in his arms two weeks after she was born. Jelli is wrapped in her soft, white blanket, her face pink; seven-year-old Salvador leans against Grampy's chair; and Stella, five, her hair flying above her head, smiles at the camera. Dad's tweed beret is on his head, and Mom stands beside him, her hand on his shoulder. A beautiful family: a joyous gift.

We spent time sitting together near Dad, telling stories. Mom said that when she was five and her sisters Aggie and Ginger nine and eleven, they would take her to Saturday matinees. Their family was poor, and the girls were afraid to ask for the nickel or dime it cost to get into the movie. Mom would open the family Bible and if she found a scripture that said, "And it came to pass," she knew her dad would give them the money to go.

Dad regained much of his physical and mental capacity, and we resumed our lives. But there is no way to safeguard against the vagaries of life. Another major transition occurred in 1991, when Bill Graham's helicopter crashed returning from the Concord Pavilion. Killer, Santana's road manager throughout the 1970s was the pilot, and Melissa Gold, Bill's companion and a vibrant teacher I had become friends with, was in the helicopter with them. The news shocked Carlos and me, ripping away the lining of our musical world. Bill had been a brother and father to Carlos and a friend to me. He had been by our side at every turning point in our eighteen-year marriage, supportive and passionately close. We were in the midst of planning a concert on Native American land to raise funds for education. I did not know how we would accomplish the project without him. Oren Lyons, chief of the Onondaga Nation in New York, came to speak at the memorial service held in Golden Gate Park. He stood in front of 300,000 people in the polo fields listening to Santana play with Bobby McFerrin and other artists whose lives had been intertwined with Bill's. Oren spoke of Bill's power to create great events in life, his philanthropy through benefit concerts, and Oren said that Bill had made a choice that rainy night of the crash. Against all advice. Beyond all reason. Maybe above his conscious will.

In front of the stage, photos of Bill, Killer, and Melissa rested on a shrine; candles, and thousands of flowers. *Could I really believe it had been their time to depart this earth? That they had chosen to go together?* Bill had taught us to put life on the line every day—with courage and daring. Whatever the greater plan, we had to carry the dreams of our friends and move forward with our own. On every correspondence, Bill signed, "Cheers, Bill." I raised my eyes to the sky and sent my cheers to Bill on his way to rest.

21

Mercy and Grace

1994

✳

$\mathcal{I}$ transferred from Dominican University to Mills College in Oakland, where I attended classes with radical feminists and strong-minded women who lived as they thought. Most of the women in my classes lived in the East Bay or San Francisco, and I saw how antiseptic and one-dimensional my life in Marin was. We studied New York Puerto Rican Nicholasa Mohr's book *Rituals of Survival;* her writing gave a cultural perspective of life in New York and expressed anger at the racism and classism she experienced. The electricity in class discussions made my Dominican days seem like kindergarten. I stretched my boundaries as a womanist and strove to develop more personal autonomy and independence.

In March, Cheryl McHale, our bookkeeper, told me I had to learn to read our general ledger. When I asked her why, she said once I would see the numbers, I would understand. Cheryl worked at our house every Thursday, and we spent a couple of hours each week going through our general ledger line by line.

Rina Medrano, a lovely woman from El Salvador, lived with our family Monday through Friday helping with chores and the children, allowing me time to sit down at the kitchen table, poring over our financial records. Besides the Santana Band, office staff, and crew salaries, there was insurance, office rent, bills from lawyers, accountants, publicist, travel agent, concert booking agency fees, and our personal expenses. Since 1973 the accountants had paid our business bills and managed our finances. I thought I knew, participated in, and understood our company and its functions because we had quarterly financial meetings and I read the quarterly reports as well as the weekly accountings of disbursements. But reading the ledgers—seeing every penny we spent—I realized I did not have all the information. I saw quite clearly that we could not maintain our lifestyle for much longer. Our investments were meager compared to our expenses. It was obvious that our accountants and business managers were not planning for our growth as a company or a family.

Carlos was in Asia touring at the time, and I told him by phone what I had found and my next plan of action. He believed I would act as wisely as possible, as he had always trusted me to interpret our business affairs to him. His grueling touring schedule and recording took all of his creative and physical energy. Yet this financial discovery was cataclysmic, so I kept him informed daily. Cheryl suggested I call our accountant's office and ask them to send all of our files to our house. The woman who handled our bill paying and day-to-day finances balked and tried to talk me out of that idea; but finally, because she has a good heart, she did what I said without trying to filter out documents or challenge me. I did not give much explanation, and she did not know why I wanted to look at our business in this way now, when I had never wanted to before. She called a moving company, and in a few days, fifty file-storage boxes were delivered to our garage. The four-foot-long cardboard files held twenty-one years of Carlos's and my financial history—receipts, tax returns, general ledgers, corporation records, concert settlements, royalty statements—all that would give me a clue to what the business managers had done and whether they had been honest as well as smart.

It was a miracle we had Cheryl: She had filed half the documents when she worked for the accountants. Because she was impeccable in her work, I had hired her as our personal bookkeeper when she left their firm. She never gossiped about why she had left; and when the boxes arrived, she took no detours from her job to organize the documents and extract pertinent financial files we needed to glean information about our livelihood. She was a perfectionist who did everything according to government regulations and tax laws—as well as her own dedication to honesty—and we sat together on the floor tackling the hundreds of sheets of paper in each box. Sometimes she screamed in frustration when she saw sloppy work or questionable receipts.

Day in and day out, often until late at night, we worked. What I thought I knew about the Santana Band business and our personal finances was minuscule compared to all that was entailed in running the corporation and our personal lives. I had had no involvement with our insurance coverage—health, dental, workers' compensation, homeowner's, equipment floaters for touring, life insurance—and its complexity and expense was mind-boggling. Our taxes were filed in every state the band played in. But all of that was relatively in order and just needed review and comparative cost investigation. The real problem we discovered was Carlos's royalties. The business managers recently had hired an auditor whose findings showed that our claim with Sony was more than $4 million for ten years. Legally we could file a claim only for the most recent three years, which was $1.2 million according to the auditor. I had had no idea that Carlos's contract with Sony Records, as with any record company, had a statute of limitations of three years for audit claims. We were told that we could expect the record company to pay no more than 40 percent of our claim for the three years. Carlos and I struggled to cope with the enormity of this financial loss. I blamed myself for not having known how the royalty system worked; Carlos was furious that the professionals we had hired failed us. We knew that the accountants would have chosen to audit because they would be due 15 percent of the settlement money, so my conclusion was that they were not as smart as we had thought, and, in fact, they obviously were not the caliber of professional we needed or that they had claimed to be.

Outside our kitchen windows, thousands of bright orange poppies sprouted among rosebushes—glorious hues of pink, yellow, and peach—in the backyard. Intoxicatingly sweet narcissus competed with the fragrance of star jasmine climbing up the side of the house. Cheryl and I would leave our files to sit outside and eat lunch, inhaling the April blooms that were re-birthing Marin. We lived on soup-size mugs of English Breakfast tea every afternoon. Salvador was eleven and busy with schoolwork and practicing the piano, imitating Thelonious Monk's wild style. Stella was nine, and she adeptly answered the phone, relaying messages to us in a businesslike voice. Jelli, four years old, played around our papers, her toys and dolls falling into the boxes; or, she sat at the computer playing math games. The children became part of our work and helped however they could, if only by being quiet so we could think.

Carlos and I thought the accountants, who were also co-managers, owed us—at least for their negligence in not having audited Sony. We intended to figure out how to collect: We hired attorneys to represent us, as our legal firm on retainer did not litigate. My desire was to not sue for what I considered ineptitude and ignorance—I believe our society is litigious to a fault. But Carlos was incensed and wanted to sue. The attorneys counseled against a lawsuit, because the cost, length of time, and assurance of outcome were all debatable.

We chose to mediate, and I am glad we did. Philosophically, I hold that coming to agreement is what life is about: It takes much more effort to work out our problems in a civil way than it does to fight and angrily hold our own position. In the long run, the process changes us in positive ways. The preparation to mediate was all-consuming, and gathering information to develop the case was a long, exhausting process due to the complexity of our business affairs. Even though I wanted a peaceful outcome, the hours of research each day were stressful, and I became emotionally entangled in the inequities I saw. From discovery to mediation took five months. I learned more than I had ever known about every single aspect of the band's business. And I held meetings with our employees to let them know how and why we were making changes and to hear their perspectives, as well as to tell them how we desired to go forward as a business. I hired a career counselor who worked with all of us to restructure our communication, and she helped staff work through the areas where they had been told they should not discuss business with Carlos and me. Cheryl helped me construct interview questions to ask prospective accountants and a new bookkeeper for the band. Carlos's personal assistant, Bruce Kuhlman, became my emotional support, helping me in every decision—he was a deep listener and a great problem solver who did not mind if I ranted and raved about the firm we had fired. He helped me find a building to move our office to and interviewed applicants with me for an office manager. Close to the beginning of mediation, I bought a warehouse in Marin, hired a general contractor to remodel the space for offices, and tried to cook and eat dinners with the children while Carlos toured Europe and the States.

In August—the time of year I adore in Marin—temperatures rose to the eighties; and at night, unseen tropical birds cawed loud cries that sounded as though we were in a rain forest. Afternoons, Rina filled up the wading pool, the children jumped in and out dumping water on the flowers from their plastic pails, and the dogs chased each other across the lawn. I attended depositions with the opposing attorneys in San Francisco, and I was grilled like a criminal. During the actual mediation, both sides stated their cases before a mediation negotiator, laying out their interpretations of facts. Carlos and I then went to a conference room with our attorneys, and our adversaries went to another with the attorneys appointed by their insurance company. Back and forth, settlement offerings were made and rejected, until at eleven o'clock at night we were encouraged to accept. My right arm was completely immobile—the stress from the months-long ordeal had frozen my body. At day's end, Carlos helped me into my coat to shield me from summer coastal fog blanketing the city.

I was relieved, but disappointed. The monetary settlement was nowhere near what we had lost. But the mediator had been soulful and aware that what Carlos and I wanted was peace more than money, and for the entire ordeal to be over. It was worth millions to have enjoyed the years I had had at home with my babies. In the five months since we had taken over the business, I was working twelve hours a day as chief operations officer, signing every check—of which there were hundreds each month—monitoring insurance, tours, and Carlos's calendar. Not only was it a job, it was also our personal lives and an investment in our future and in our family.

At the end of August, I was cleaning Carlos's studio in preparation for his return home from the road. I dusted the bookshelves and my cloth swept a small stack of color photos onto the floor. The glossy images revealed three Asian women with lithe bodies, long black hair falling over their shoulders, and dark, sultry eyes. Carlos was in a couple of the pictures. *Who had taken the photos, and why?* There was nothing risqué or outwardly abnormal in the photos, but with one look I knew Carlos was not living on the road with integrity toward our marriage. My spirit collapsed under the weight of knowing. Carlos's infidelity diminished my view of myself. I was unable

to look at it as being about him, and I assumed his conduct had
something to do with me.

I picked up the photos and carried them back to the house.
In my office, I wrote a letter to Carlos telling him of my devastation, and sealed the photos in an envelope with my words. I
filled out a Federal Express form and mailed my broken heart
to Carlos. Feeling disconnected and in shock, I sat at my desk,
staring into the garden. Salvador's giggles rang from downstairs; I heard Stella singing and then Jelli saying, "Up, up," to
Rina. *What will we do? Where will we go? How can Carlos reject us, his
family?*

I had a meeting scheduled with a prospective designer in
one hour at the new office space. Smiling and hugging the children good-bye, I picked up my car keys and purse and drove to
the office. I conducted the meeting, asking the designer's ideas
for furnishings, paint, and carpet, barely surviving the hour of
acting businesslike. I got back in my car and drove around
Marin, looking at neighborhoods to see where I would want to
live with my children. This was my answer to being so hurt that
I could not even look in the mirror: Keep busy, make a new
home, try to stay alive.

Carlos called as soon as he received the package. All he
could say was, "I'm sorry." It was not enough. I had no idea at
the time how afraid he was, how exposed in the life he'd kept
secret from me. I moved the business into the new office building and concentrated on the children while rebuilding our management company. When Carlos came home, I was withdrawn
and angry, ready to snap. We tried to talk, but his explanation of

the photos struck me as feeble: He said that other women did not mean anything to him. It was just a physical release; I was whom he loved.

Love meant something very different to me—it meant commitment to one person and being devoid of desire for someone else because of feeling complete inside. I did not need attention from men to make me feel worthy as a person; my marriage was enough, and my children were my treasures. It was unfair for Carlos to live as though he were single and not tell me who he was, that this "release" was important to him. I could have made my own decision about staying in our relationship if I had known the truth.

My needs were so different from Carlos's. Trust and loyalty were part of my existence. *How could I ever trust him again?* Hours and hours of talking and trying to figure it out with my mind just made me crazy. Staying busy did not resolve the bitterness I felt at his infidelity. My anger almost destroyed us. I knew Carlos's struggle was graver than what it appeared to be. Really, all brokenness is a lack of oneness with one's own spirit and light. The real mountains to climb were my anguish and Carlos's confusion and lack of understanding that marriage— or even great love—must be treasured and honored on every level if it is to last. It took months for us to talk through the elements of the issue: what I wanted from marriage; the sacred unity of husband and wife; why Carlos felt he needed or desired sex outside of marriage; and my point that he would feel as betrayed as I did if I had lived as he had. He pleaded with me to not give up on him, but to work together on our marriage. At times the effort was so exhausting that I thought I should run away from the problems, with the children, and start anew. The solution seemed so simple to me: Live with honesty and integrity. But I had come from a strong home with parents who talked to Kitsaun and me and gave us spiritual values on which to build our lives. Carlos's parents had tried to give their children the best they had; but Carlos had gained a much different set of values from seeing his dad stray and from not receiving a foundation of unconditional love. When he was a young boy in Tijuana, Carlos had been molested. The American man gave him candy and toys, and the shame Carlos carried in his body had devalued his existence and manhood. I connected his feeling of lack to these experiences of abuse, and that made me believe our relationship could be healed if we could work through the pain.

We tried to protect the children from hearing our arguments and suffering, and we walked gingerly around each other. In therapy together, Carlos talked honestly and began to dig his way out of the underlying drive that allowed him to disconnect from our marriage and that fed his infidelity. I was able to vent my anger and frustration at trying to forgive what I could not trust. I knew I was holding on too tightly to the ideas and beliefs I had about marriage as partnership. Equality was my goal in marriage as well as life. I cultivated an image of two people sharing every responsibility and buoying each other up in their lifework. We discussed and questioned what we believed about love and our nature as humans on the path of life. Carlos had never received the lessons I had about fidelity and keeping promises. He said, "I love your family and your standards. I want to live up to them."

I admitted that I resented the years spent chasing my husband around the world to have a relationship. Our marriage was crying out for reciprocal attention and commitment from Carlos. He responded by canceling his commitments and staying home for four months. It was the longest amount of time he had been off the road since we married.

This time allowed Carlos to practice a simple existence completely foreign to our family. Rather than rushing to interviews or band rehearsals, Carlos picked up the children from school, ate meals with us, and experienced our world. He videotaped the children dancing and clowning as they performed for the father they worshipped but were usually waving good-bye to. Through my sessions with the therapist, I faced the realization that I could not live in fear of losing Carlos to another woman, of my life changing, of a loved one dying, or of the unknown: Fear paralyzes. My goal needed to be to live in each moment, forgive the past, and be the best person possible by meditating on God and following my heart. I could not magically or easily transcend the hurt I felt, but somehow I had always known that being in a relationship is work, and that marriage needs care and the commitment of time, love, and sacrifice.

My parents had weathered their storms. I had heard them argue, but never had been party to significant discussions or turmoil. Perhaps their marriage was different from ours in some way. But I thought not. Their stakes were the same. Perhaps I would always be a romantic. I had fallen so deeply in love with Carlos—without inhibition or insecurity, wearing my love openly for him to see. Our family was sacred to me, and Carlos and I united in maintaining the communion between our children and us. There was nothing that could abolish my commitment to our tree of life.

Our office complex had a large room in the back, where the band rehearsed. One day, before rehearsal began, Carlos stood in the front doorway with Chester, the keyboardist. I watched him from my desk. His black knit cap was pulled low on his forehead, and he looked tall and slim in a black silk shirt, exquisitely handsome, his full lips drawing me to him as he talked to Chester. I felt a familiar spark inside, like I'd felt when we first met and he was all I could think about. It was instant recognition, without words, of something reaching inside to claim my heart. Carlos's innate affirmation of spiritual truth, his dedication to seeking God, made me love him as I had when we first met. I remembered our conversation from a day earlier, when we drove into the city to pick up Stella from school.

"I was so nervous when we first went out," Carlos had said. "I thought you were so hip and so cool and that I was such a dork. I was careful not to breathe too hard so that my nose wouldn't wheeze."

I laughed. "Come on," I said.

"No," Carlos replied. "I was so scared. Then, later, when I got to know you, I saw you were as dorky as me."

We looked at each other as Carlos drove past the marina, sailboats bobbing in their slips, joggers huffing along the bay. Just like in 1973, when we met.

"You're so beautiful—your arms, your neck, your hands, your face. I just love everything about you," he whispered.

I looked over at my husband as he said those words, and I

pictured us twenty-three years earlier. Who would have thought he was worried about being cool? The tall, quiet guitar player in sunglasses and full-length snakeskin coat with cowboy boots, gliding across the stage, hitting notes that fell like rain inside my body and awakened the one great love in my life.

The sun was falling across my face, making me glow as he offered me his ardent praise. I smiled. I couldn't help myself. "I adore you," I said.

By 1996, our family was back to a semblance of serenity. The children and I traveled to Montreux, Switzerland, for the annual two-week Jazz Festival, where musicians from around the world performed together and created exciting music by playing cutting-edge jazz and big-band arrangements. Kitsaun and a friend, Aaron Estrada, who was a couple of years older than Salvador and the son of Santana's first road manager, came with us. We hiked the hilly city and took the tram to the Alps, where we gazed over sparkling Lake Geneva. We went to Château de Chillon, an eighteenth-century castle, and walked back to our villa, Stella complaining the whole way that her feet hurt. Jelli rode on my back or on Auntie's, and sang little songs. Santana arrived and played in the Festival Hall; Van Morrison was the opening act. After the concert, we traveled to the south of France, where the band would play in Nice. Carlos and I laughed when Salvador and Aaron grabbed towels from their room and said, "We're going to the beach!" as soon as we checked into our hotel. All beaches in the south of France are topless, and we knew the boys were not swimming with their bodies as much as with their eyes.

On our way to the venue, Kevin, our tour manager, came

onto the tour bus, his face a tangled storm. "A plane went down last night . . . ," he said, pausing with a heavy sigh.

Carlos and I looked at him, waiting.

"I think Wayne's wife was on it," Kevin said, dropping his head.

"Kevin. Are you sure?" I asked.

"It was TWA Flight 800. The promoter said Ana Maria was on the flight."

Carlos put his head in his hands. Wayne Shorter, the man of ten thousand hearts, who gave love and joy through his horn, had played the Nice Jazz Festival the night before. I wanted to jump off the bus and run back to the hotel where Wayne was staying. *But what could I say? What would it matter?*

Kevin's head was still hanging. "Wayne is on a flight home."

What would he go home to? My heart broke for him. I remembered the last time Ana Maria and I were in Antibes shopping in boutiques, her soft, dark brown hair falling sexily into her eyes. Her voice was low and husky from years of smoking, and her eyes were bright. She tried on a tight skirt and cropped blouse, turning to the side in the mirror. "I look too fat, don't I, Debbie?" She pushed her stomach in with her hands and turned to face me.

How could someone with her luscious golden skin and gorgeous legs ask such a question? "You look wonderful, Ana," I said. "Buy it."

I walked through the trees behind the venue, thinking about Ana Maria's spirit, her smile, her joy and fire. She and Wayne had been together since she was seventeen. Portuguese and black. Both brilliant.

The next morning the children and I were scheduled to fly back to the Bay Area. They were amazingly brave on our ten-hour flight. During every bump in the air, I knew they were thinking of Ana Maria and fearing we were going down, too. I was searching the clouds with reverence and faith to see her soul dancing by.

22

Vision Fire

1995

✳

 $\mathcal{S}$ moke billowed behind Bald Mountain—gray, red, and yellow—the acrid smell of dry California shrubs and grasses burning. From our house, the plume of smoke covered half the sky in the west, above Stinson Beach. I drove to pick up the children from school and listened to the news on the radio. The fire was in Point Reyes, the pristine national park and seashore where gray whales migrate in the winter. The burning began on Mount Vision; and residents of Point Reyes, Inverness, and surrounding towns worried as ashes fell on their homes and cars. After twenty-four hours, nine thousand acres were burned and four teenagers were suspected of starting the devastation. I watched and listened with concern and compassion for the boys. *What must it feel like to have something in your care rage out of control, leaving you helpless?* News reports said that acres and acres of burned trees and flora would be scarred for years, as well as the animal population. Yet, just a few months later, after winter rains, regeneration began. Grasses sprouted rampant across the land, songbirds birthed in record numbers, and abundant new seeds sprang up from beneath the charred ground, turning hills and trails green again.

African traditions impart the belief that fire can remove a block and keep one's vision alive. The Vision Fire represented what happened in my life after the personal changes and growth I experienced in 1994. Everything I knew about myself, my marriage, and life had been burned to ash—and a new energy and concept of who I am was born. I connected with a spiritual awareness that was outside the constraints of all I had followed before, and I searched for a spiritual place of worship that would not dictate but inspire. I visited nine churches in Marin, looking for a haven that would not tell me to love and obey my husband while forsaking my female power, and that would not have a limited view of women. Finally, I found Unity, whose belief is that God, Divine Mind, is the Source and Creator of all and that we are spiritual beings with the breath of God within us, a church that embraces the world and people's varied beliefs. I breathed in the power of my body, spirit, and mind, further exploring my soul.

There was not enough time for me to study, raise our children, and manage Santana. With a heavy heart and a sense of duty to our business, I decided to leave Mills College. It was as if, once more, I had to choose between serving others and developing myself. I felt creatively starved, so I enrolled in a six-week writing course on autobiography taught by Melba Pattillo Beals at an independent bookstore. She had written the acclaimed memoir *Warriors Don't Cry,* about her year trying to integrate Central High School in Little Rock, Arkansas, and the brutal racism she had lived through. With her encouraging instruction, I wrote about hearing the hurtful words of the children on the playground when I was eight and discovering that I was biracial. For the first time, I comprehended how deeply that event had affected my life.

After the bookstore course ended, Melba asked those of us interested in continuing our writing to attend a class at her home. A new vision for my life opened as I began to write my story. Each week we wrote a chapter and then took it to class and read it out loud. During the week, we rewrote, using the comments from other class members to clarify and change the writing. Pouring out my thoughts was liberating and exhilarating, but Melba would ultimately ask me when I read aloud, "What did you feel?"

I wanted to cry, I was so frustrated. I thought I had emptied my heart and guts, but she questioned my feelings week after week, finally breaking through my system of self-control. For years I had protected myself behind a stoic smile, burying everything that had hurt me or that I had inflicted upon myself: not finishing college; loving Sly; following Sri Chinmoy. All the uncomfortable experiences of my life were pushed down into the center of my chest and covered over with a layer of hardness. My recognition of this was the first step in releasing my voice. I began to notice why I was not living my truth or allowing my essence to burst forth in the way that dozens of women I admired had done. They stepped out and lived in their power. I kept at my process, with Melba forcing me to leave excuses behind and write, no matter what the cost to my heart.

Writing flavored my relationship with my family and strengthened the acuity of my parenting. As I exposed my experiences and revealed my hurts and stumbles through life, empathy and understanding released me from fearing negative experiences the children were facing. Watching our children maneuver through life situations similar to ones I had experienced caused me to grapple with "truth." As they felt normal adolescent angst and pressure from their peers, Carlos and I learned that drugs and alcohol were popping up at parties. *Should we tell the kids what we did as teens, or should we isolate and protect them—or even pretend that we bypassed everything that was appearing in their lives?* Every parent has been faced with this dilemma, but I had never felt so uncertain. I chose to reveal the facts of my past only if asked, and I would openly discuss and try to listen to the children's stories like a comfortable piece of furniture on which they could relax and explore the choices before them. Sometimes, this posture was possible only because I was receiving information from them that let me know where they stood on the issues. Other times, keeping my mouth shut while they talked was one of the hardest challenges I faced.

My parents had told me what not to do without revealing what they had experimented with or how they had lived. I had no frame of reference in telling my children my stories. "Don't lecture," the counselor said. "Tell them why you're worried, what the dangers are, and the possible negative outcomes. Try to remember how you felt at their age." I had been exposed to much less when I was in middle school and high school. My interests had been friends, cheerleading, and music. I knew that keeping my children busy was important for their success as teens. My technique was to keep the children engaged in activities they loved: Salvador, music lessons and camps; Stella, volleyball and tutoring young kids; Jelli, art and writing. I bumped along, trying not to break their spirits yet keep them healthy and whole. I often felt as though I were riding a wild bull in a rodeo—I held on as tightly as I could, sometimes getting thrown off, but never trampled.

Carlos and I talked about what we would say if one of our children came home wearing shorn hair, a sari, or a ring with a guru's face on it. We knew we could not stand mute and allow them to follow blindly. Carlos and I had sought meditation to bring our lives into balance, but because Sri Chinmoy had tried to control our lives and spiritual growth, we wanted to make sure our children understood the difference between listening to their own souls and an outside teacher. We meditated with Salvador, Stella, and Angelica, and I told them, "You house the truth of God's essence inside yourselves, to be heard in the whisper of silence. All that a guru can offer your soul is a guide-book to the trail of enlightenment. All teachers are imperfect, as each human is. The same desires, judgments, competitive nature, and ego reside in him or her. At times you may feel divinity's presence, especially when meditating, but remain aware that it is the effort of your own soul that calls this light to you. Only the invisible, omnipotent Spirit of God can bestow grace and wisdom. A guru may lead you astray. Follow your own connection to divinity."

Carlos told the children that they were born with the same light-wisdom of Jesus, Buddha, Krishna, and Allah. They have the same capacity to look at life and make conscious decisions to benefit people, the planet, and themselves. "It is important to question authority," he said.

My writing classes became a time I savored just for me, and I craved to deepen my experience. An advertisement in *Poets & Writers* magazine—for a one-week writing workshop in New Mexico with Natalie Goldberg—caught my eye. I had read her book *Writing Down the Bones,* which promised to "free the writer within," and I had begun her system of writing practice, scaring myself with what came out when I put my pen to paper and let go of my controlling mind and conscience. I loved Natalie's writing and related to her because she had a spiritual teacher, Katagiri Roshi, with whom she studied meditation and life. I signed up for the course with Lynn, my confidante and writer-friend since Los Angeles. After all, we had begun our journey writing poetry together.

The workshop was called "Fast Writing, Slow Walking" and took place at the Mabel Dodge Luhan House, a historic artist colony in Taos. Lynn and I arrived at nightfall, snow glistening on the ground, and the branches of bare cottonwoods sticking akimbo from shimmering trunks. Sixty-five writers were gathered in the dining room and living room of the lodge, talking and greeting one another as they lined up to eat in the kitchen. I heard Natalie's voice before I saw her, and my heart beat a little faster. I was a little in awe, and nervous to write with someone I held in such high esteem. I had swallowed her words as though they were honey, and I knew she had writing technique and profound philosophy of life to teach me. Anticipation pumped through me, and Lynn and I shared smiles as Natalie dismissed us to the classroom.

I clutched my notebook in my arm and followed the line of writers, snow crunching beneath our boots, to the two-story adobe building down a path. The sky was open, and stars a million years away blinked slowly. Natalie told us to count off into small groups of six. Lynn and I cheated and said the same number so we would not be separated, giggling like teenagers that we had disobeyed and not been caught. The rules of writing practice were recited by a student: (1) keep your hand moving; (2) don't cross out; (3) don't worry about spelling, punctuation, or grammar; (4) lose control; and (5) go for the jugular.

We were given topics to write about for ten minutes, following these guidelines. Then we would read our pieces out loud and no one was permitted to comment. No "Your writing is beautiful" or "I don't get what you mean." Just read and be silent. That was the hardest part; to let another's words—her guts spilled onto a page—hang in silence. The first night, our topics were "corn on the cob, snow, knuckles, and summer." We broke into our small groups and went to someone's bedroom, where we wrote and read until late at night. Lynn and I walked in the starlight with the glowing blue light outside the kitchen guiding us back to the main building. It was freezing cold outside, but our room, named "Placitas," was warm, the wall heater clicking through the night.

Each day we began in the classroom with Natalie teaching about writing and telling us that we "have to keep our arms in the fire" to be connected with a writing community, because "writers don't do it alone." She rattled off topics, and we would break into our small groups to write and read out loud over and over. I loved the intense discipline; but after two days I began to break down, trying to think of a way out, because the writing began to "crack me open" as Nat said. And that brittle place in my chest was letting out pieces of my soul. When I wrote about "what I carry," my eyes overflowed from years of not living my art, writing my life. Words spilled out and flowed from me effortlessly because my hand moved more quickly than my mind could control it. Natalie's example of accepting herself allowed me to accept myself—my imperfections, my past—and I felt peaceful and wild.

The Taos pueblo lay directly behind Mabel Dodge, a flat expanse of snow and ice where dogs ran in packs, their tongues hanging out and tails wagging. Out from the mesa rose Taos Mountain, sacred to Native Americans, and holding the power of generations who walked and blessed the land, traveling gently through the seasons. I absorbed the wisdom that floated from the pueblo, renewed by the scratch of pens moving across the page.

Natalie had given us a reading list, and in the large group we discussed Jamaica Kincaid's *A Small Place* and William Styron's *Darkness Visible*. Writers have been notorious drinkers and sufferers of depression, she told us: "Be careful." She read Flannery O'Connor out loud to us, the writing zinging through the classroom, vibrant and sharp. My skin breathed it all in, and I was filled with the lineage of writers everywhere. In the shuttle returning to Albuquerque, the Rio Grande flowed swiftly beside us. The writing had grounded me in the direction I wanted to travel. I felt whole. Natalie said Katagiri Roshi had told her, "Continue under all circumstances. Do not be tossed away." Returning home, I carried this with me. As life became busier and busier, and when the children needed me but I needed to write, I tried to put a boundary around my space so that I would not throw away what I had learned at the workshop. I continued with my weekly writing group and applied my newfound freedom to what I wrote.

In business, Carlos needed to find a new record label. Touring was the band's mainstay and Carlos's great love, but people constantly asked whether he had released new records and CDs. Radio only played classic Santana hits, such as "Oye Como Va" and "Black Magic Woman," and there were at least two decades of songs that only devout fans knew about. We needed to shop record labels to see whether there was interest in Carlos's talent.

We flew to Los Angeles to attend a tribute to Quincy Jones. When our car pulled up to the front doors of the Century Plaza Hotel, Clive Davis was standing outside. I said to Carlos, "You should be back with Clive." He had signed the original Santana Band to Columbia Records in 1969 before it had become Sony. Clive had started his own record company, Arista, and was legendary for picking Top 40 hits for his artists. Carlos's eyes followed my voice to Clive's figure.

We left the car and enjoyed the evening celebrating Quincy's outstanding musical genius. A few months later, Island Records released Carlos from his contract, and he met with record executives to investigate working with them. Carlos's sound was recognized everywhere in the world, his unique guitar sound undisputed—but music was an industry of numbers, Top 40 hits, payola, and luck. It was not the sixties anymore.

Carlos met with Clive Davis at his bungalow in the Beverly Hills Hotel, and they talked more than two hours about musical vision and ideas for getting the band back on the radio. Clive went back to his label, and they made an offer. With tremendous excitement, the contract was signed to record with Arista. Guest artists were called in to write songs on which Carlos collaborated, and the Santana Band recorded their vivacious, rhythmic anthems. Recording took fifteen months, and during that time, Salvador, Stella, Jelli, and I watched Carlos pack and repack his suitcase while he recorded—sometimes six days a week—toured, filmed videos, and gave hundreds of interviews. Without Carlos beside me, I started Salvador's college search, wobbled precariously through Stella's first bad choice in a boyfriend, and prepared Jelli to move to a new school. I tried desperately to control Carlos's calendar, approve tours, sign every check for each employee and vendor, oversee the staff's duties, and keep our corporation efficient. As chief operations officer, I structured the way our office was run and the amount of time the band toured—trying to keep a balance between fame and reality, work and family. It wasn't easy. If I didn't say no to many requests, Carlos would never take time off. Every week of the year there seemed to be an award show or a benefit or a concert he was asked to play. I had fashioned a system that required him to take time off equal to the time he worked so that we could have a life away from Carlos Santana the guitar player. Most of the time I stood alone against the demands, holding on to my goal to have a household with a father present.

I cannot really say that this time was more intense or hectic than other times in our lives, but in the scope of my seeking to write, a new scrutiny of time was necessary. *Could I hold the family together, manage the business, and have time to quietly write?* I awakened at 5:00 A.M. to write, or I wrote when the children were in school, or after they were asleep. My writing time was fragmented and unreliable, but I continued under all circumstances—as Katagiri Roshi had advised Natalie.

Supernatural was released in June 1999. Santana was on the road, opening for the Dave Matthews Band when *Supernatural*'s first single, "Smooth," hit radio stations across the country. It climbed the charts and, for the first time ever, we had a number one song on the Top 40. The majority of young teens who loved the CD had never heard of Santana. Only their parents remembered "Black Magic Woman," which had reached number four in 1970.

Wherever we went, we heard "Smooth" or "Maria Maria" playing—in restaurants, at basketball games, in cars passing by on the street. In our October goal-setting meeting I had voiced my dream of *Supernatural* reaching platinum, which would mean the sale of one million CDs in the United States. By November, *Supernatural* went platinum, and we celebrated that Santana was back on the radio.

When the Grammy nominations were announced, one of our business associates called us from L.A. "Guess how many nominations we received—two, four, six, eight, or ten?" he asked.

I was smiling because his voice was so excited. "Ten," I said.

"How did you know?" he exclaimed.

"I didn't. You said 'guess.' "

The music had moved like a spiritual locomotive on a rail of light. It was vibrant, soulful, energetic, and new—filled with Santana's poly-rhythmic drums and passionate guitar melodies, yet with the voice of hip-hop and lyrics of young musicians on the current scene. *Supernatural* birthed a multitudinous experi-ence that dramatically shifted Carlos's influence in the music world. Clive had taken a risk because he had believed in Car-los's talent, and he had been dedicated to the CD's success. The multilayered, artistic sounds of the band were being heard by a new generation carried along on our pilgrimage.

2000

In February our family traveled to Los Angeles for the Grammys. The night before the award show we attended Arista's pre-Grammy party at the Beverly Hills Hotel showcas-ing Whitney Houston and Santana. Paparazzi swarmed the red-carpeted entrance and lobby. While Carlos strolled the press line giving short interviews, the children watched musicians and producers gathered in their glittering finery. I went upstairs to the suite Arista provided for our family—a luxurious two-bedroom, three-bath apartment—lit the gas fireplace, and ex-plored the bedrooms, walking across marble floors and thick carpet that felt like marshmallows when I stepped out of my three-inch heels. I relaxed on a chenille chaise lounge, opened a small ten-dollar jar of cashews, and waited for Carlos's inter-view on *60 Minutes II*. After twenty luscious minutes of quiet, Carlos and the children came up to the suite and lay across the king-size feather beds. Charlie Rose began rehashing the old news of Carlos being high on acid during his Woodstock per-formance, and I was sorry the girls were watching the inter-view. Salvador was sixteen and aware of his dad's past. But the girls were nine and fourteen, and I didn't want them to hear about the drugs or, later in the piece, Carlos's sexual abuse when he was a child in Mexico. Why couldn't the report focus on Carlos's spirituality, his knowledge of African rhythms and Mexican melodies, and how he had toured when the band was hot as well as when it had been forgotten by mainstream media? What about Carlos's tenacity to perform in small venues, the overnight bus rides, and how the band had sometimes stayed in hotels that didn't have hot water? My fondest memories were when Santana performed in bullrings in Madrid and San Sebastián, Spain—walking from the dressing room to the stage across a bridge of wooden planks with bulls snorting below.

During concerts, from the wings of the stage, I had watched Carlos's dark eyes peer out from his buttermilk skin beneath the spotlight circling his body. After seeing thousands of shows, I had my own ideas about what was important about Carlos, and it seldom was what the media chose to focus on. The children watched the program without comment, and when we left the suite for the party in the grand ballroom, the flash of cameras and flurry of ball gowns and stars with their entourages made us all forget what we had watched.

Whitney Houston performed for more than an hour, her voice strong and sure; each beautiful note was a thief pursuing our hearts. She sang to Clive Davis, who had groomed her from a teen, giving her voice the hand-carved songs that catapulted her star into unreachable galaxies. Arista had been built by Clive, and now, according to industry talk, he was being pushed out of his reign.

*NSYNC, our daughters' favorite band, sat to our right. Babyface, Mary J. Blige, Stevie Wonder, Britney Spears, Jennifer Lopez, P. Diddy, CeCe Winans, and many I didn't know sat crowded around the tables. Whitney ended her set. While Santana's equipment was being set up, at least fifty people drifted out of the room, as if they had only been there to hear Whitney. I was shocked and felt an industry snub, but knew we were not part of the music social scene, nor did we really know all of these artists. Seeing someone socially doesn't make you friends. Santana went onstage close to midnight—a torrent of rocking, high-energy songs poured out as though the ballroom were full. By the time the bass line of "Maria Maria" crashed through the room, Stevie Wonder was on his feet clapping and Clive was smiling like a proud father.

In the limo ride back to our hotel, the kids talked excitedly about meeting Chevy Chase. "He said he had three kids, too," Salvador said, laughing. "His wife said, 'No, dear, we only have two.' " Stella and Jelli fell forward giggling. I missed the whole exchange sitting upstairs in the quiet of the hotel room before the party, and was glad the children had gotten to meet someone they admired.

Early the next morning, I sat in the living room, silently meditating on my heart, asking God's Spirit to fill me with peace. Rain pelted the windows of our villa at the Sunset Marquis Hotel. Rivers of water spun down the Hollywood street, banking into a gutter beside the driveway. The sound of drops against the window tossed an echo inside my body, steady and forceful like a drumbeat. Salvador, Stella, and Angelica slept in the rooms upstairs. Carlos was in our bedroom dressing to leave for sound check at the Staples Auditorium. I pondered the past and the future, not knowing what the day would bring.

Twenty-eight years of being married to Carlos, being part of his musical life, being a mother, business owner, and spiritual seeker—yet I was still searching for my own place in the world.

The phone rang. I picked up the receiver to hear our publicist's voice.

"Carlos is getting dressed, Michael. No, he's not giving any interviews before the telecast."

Plop. What was that? Rain dripped from the ceiling onto the staircase. "Michael, you won't believe it. There's a leak in our room. This place is falling down around us. I'll see you later."

"Who was it?" Carlos stood in the doorway.

"Michael Jensen. I told him no interviews."

"Thanks, *muñeca.*"

Carlos wore a knee-length black jacket and matching Italian wool pants. His face gleamed from the aloe vera lotion he had smoothed on after shaving.

"You look great," I said.

He bent down, his arms circling my back. "Thank you."

I stretched my arms around his neck and hugged him close.

"Are you coming with me?" He leaned away and raised his right eyebrow.

"No. The girls and I are having our hair and makeup done here. We'll come with Salvador after sound check." I knew he was worried because I wasn't dressed. Carlos was never late for anything, much less the Grammys where the band would perform "Smooth" with Rob Thomas. His anxious mood was not due to the anticipation of winning an award, but because he was playing—that was his passion, and he was pulsing with adrenaline.

He walked back to the bedroom. "Okay." Carlos knew I would arrive at the show on time with the children. He never had to worry about my being where I needed to be.

After Carlos left for sound check, the children and I finished getting ready and rode in the limo to the entrance of the Staples Center. We walked inside the cavernous arena to the dressing rooms, feeling as if we were backstage at a show on a Santana tour. The band was talking and eating, waiting for the ceremonies to begin. My chocolate-brown sequin formal hung in a garment bag, and I found a small room to change in. I was just slipping my feet into my gold heels when Carlos was called to go into the audience for the pre-telecast show. Of ninety-eight Grammy categories, only seventeen awards are televised, the remainder given in a sparsely attended afternoon program. Blues, classical, country, gospel, new age, and jazz receive Grammys at this time, and Carlos and I stepped onto the royal blue carpet leading to the folding chairs in the front row to watch the show. The first category in which Santana had a song was "Best Instrumental Composition" for "El Farol." It went to Don Sebesky, and I wondered, *What if we don't win any?* Carlos and I clapped while producer David Foster kept the program moving. Our friend Wayne Shorter received "Best Jazz Instrumental Solo," and we hooted with love. The next category that included a Santana song, Carlos's name was called as recipient. The roll was on. Six Grammys went to Santana in the pre-telecast program. Carlos and I both felt light-headed. Each time he mounted the stairs to receive his award, years of studio sessions, sound checks, thousands of concerts, and scores of musicians who had played with Carlos and traveled on buses, trains, and planes were receiving acknowledgment through him. Musicians receive Grammys at different times in their careers; Carlos had received the "Blues for Salvador" Grammy years earlier; there are ten Bammies from the California awards show on the bookcase at home and numerous international honors. With this recognition we felt that we could expose younger listeners to the sounds of Tito Puente, Gabor Szabo, Flora Purim, John Coltrane, Miles Davis, Kenny Burrell, and Mahalia Jackson—brilliant composers and musicians who are not played on pop radio but who hold treasure chests of notes and rhythms that transport us above daily struggles and lift us into sublime joy.

During the break before the live telecast, ticket holders were let into the arena, musicians walked the red carpet, and Carlos and I stayed in the dressing room with the band. We had brought our entire staff to the Grammys because I felt they deserved to participate in what they had also toiled so hard to produce, coordinate, and promote. When we were taken to our seats, they sat high above us in the balcony, out of our sight but in the effluence of the night's adrenaline. The three hours went by like a streaking comet, and Bob Dylan and Lauryn Hill walked out to read the last nomination: "Record of the Year." Bob opened the envelope and pointed at Carlos when he said, "Smooth." Carlos stood and grabbed my hands, attempting to pull me to my feet. I pulled back, thinking he was trying to take me onstage, and we had a mini tug-of-war. My role had been behind the scenes, where I liked it. The last place I needed or wanted to be for my soul to shine was onstage. What I care about is establishing a spiritual foundation of open communication, integrity, and kindness to support the music. When I finally stood with Carlos, he kissed me and then climbed the stairs to accept the final Grammy of the night. I applauded with everyone else in the audience, my body trembling from the intensity of the attention and the long day of smiling.

It was an exhilarating experience. We hosted a small, private after-party at the Conga Room, avoiding the record companies' extravaganzas, and returned to our hotel room to a pile of gifts. Quincy Jones had sent ten small bottles of champagne engraved with one Grammy nomination each. A tray of giant chocolate-covered strawberries sat beside a bottle of champagne from the hotel. It was too early in the morning to make another toast, and Carlos was still on an adrenaline high. He sat looking at the television screen, but I suspected he was recalling the scenes and words of the day, tumbling end over end through his head. I climbed into bed, deliciously spent and full of dreams. All we had set out to accomplish, from believing we could self-manage our company to signing with Arista, had culminated on this spectacular night of winning nine Grammys. *Supernatural* continued its magic, selling over 25 million copies worldwide.

In August, after the Grammys had arrived and been placed on shelves in our home, Dad, at ninety-one, grew visibly weaker. I could see his body shutting down as he leaned to the side in his wheelchair. Mom had tended to his needs for ten years since his stroke, making sure he took every recommended vitamin, driving him to physical therapy, and reading favorite Bible verses to him daily. In the beginning, she had even tried to push his guitar into his arms, although the stroke had erased seventy years of music from his mind. Tirelessly, she spent every minute she could with the love of her life. The last few months, Dad had not been able to speak well at all—his voice was shaky, and the aphasia had taken away his ability to match the words in his mind with what he was experiencing inside. He often shook his head in frustration.

Carlos and I were out of town when Kitsaun called to say, "You'd better come home. Dad doesn't have long." We caught the red-eye, solemn, remembering Dad on the tennis court slamming the ball at us, his pure tenor voice singing "Danny Boy" or "SK Blues." We arrived home at 6:40 A.M.

Salvador and Stella were getting ready to leave for school, having said tearful good-byes to Grampy the night before. We hugged, and I let them go—as I would have to let Dad go. Jelli awoke and ran into my arms. She was nervous but courageous as she watched me walk out the door.

Mom stood looking out the kitchen window when I arrived, her body a wisp of grief as we embraced. Dad lay in his bed, the artery in his neck bulging and receding.

"Hi, Dad," I whispered, and laid my palm on his forehead, thinking, *God Bless you, great person, my father, my friend.* Ginette, the health care worker, was sponge-bathing Dad. Kitsaun and I carried warm water, wiped the floor, helping however we could. My sister's serene strength and benevolence emanated throughout the room, providing a berth for my sorrow.

Ginette spoke: "Your dad is going. Talk to him."

"It's okay, Dad. We'll take care of Mom. You had a magnificent life. It is okay to leave."

When he gasped his last, it was an enormous, holy moment that closed an era. I stood looking at my father's shell, the Spirit already transcending heavenward. Memories of summer trips to Chowchilla where the sun fried us to a crisp; Sundays at church in Oakland with Uncle U.S. preaching until perspiration poured down his face; Aunt Daisy's rich gumbo, fried chicken, and sweet potato pies, her tiny waist cinched into dresses from Lanz, a box of violet gum in her "pocketbook"; the image of my mother and father standing together with luminous light in their smiles as they guided my life—these all clutched my heart. Saunders King, sophisticated, elegant, dressed in Italian suits I loved to buy for him, bent over his Gibson guitar, hands moving over the frets, his keen eyes firmly on Kitsaun and me, never letting us slip.

Dad had given us straight backs and strong handshakes, and he had taught us to look people directly in the eye. He was the last King of the generation that bore us. I felt a shattering emptiness left by the departure of Dad—a steadfast, dependable model of courage in my life. It was inevitable, part of humankind's trail, and I faced being the grown-up now. I stood in the presence of his flowering soul after he exhaled his last earthly breath and felt him lightly touch my heart.

Dad embodied all of the melodies that were important to me: power, Blackness, loving everyone no matter what their station in life, and upholding Truth. From the day he stood outside San Miguel Elementary whistling a song of freedom while he waited to hold my hand, he hovered over my life, teaching me to be an individual. I can feel him today. He has woven multifaceted threads of brilliance into the heritage I pass on to my children and the world.

Life burns a pattern no one can predict. Gurus try. Preachers prophesy. The wind moves the flames that completely incinerate one tree yet leave another untouched right at its side. Dad's death imbued our family with momentary pallor. He and Mom were the babies of their clans' five children, both the only ones remaining—and now Dad is gone. His legacy of song, the tenor vibrato in his voice and the sweet strumming on his guitar, are seeds planted in Kitsaun and me, Salvador, Stella, Angelica, and his son-in-law, Carlos. His sense of justice and individuality, joined with Mom's bravery and disregard for the ignorance of others, lives in us. Dad led with his chest out, noble and ready to defend all that he believed. He was an ultra-cool blues musician whose innovative style influenced many. We stand tall with his boldness.

There are times when Carlos plays his guitar and I hear Dad in his notes, like jewels of love. I heard it the night Archbishop Desmond Tutu and his beautiful wife, Leah, sat in our home. Carlos, with Chester on keyboard, played "Victory Is Won," which Carlos wrote after hearing the archbishop speak of black South Africans' transcendence of the torture and oppression they endured during apartheid.

And in Florida, on Carlos's birthday, I stood on the side of the stage as a cake was taken out to him. Carlos blew out the candles and began the beautiful ballad "Apache," which introduces "Smooth," and then raised his right arm, guitar pick in hand, sustaining the note, and touched his heart, reaching his arm out to me. "I love you," he mouthed, bowing deeply. I bowed to him and mouthed, "I love you." Such a sweet, gentle gesture of deep waters, years together, the landscape of our marriage. Lifetimes of power sustained each note, producing waves of tones—some sharp, most soft and full. Carlos's butterscotch fingers bent the steel strings, pushing against the frets and causing notes to stream from the hard-body guitar and stop my breath. His playing is a crying sound that climbs in pitch, then descends with the slow vibrato of seeds shaken in an African gourd. Every note is chosen with the hope that in the listener it will sing a story, spark a journey to goodness and mercy.

When I look back at my life and compare it to what I had imagined it would be, it has been a strenuous journey along a mountainous path with breathtaking views. I was taught to look toward heaven to find God, but I searched my own heart and found light, joy, and God's breath of truth inside me. I believe in the connectedness of us all with our own luminosity humming a story of truth and love in the space between the stars. What glows, even in the dark, is the power of Divine Presence.

Portions of who I am have died hundreds of times. Whenever I transcend an outdated belief or change my focus and expand my dreams, I become a new person with a transfigured body. My family's history tells me to value the incontrovertible truth of my strengths, foibles, choices, and vision. I am a bridge to my parents and the generations of humans who have come to earth to learn what life is truly about. It is not material riches or perishable wealth. Life is good works, art, faith, and love—with people of all nations moving through sky and clouds, drinking the nectar of God. Life is believing that within each of us lies every answer to the questions of the universe, that the unquenchable fire of our existence is within our grasp if we only open our hearts.

$\mathcal{N}$ote

Angelica wrote this poem about my dad three years after he died. She never knew her grandfather before his stroke when he walked with the stealth of a panther, nor had she the privilege of hearing his resonant tenor voice in song. Yet their bond was tender and immense, and she embodies his spirit.

SK Blues

as he grew older
he smelled fresher more pure
like a baby
cozy in the mother's arms
his scent lingered in the air
even when he was miles away
as he went out
i came in
as he spoke less
i spoke more
he is in me
his eyes soft like a bunny
his embrace warm like his easy chair
in front of the fire
his dark-as-dark-gets skin
worn and yet
still as tender as his granddaughter's heart
his gentle-as-the-breeze hand
resting on top of his wife's
i catch myself
sitting watching the giants
winning another game
just like he and i used to do
i find myself
shuffling my knuckles
just like he used to do
and i cry
because i know
that he is in me

Angelica Santana
September 4, 2003

Glossary of Spanish Terms

campesino	farmer
chile relleños	cheese-stuffed chili pepper fried in egg batter
cuidando	take care of, to care for
horchata	rice beverage, with sugar and sweet spices
muñeca	doll
niño	child, infant
tío; tíos	uncle; uncles
tía; tías	aunt; aunts
Virgen	the Virgin; Virgin Mary
zócalo	public square

Acknowledgments

✳

I am grateful to many friends who have supported me in telling this story. Melba Patillo Beals started me on the journey. My writing sisters, Susan Adelle and Judy Hebert, lived through countless drafts. Natalie Goldberg gave me writing practice. Rob Wilder graciously read an early version.

My parents Saunders and Jo Frances King, and my sister Kitsaun King, gave me love to stand on.

Thanks to Jillian Manus, my agent, and Melody Guy, my wise editor, for believing in my voice.

About the Author

DEBORAH SANTANA is vice president and chief operations officer of the New Santana Band, Inc., and has been managing the Santana Band full-time with Carlos Santana since 1994. She is also vice president of the Milagro Foundation, which was started by the Santana family and which has given almost $2 million to charities and nonprofit agencies that support children and youth in the areas of health, education, and the arts. She has been married since 1973 to Grammy-winning musician Carlos Santana. In 2000 she received the UCLA César E. Chávez Spirit Award, which honors individuals who have continued to pursue Chávez's vision of social justice. In 2004 she received a "Women of Distinction" Award from the Founder Region Soroptimist International Organization for her work with the Milagro Foundation, and in September she and Carlos received the Youth AIDS award for their commitment to fighting the AIDS pandemic in South Africa. For more information about the Milagro Foundation, please visit www .milagrofoundation.org.

About the Type

This book was set in Perpetua, a typeface designed by the English artist Eric Gill, and cut by The Monotype Corporation between 1928 and 1930. Perpetua is a contemporary face of original design, without any direct historical antecedents. The shapes of the roman letters are derived from the techniques of stonecutting. The larger display sizes are extremely elegant and form a most distinguished series of inscriptional letters.